Mr Cool's Dream

THE COMPLETE HISTORY OF THE STYLE COUNCIL

"Painstakingly accurate" - Paul Weller

IKON ORIGINAL

A Wholepoint Publication 2008

www.wholepoint.co.uk

MR COOL'S DREAM
THE STYLE COUNCIL

"Probably the best pop group in the World"

by Iain Munn

Fully revised and updated, October 2008

Mr Cool's Dream
The Complete History of The Style Council

Published by Wholepoint Publications

Copyright © 1996 - 2008

First printed in Great Britain, March 1996

This edition printed in Great Britain, October 2008

© Iain Munn, 2008

info@wholepoint.co.uk

A CIP catalogue record of this book is available from the British Library

ISBN 13: 9780955144318

Printed and bound by CPI Antony Rowe, Eastbourne, UK

AUTOGRAPHS

It's a tough challenge …

Paul Weller   Mick Talbot

Steve White   Dee C Lee

"and don't sign what isn't true …"

REVIEWS

Genuine comments on the 2006 paperback

"MCD is a fine achievement. The dedication in keeping the torch burning is second to none and the book is a fitting tribute. The return of the Cappuccino Kid is a masterstroke. On behalf of Councillor's everywhere, we are grateful."

"Painstakingly Accurate." - Paul Weller

"Meticulous day by day guide." - MOJO magazine, Rated ****

"There's no better companion." - Virtual Brighton magazine

"A very accurate account of the bands history. It brought all those memories flooding back of an amazing few years at the very start of my musical career." - Anthony Harty, The Style Council Bass player

"The definitive record of a great band." - Steve White, Style Council drummer

"Very detailed and a real labour of love." - Paolo Hewitt, Author

"The last word on The Style Council." - Paul Weller

"Sat down for a little skim through ... and started to get absorbed in the diary of my life!!" - Tracie Young, Style Council vocalist

"Very Impressive." - Mark Baxter, Author

"The book is a fabulous, exhaustively researched and fascinating chronicle of the most intriguing and unpredictable pop group of the 1980's. It's also that rare thing, a band biography which is actually lively, readable and not embarrassing to be seen with in public." - Dickon Edwards

"Brilliant stuff, well written." - Barry Mason

"The combination of facts and quotes worked very well for me." - K.P. Norway

"A highly professional and exhaustive account." - Martin Ling

"A train spotter's guide to TSC, a must for any Paul Weller fan." - Dave Porter

"The amount of research that went into it must've been brutal, you should be proud of all of it!"

"A great read, an indispensable reference guide, I thought I knew a lot, but I learnt so much more. Congratulations."

CONTENTS

The Complete History of The Style Council

Assistance

Mr Cool's Dream contains a wealth of information. However, if you have any suggestions, additions or corrections then please get in touch.

Phone/Fax: 08712 115510

info@wholepoint.co.uk

www.wholepoint.co.uk

All illustrations are © Dodger, 2008

Photographs

Reviews for the 2006 edition often suggested the book was missing the official, professional photographs from Peter Anderson, Tom Sheehan (true gent) and Nick Knight. While this is accepted, their photos command prices that would easily double the cover price of this publication. Whilst *Mr Cool's Dream* remains an independent publication their inclusion will not be possible. As an alternative all of the photos used have been donated to the project for which I am grateful. No photo or illustration used within this publication should be reproduced without the specific owners permission.

PREFACE

Back in December 1982 at just 24 years old, Paul Weller split up one of the UK's biggest bands, The Jam and has never been pardoned. Forming The Style Council with Mick Talbot done him no favours and gave him no kudos - he had to prove himself once again. Today at 50, Paul *is* as successful and acclaimed as he was back in The Jam - but what happened during the "lost years" in-between?

Mr Cool's Dream dedicates itself to The Style Council, the only book to offer an accurate and highly detailed insight into Weller's "forgotten" group. Time has been very kind to The Style Council and many of their songs are still relevant, inspiring, radio played and fresh - without the ridicule that came with admitting to listening to them back in the 80's. Oh how I was frowned upon!

On the back of Paul's continued achievements - most recent being another number 1 album, *22 Dreams* and *Mojo's* 'outstanding contribution to music' - more people are now delving into his past and now appreciate what he was trying to accomplish in the 80's and where he was heading, musically at least.

If you are still unsure, then alongside *Mr Cool's Dream,* the 5 CD *Complete Adventures* box set and *TSC on Film* DVD is your instant path to a fascinating 7 years of Jazz, Politics, Soul, Classical and House music. Worth it? Absolutely!

MR COOL'S STORY

Mr Cool's Dream, The Complete History of The Style Council is recognised as the absolute guide on "probably the best pop group in the world." It first appeared in 1996 before one of the world's leading music stores, HMV, stepped in with an exclusive deal where they released a cut down edition inside the 1998 *Complete Adventures* box set. Eight years later the mysterious and elusive **Cappuccino Kid** came out of retirement alongside many high profile Style Councillor's to offer their stories in an updated edition. **Paul Weller** called it, "painstakingly accurate" and **Steve White**, "the definitive record."

This edition has been fully revised and updated, expanding on the now out of print 2006 release by adding new features and talking to many more relevant people. One thing is certain, you will not find another Style Council book like it. Ever!

Is *Mr Cool's Dream* the "missing" 22nd Dream?

FOREWORD

"LIKE 2 GRANNIES AT A JUMBLE SALE!"

"A WONDERFUL TIME IN MY LIFE"

The Style Council for me represents a wonderful time in my life. I was still a young man, still discovering myself as a musician and a person.

I've only got good memories really, at least up until the end which got to be a bit drawn out and negative. But on the whole it was just fun. We had so many laughs, made loads of good music, turned people onto lots of other good music too, I like to think.

My favourite bit outside of the music was me and Mickey Talbot shopping in Rome for clothes like 2 Grannies at a jumble sale! Getting very well fed and watered in all sorts of countries. That was another thing for me – we really got to travel and see the world and that was an eye opener for me.

For me T.S.C. will always represent youth, vitality, sunshine and friendships made that have pretty much endured. I loved it.

Good luck as always,

Paul Weller, 25th June 2008

ACKNOWLEDGEMENTS

I would like to thank the following for their support in my quest to create an unsurpassable and acclamatory reference guide on The Style Council.

Paul Weller for finding the time to contribute a foreword at the same time as *22 Dreams* was topping the charts. I appreciate the encouragement and acceptance of my *Mr Cool's Dream* project. For you, the complete story of someone's loafer …

The Cappuccino Kid, **Gary Crowley**, **Paolo Hewitt**, **Camelle Hinds**, **Dennis Munday**, **Eddie Piller**, **John Reed**, **Steve White** and **Tracie Young** for exclusive information and their untapped knowledge.

Lifetime friend **Kenny Lam** for the excellent work and countless hours spent on the dust jacket. **Dodger** for the superb illustrations. **Mark Anthony, Graeme Atkins, Mark Baxter, Andy Davis, Barry Mason** and **Tony Pacey** for their on-going support. **Tom Sheehan** for his kindness.

To many genuine **Honorary Style Councillor's** for their on the job knowledge and memories; Freddie Bastone, Billy Chapman, Anthony Harty, Camelle Hinds, Chris Hunter, Kevin Miller, Dennis Munday, Mike Mower, Stewart Prosser, Audrey Riley, Steve Sidelnyk, Joe Smooth, Barbara Snow, Helen Turner, Steve White, Jaye Williamson and Tracie Young.

Fellow Internationalists from Cairo to Honolulu and beyond who have contributed to this or previous editions; John Adamson, Andrew Allen, Mark Anthony, Graeme Atkins, Louisa Bosworth (IKON), Brian Burroughs, Flavio Candiani, Brian Flynn, Simon Franklin, René de Hey, Jon, Debbie Kruger, Martin Ling, Sananda Maitreya, Barry Mason, Carl Meyer, Kevin O'Conner, Mel O'Toole, Giovanni Parmigiani, Shaun Perkins, Niels Petersen, Steve Rinaldi, Eric Stephenson, Christopher Strupp, Sandra Sully, and Arnie Zeigler.

Michael 'editor' Alexander, Bob 'Robert' Brewster, Fergal Crean, Darron Connett, Elaine Dickson, Iain 'Burpo' Harper, Paul Kiddie, Kenny Lam, Myles Marshall, Shona Marshall and David Whiteley.

Past or present visionaries of the book at Acanthurus Leucosternon; Andy Bartlett, Erik Brunskill, Bob Cameron, Johnston Craig, Mark Downey, Alana Drummond, Scott Drummond, Kareem El Farargy, Thomas Guild, Andy Kerr, Charlie Lodge, Kevin MacIver, Iain Macleod, Dougie Ramsey and Robin Warnock.

Continue to spread the word and keep sending in your photos of *Mr Cool's Dream* on location in far and distant lands, or just down the local.

Iain Munn, October 2008

DEDICATIONS

William Munn (1933 - 1998). The much missed Munnfather may have left us 10 years ago but the legend lives on. Is there a cinema showing *The Quiet Man?*

Mum for your constant wise words and extraordinary energy, I am always grateful. Remember to keep removing your (well deserved) college shoes! **"COOL IT"**

Darren at 8 summers old you tell me, 'Mr Cool is a fool' - Maybe! But once you discover this great music the book will all make sense. You always put a smile on my face dude. 3 goals with 3 shots in the sticks - Keep trying …

Karlynn for everything and allowing me to get on with this 2 year project, when I really should have been dancing through the fire, just to catch you're flame …. just close enough to tell you that …..

Ann (Graduate!), **Catherine**, **Colin** (the 'man in the corner shop') and **Willie**. Not forgetting the in-laws, **Jim** (top joiner for dwarfs), **Lynn** and **Mark**.

Lets hope for a bright future and peaceful times for the following apprentice's lead by **Hannah Miik**. They are **Callum, Emma, Katie, Kyle, Lewis, Robbie, Siobhan** and **Sophie**.

Finally this book is dedicated to everyone who has been touched by The Style Council and to this day promotes the music of Paul Weller 1983 - 1989.

INTRODUCING THE STYLE COUNCIL

Why are you called The Style Council?

'A friend of mine thought of the name. They thought it was really pretentious but you can get lots of great puns out of it.' (*Internationalists*)

'Some cat I know came up with it. I think he got it out of a shop window.'

One classic suggestion following on from the creation of The Jam at the breakfast table was the letters on the Tea, Sugar, and Coffee Jars!

Twenty years later Paolo Hewitt confirmed it was 'taken off a tube advert.'

Further information courtesy of the Autumn 1984 *Council Meetin'* tour programme;

The because there's only one; **Style** is an expression, each individual has their own style. Style isn't just clothes and cosmetics it's soul, it's attitude, it's spirit and thought. It's also care; **Council** is a bond of people, a collective. People working together because they have a common interest. Showing that people can do it if they want to.

This was expanded upon in the fan club magazine *The Style Population*;

Music Optimism, vitality, feeling and a great hope and strength; **Description** Take a pinch of white or a pinch of black, add funk, soul, r 'n' b, a squeeze of modern jazz and mix, then blend with socialism, love and emotion. Drink it down and feel better y'all.

The official Style Council fan club membership card

Paul Weller (25th May 1958)

'One of the most greatest enjoyable times of my life' (Radio 2, 2003)

'I had this whole thing planned for months. I wanted Mick in my new group because I believe him to be the finest young jazz/soul organist in the country and also because he shares a hatred of the rock myth and rock culture. I haven't any plans for an album. I'll just collect up tracks as I go along. I'm more interested in releasing 45's really. So people will have to bear with me, expect nothing and I'll give as much in return.' (Jackie, 1983)

Mick Talbot (11th September 1958)

'It is great to be part of the ultimate group' (Internationalists)

"I started playing when I was 7 or 8. We lived with my grandmother when I was young and she showed me some things on the piano. My dad played a bit too but was better on guitar. After a while my grandmother said she couldn't show me much more as she hadn't learnt formally. So she sent me to lessons, which I was a little scared about, but I stuck with them for about 3 or 4 years and in hindsight I realize how important they were. I had ambitions to be a musician, but the first time I thought I could make it was when I was in a band that got paid to do it and wasn't being put on as a favour like school bands.

I got called by Paul Weller towards the end of summer 1982. The Bureau had run its course and lost its contract and I was on the dole, pretty much at a loose end. I hadn't seen Paul for some time. I'd done a few live shows with The Jam and recorded on the *Setting Sons* LP. He thought I might be right for his new project. In the course of a long lunch meeting we seemed to have a great deal in common and that's pretty much where we started from. We became close through our shared experiences of music and fashion and the fact that we were born in the same year which gave us a similar history. The best thing about Paul when I worked with him was his encouragement of other musicians and his own musical bravery."

Flavio Candiani, 2004.

Steve White (31st May 1965)

'I was more over-awed it was Mick Talbot, one of my sort of heroes'

Steve White was influenced by Keith Moon, 'to me the greatest Rock drummer there ever was,' Lee Morgan, Jimmy Smith, Art Blakey, John Coltrane, Georgie Fame, Stevie Wonder and Aretha Franklin.

On 4th May '83 Steve got 'a phone call from a dear departed friend at Polydor Records, the legendary Dennis Munday' who informed him that a band were after a Jazz influenced drummer. Upon arrival, Steve said, 'I was more over-awed with the fact it was Mick Talbot, one of my sort of heroes.' He was asked to appear on the first Radio 1 session and remained with The Style Council until 1987.

Dee C Lee (6th June 1961)

'6/6/61 - Yes 666, call for an exorcist' (Smash Hits)

Diane Katherine Sealy from Balham, South London will thank us when we say she was NOT a model. Dee hated getting tagged as an ex-model when she was simply modeling her hands (false nails) and feet (platform shoes) when she was 16. Dee then went through a feast of jobs - secretarial, bar maid and a telephone canvasser were just a few. She then went to the Far East with a group Body Heat to sing and dance over backing tracks influenced by 70's soul and pop music like The Jackson's, Osmonds and the Sweet. Her break into music was session work with the then unknown Wham and Animal Nightlife when she was 21. Dee's contribution to Wham was a number 1 album and two top three singles before joining TSC.

She told *Smash Hits* she was, 'very unsure of myself. People kept saying I had a good voice but I wasn't confident enough to push myself. I was a bit of a quivering wreck. But it was make or break time and I decided to make.'

On her first visit to Solid Bond Studios Dee saw gold discs on the wall and asked Paul who The Jam were, 'Some crap group who record here' he replied. (*Radio 1*)

Dee first appeared on *Money Go Round* and remained to the end. In between, she had a top 3 solo hit with *See The Day*. Paul said, 'She is great because she has character in her voice, she is not just a backing singer but actually adds something to the band. She's also a great performer as well.'

TRACIE YOUNG

At barely 17 I never expected for one moment that someone like Paul Weller would give me the time of day or encourage me in my ambitions. But, with hindsight, I understand more now than I ever did then, exactly what he tried to achieve with Respond Records and The Style Council. Possibly Paul himself believes much more could have been achieved with both if he had been older and wiser. The beauty is, he at least had the belief. His vision of a stable of young artists, working on projects diversely and together, was as inspired as Motown. I honestly believe that the idea would be better received now.

These days, teen chart stars are two a penny. Many have longevity and whilst they may not have credibility they do, at least, make a few quid. With The Style Council some prospered, some fell by the wayside and some used it as a platform to go on to other things. I like to think that we had a passion that is lacking now - a real sense of excitement and most importantly, not a desire to just "be famous" or rich.

For my part, I never once achieved what I hoped for, but the time I spent with The Style Council and Respond compounded my attitude to life. To this day, I still embrace opportunities not seen by others as the obvious or most lucrative route. I am persuaded by other people's passion for what they are striving to achieve and I find it infectious. Whatever the disappointments, I still believe that genuine passion makes anything worthwhile.

The "celeb culture" is an out of control animal now and, in that sense, Paul was way ahead of his time. The Style Council and Respond Records would be such a refreshing antidote today.

STEVE SIDELNYK

On a sunny day in 1983, I got a phone call from Tracie Young who was auditioning drummers for her band. I had actually applied for the job with Respond act A Craze but didn't get it. I thought it was a little funny that I got a call, but that single phone call changed my life! I went down to the audition in a rehearsal room and Paul Weller was there with Tracie so I proceeded to bash the living daylights out of a kit playing along to a cassette over a PA! I got the job! I thought I was a pretty good player, but I hadn't met Steve White by then! The time I spent playing with The Style Council after then was amazing - tours, Lacostes, the never ending search for White 501 Levis, Live Aid, The Old Grey Whistle Test, Red Wedge, Australia and Japan. Every show I played with TSC was a unique experience. I'm so proud that I was a part of the whole scene and in these days of homogenised pop music, it just emphasises just what a great band TSC were!

HELEN TURNER

Dennis Munday walked me the entire length of Oxford Street, from Polydor to Solid Bond at Marble Arch, where I auditioned, accompanied by my own rudimentary guitar, as a singer! Paul was deadpan, dead polite and asked me how my piano was. A few days later, I was in an office at Polydor with Dennis, Paul and Mick, (just) getting my digits round *Mick's Up*. I got the job, although I had to phone a few weeks later to check!

The final rehearsal was a dress rehearsal at Ezee Hire in North London and at the end the entire Respond rostra turned up. It was a bit overwhelming at the time, but friends were made, particularly as the whole thing went straight to Europe the next day. I'd say that a year from then, The Style Council were the best live band around and not a session player in sight!

ANTHONY HARTY

TSC gave me a career start that most young budding musicians could only dream of. Along with Steve White and Steve Sidelnyk, I was one of the youngest musicians at that level as we were all fresh just out of school. It was amazing that Paul gave some seriously young, inexperienced players the chance to play in his band. I got the gig by writing to Paul and within a couple of months I was playing with one of the biggest names in British music. It gave me a wealth of experience, whilst the group and surrounding people gave me excellent grounding in the industry - the ways to be and not to be!

I think the period I played with the band 1983 to 1985 was the era that typified The Style Council's sound and was their best period. Shame it didn't last any longer!

.

STEVE WHITE

A better, more informed book you will not find on The Style Council. Reading this put me right about times and dates. For myself I will keep it as an excellent reference to something I was really lucky to contribute too. Mick (Talbot) got a copy and was also impressed.

Hindsight is a beautiful thing and with this in mind I think we can safely say that the songs and spirit of the "Council" have matured to a fine legacy. *Mr Cool's Dream* is the definitive record of a great band, dedicated and put together with love, well done Iain.

KEVIN MILLER

I recently saw a website that claimed, "The Style Council, probably the best pop group in the world!" Not sure about that but looking back I do remember having this feeling at the time that there was just no other band around that came even slightly close in the coolness stakes, plus the musicianship wasn't bad either! I will never forget a gig at The Royal Festival Hall in 1984 in aid of the striking miners. TSC appeared on the same bill as Wham. We played live of course but they mimed. The headline in NME that week was "Mimer's Benefit!" Excellent! The days spent at Marble Arch drinking take-away cappuccinos and eating toasted peanut butter and banana sandwiches from the Italian coffee bar just up the Edgware Road were some of the happiest of my life. I was, and still am, immensely proud of having played a part, albeit very small, in the history of one of the UK's finest musical acts.

A VIEW FROM STAGE LEFT STEWART PROSSER

Mention The Style Council to people of a certain age and a nostalgic mist settles over them as they remember the songs and sounds of a band that, while standing out from the crowd, also managed to define life in the early nineteen-eighties.

I'm just the same. Standing back and remembering all of the excitement, creativity and relentless charging around in the few short years I was with the band has me reaching for my copy of *Our Favourite Shop* and I remember fondly the fun of playing in such a close-knit team of talented players.

Brass was an integral part of The Style Council's sound and from day one we were treated like band members, not session players, playing an active role in working out arrangements and taking solo spots. During those years, playing alongside saxophonist Billy Chapman from Animal Nightlife and Dexy's trombonist and friend Chris Lawrence was a great buzz. It felt good to be part of something that grew so fast. It seems as though one minute we were playing smallish clubs around Europe (I remember a particularly sweaty, adrenaline-soaked night in a tiny club in Berlin) and the next much larger venues in Japan and the USA, finally arriving at Wembley complete with a string section and celebrity special guests. A real evolution. My audition for the trumpet spot was held at Solid Bond Studios in Marble Arch. I had stayed up for a few nights beforehand playing along to every Jam track I could find and felt well prepared, so was quite surprised to be asked to improvise a solo over some blues chords that Mick put down while Paul listened intently; following up later with questions about who I listened to. Very relaxed, friendly and un-rock and roll. Later I came to realise that that approach characterised the attitude of the whole band.

From that moment on it was literally a life-changing experience. I had been in a stable day job playing every spare moment in bands at night to develop my abilities. So being plucked from that obscurity and sucked into the whirlwind of a major league tour in my early twenties was electrifying. I remember our first gig vividly. No gentle warm-up outing for us. Straight in with a live TV show on *Sight and Sound* in Concert for the BBC and to cap it all it would be the first time that I had played the flugelhorn solo I had written over Mick's fabulous *Le Depart*.

The walk across the darkened stage to the mic as Mick began those arpeggios on the piano was the longest of my life! To cap it all as I played the first note, the audience spontaneously burst into applause. A real spine-tingling moment that stays with me.

Looking back, it all seemed to go very fast and later, it felt like a natural step to leave to do other things after the final Wembley show in 1985, when the band was at its biggest physically. So I'm as nostalgic as anyone else and will always be grateful for the opportunity to have been part of something that was truly era defining.

DENNIS MUNDAY

THE NEW GOSPEL ACCORDING TO DENNIS

It is now 25 years since Paul pulled the plug on The Jam and formed The Style Council. History has now proved beyond doubt that it was the right decision. At the time, it was difficult for Jam fans to get their heads around Paul's decision, but there was only one way for The Jam to go! They had run their race and won convincingly, and are now held in the same esteem as the very bands that Paul idolised as a teenager. After the claustrophobic atmosphere of The Jam, the hedonism and the joie de vivre of the Council was just what the Doctor ordered, and to be taken in large doses and as often as possible.

With The Council, Paul took far more chances than he had previously with The Jam, mixing various styles of music, incorporating a hard political edge. Their support of the miners and the other contentious issues of the day, could have had a devastating effect on their careers. This never stopped them, they never wavered, or held back.

The funny thing is, the eighties are now fashionable (even here in Italy) and the Council are looked at in a more favourable light. The very people who stated that this part of his career was Paul's lost years, now speak far more flattering than they did all those years ago. No doubt, this is down to his enormous solo success and the fact that he has become an icon of the British music scene.

Whatever is said about The Style Council, there is no doubt in my mind that Paul's current solo success owes as much to the Council as it does The Jam, and at last the Council are getting the recognition they richly deserve. When he formed the Council, it gave him the opportunity to record what music he wanted, and with whom he wanted. During the first two years, the Council's output was phenomenal, different, and for me, an exciting time to be working with Paul.

The Council underwent a change after *Our Favourite Shop*, and the idea of the Council remaining a project band, was thrown out of the pram. This format worked successfully during the early period, with a mixture of artists coming and going, and it gave the Council's singles and albums variety. When they recorded *The Cost of Loving*, the group had a fixed line up (Paul, Dee, Mick and Whitey), they were hearkening back to a typical group sound, and with this album the Council lost their carefree spirit that permeated throughout the first two years. Even *Our Favourite Shop* with its explicit political overtones, still had a diversity of songs and line-ups.

I never understood the fuss that was made over the 'orange' album, after all it went to number 2 in the charts. It might not have hung around like *Our Favourite Shop*, or sold as many copies, but a number 2 album ain't that bad.

This album saw the crack in Paul's relationship with Polydor widen to a chasm. The next offering *Confessions Of A Pop Group* was, perhaps, a step too far, and too excessive. Having said that, the whole point of the Council, was to allow Paul to gratify himself in his excesses, something that, with perhaps the exception of Bob Dylan, David Bowie, Neil Young and Van Morrison, most artists have not been able to indulge themselves as Paul did during the Council years.

Looking back it was inevitable that Paul would leave Polydor as his relationship with them since the days of The Jam had been tenuous, to say the least. When he delivered *Modernism: A New Decade,* they were not ready for such a change of direction, although I am certain that the company dropping him from the label had more to do with having to pay him a huge advance, rather than the quality of the record.

I get pissed off when I read demeaning pieces on Mick, written by ill-informed pundits who have trashed his role in the Council. Mick bought a lot to the table and he certainly doesn't deserve this kind of criticism. Embittered Jam fans even accused him of being responsible for the break up of the band, which was absolute crap as Mick's part in this was no more than a walk on role. It wasn't just music Mick had in common with Paul, his tastes in clothes were similar. Mick was always subtly different, and he stamped his mark on what he was wearing, like the Embassy coupon in the band of his titfer.

Mick's contribution to the Council songbook has always been understated. His touches at times were uplifting, and he was responsible for many of the more subtle contributions to the tunes the Council recorded.

During the early days of Wham, it was said that Andrew Ridgeley was George Michael's crutch; this could not be said of Mick's role in the Council. Whilst his contribution may not have had the same weight as Paul's, it was nonetheless crucial and his 'organ' was one of the trademark sounds of the Council's songbook. In Mick, Paul found a genuine 'soul' brother, a person he could he relate to, not only musically, but also as a mate.

I recall Paul asking me to find a drummer to augment the duo, and he was forthright in what he wanted. They had to be talented, good-looking, and play all styles of music, particularly Jazz - a tall order to fill. Fortunately, I found Steve White who lived in Eltham, which was in the same neck of the woods where I had grown up in the sixties. Coincidentally, we attended the same school, Crown Woods comprehensive. On the phone he sounded incredibly young, but the more I spoke to him, the more he convinced me he had talent and the diversification to give Paul and Mick what they wanted. The audition took place, he became a Councillor at the tender age of 17 and the rest is history. Even at this young age one could see that he would develop into one of the best, if not the best drummer in the UK, and he has been one of the lynch pins of Paul's solo career.

Paul wrote many endearing songs during the Council's career that stand the test of time, and like good wine, they have improved with age. *The Whole Point Of No Return, A Stones Throw Away* and *It's A Very Deep Sea* are comparable to anything he wrote with The Jam.

The pinnacle of my association with the Council is undoubtedly the box set. I got a real thrill working on this, and I hope I did justice to the Council and their fans. Working with the Council I had some great times and acquired some good mates along the way. Their music, unlike the Olympic flame, will never go out.

Keep the flame burning.

Dennis

Dennis released *Shout To The Top* - his story on The Jam, The Style Council and beyond. Available on hardback and now an updated paperback.

THE CAPPUCCINO KID

The unfathomable Cappuccino Kid's sagacious chronicles adorned the sleeves of many releases and he rarely if ever appeared elsewhere. It was then to my surprise and excitement that he pronounced this publication meritorious enough to leave *The Diary of A Farm Hand* behind and voyage to the Tour De Eiffel for these concluding words ………

WHEN THE CLOCK CHIMES I SHALL BE GONE

Idling down one of life's little highways one crisp-autumn day, walking stick and blazer to hand, shoes loafered and crisp, buttoned down but spirit up, a white dove unexpectedly came and settled on my shoulder and asked in my ear the following question. 'What sir do you recall of those hot summer days with your great links, The Style Council, and what indeed became of that very fine ice cream combo?'

As the words slowly tumbled into my ear, their effect was to bring my whole being to a complete standstill as my mind switched on the film from and ran images from that joyous time which were so strong they took me back to my youth, a youth set to music of a wondrous, Council nature. The past suffused my body and I felt as if all of life's five pipe problems had suddenly been extinguished and I now existed in dreamland.

Ah, if such beauty could only hold but in truth I could not visit that land anymore for now I walked in a different manner, thought in different ways, dressed with new aims. To return in detail to that time right now would be to betray the promise of forward motion that all who know such things have made with each other.

I know only this.

That there on those vinyl works, collected in sound and made with love, are the creations that still thrive, still breathe, and are there for all new flowers to find, to discover seeds that they may fruitfully plant once more and thus again colour the world up in a manner fantastic.

To do so will be to know so and thus we go forth, truth by our side, the make up of beauty in and on our make-up, salvation painted in the rainbow rays that lie at the end of our roads.

THE CAPPUCCINO KID

To this day his identity remains a mystery. All Paul would say was, "I've been called The Cappuccino Kid but it's not me. It's a geezer we bump into around the café's and restaurants of the West End."

JOHN REED

is the author of *My Ever Changing Moods*, the best selling Paul Weller book. He exclusively looks at the now 20 year old misunderstood 'concept' album.

CONFESSIONS OF A POP GROUP

Paul Weller summed up where his career was heading in 1988 with the opening lyric to that year's Style Council album: "I'll keep on diving till I reach the ends/Dredging up the past to drive me round the bendz." Haunted by his past glories with The Jam, he was heading for rock bottom. *Confessions Of A Pop Group* proved to be the least successful album of Weller's career. His record label, Polydor, duly rejected a bizarre, house-flavoured follow-up LP and, within a year, The Style Council were no longer in session. Woking's most famous musical export found himself aged 30 with a wife and kid and no recording contract - and *Confessions of A Pop Group* proved to be his last album for four years.

The Jam had been a tough act to follow, of course. Their '60s-tinged, kitchen-sink punk-pop had won the hearts of a whole generation - many of whom had never forgiven Weller for splitting them at their commercial peak in 1982. Where The Jam offered an earnest, passionate, serious view of the world (and some great tunes to boot), The Style Council seemed hell-bent on confounding their audience via self-indulgent humour and an unhealthy obsession with... well, you name it: shoes, French cigarettes, jumpers, coffee, jazz. Jazz! It was hardly the stuff of Saturdays' Kids and yet The Style Council's hit rate between 1983 and 1987 (14 UK hit singles, to be precise) rivalled that of Duran Duran, Madonna and George Michael.

At first glance, *Confessions* was a bit off-putting. Each side had a subtitle, hinting that this might be a, whisper it, concept album. *Confessions Of A Pop Group*, confusingly, also lent its name to Side 2, with Side 1 carrying the strapline 'The Piano Paintings.' Indeed, each song was accompanied within the packaging by a specially commissioned illustration, presumably to complement the album's pseudo-classical bent. Was this some grandiose attempt at mixing high art and pop? The promotional angle for *Confessions* was baffling, too. A low-key launch for the LP consisted of a cheese and wine bash at a high-brow London art gallery. How odd.

The album was fan fared by the single, *Life At A Top People's Health Farm*. Weller described this oddity as an update of Bob Dylan's *Subterranean Homesick Blues*. True, the witty, punning lyrics name-dropped icons as diverse as Margaret Thatcher, The Archers and Leon Trotsky. But within this ramshackle mess, whining vocals were drowned by murky horns and crass drums. It barely scratched the Top 30.

Confessions stalled at No.15 on its release in June 1988 and dropped out the charts after just three weeks. Compare that with, say, their debut platter *Café Bleu* from 1984 (number 2, Top 40 for 9 months) or its chart-topping follow-up, 1985's *Our Favourite Shop*. Even *The Cost Of Loving* reached number 2.

TSC were no longer the commercially acceptable face of UK pop-soul, losing ground to Terence Trent D'Arby and Wet Wet Wet. Meanwhile, as Weller's star dimmed, another very English institution, Morrissey, hit paydirt with his first solo album, *Viva Hate*.

Despite these drawbacks, though, *Confessions Of A Pop Group* remains a high watermark in Weller's 30-year career. Ignore the clinical exterior. For The Style Council's look of total disinterest on the cover, blame Polydor for scrapping the original design which omitted (like its predecessor, "the orange album") an image of the trio. (Dee C. Lee was heavily pregnant, having married Paul a year earlier, and is tactically hidden behind a grand piano.) Now suspend disbelief for a second while the album's bassist Camille Hinds compares it with *Fulfillingness' First Finale*, the final instalment in Stevie Wonder's majestic trilogy of mid-'70s albums. "During this period," he says, "[Paul] was absorbing composers like Bacharach and Michelle Legrand, Dance was on the horizon and *Confessions* seemed like a semi-conclusion."

The Woking Wonder embarked on *Confessions* with grand ambitions, safely ensconced within his Solid Bond Studios. Like its predecessor, the album was self-produced and betrayed a debt to contemporary US R&B (from the work of million-selling producers Jimmy Jam & Terry Lewis to indie Funk like Osiris' *War On The Bullshit*). But the range of music on offer here, the sense of adventure, set it apart.

It's A Very Deep Sea was a beautiful, poignant lullaby, reminiscent of smile-era Beach Boys. Self-questioning lyrics also defined *The Story Of Someone's Shoe*, setting this tale of one-night stands to the soothing if impersonal harmonies of the Swingle Singers, with a polite nod to MJQ. *Changing Of The Guard* was more specific: a paean to Paul's former long-term girlfriend and *The Gardener Of Eden (A Three Piece Suite)* was a serene, 10-minute-plus composition split into three parts: a cinematic mix of moody, quasi-classical piano interludes (think state school Michael Nyman) between intelligent lyrics which cast a weary eye over the world's ecological ravages.

Side 2 was more upbeat, from the sunny *Why I Went Missing* to jaunty summer single *How She Threw It All Away*. But the spine of the album was provided by the closing nine-minute funk workout. Unlike The Style Council's earlier stabs at white-boy funk, this reinvented Funkadelic's anthemic *One Nation Under A Groove*, but with the latter's unifying optimism replaced by a cynical, hard-bitten outlook in the wake of another Tory victory. Think of their 1983 hit, *Money-Go-Round*, only made by grown-ups.

Looking back now, *Confessions* seems to capture the period perfectly. As the country entered a major recession, and a year on from the failed Red Wedge initiative, Weller painted a vivid picture of a bleak, hopeless world, his previous idealism replaced by pessimism and personal regrets of hollow one-night stands, of fraught relationships and feelings of guilt and shame. Coinciding with the death of political idealism in pop, this was arguably Weller at his most honest and, yes, soulful.

During the sessions, relations between artist and label soured. Rumours abounded that Weller had delivered the finished record on a cassette with a defiled mugshot of Polydor's A&R chief attached.

Within a year, The Style Council had disbanded, and Weller – although re-energised by the nascent garage/house scene - had been unceremoniously dumped by the label.

Confessions of A Pop Group might just be the most misunderstood album in recent pop history. It's tempting to draw parallels with Dexy's *Don't Stand Me Down*. Its potent mix of musical ambition and soul-searching proved too unsettling. Weller's self-doubt soon spread to a wider lack of confidence in his ability to make music. The man was in crisis. Of course, Weller eventually picked up his guitar again as a solo artist and was re-born, creatively and commercially, in the '90s. And yet *Confessions Of A Pop Group* towers over even solo pinnacles like *Stanley Road*.

Paul Weller's previous confidante, Paolo Hewitt, describes *Confessions* as "Paul's attempt to forge a space that all serious musicians crave: complete musical freedom, not answering to anyone. It's the strangest record Weller ever involved himself in". Maybe TSC's time was up. As Weller later remarked, "We could have made the best record ever and no one would have noticed."

CONFESSIONS OF A POP GROUP

It's A Very Deep Sea *****

The Story Of Someone's Shoe ****

Changing Of The Guard ****

The Little Boy In A Castle **

The Gardener Of Eden (A Three Piece Suite) ***

Life At A Top People's Health Farm **

Why I Went Missing ****

How She Threw It All Away *****

Iwasadoledadstoyboy **

Confessions 1, 2 & 3 ***

Confessions of a Pop Group *****

Score: 39/55 (Rated: 71%)

© John Reed, 2008

John is the author of the best selling *Paul Weller: My Ever Changing Moods.*

THE COMPLETE HISTORY OF
THE STYLE COUNCIL

1983 - 1989

A WHOLEPOINT PUBLICATION

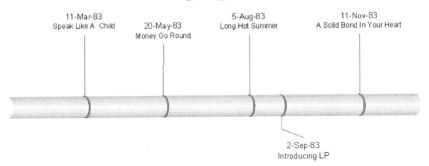

1983

11-Mar-83
Speak Like A Child

20-May-83
Money Go Round

5-Aug-83
Long Hot Summer

11-Nov-83
A Solid Bond In Your Heart

2-Sep-83
Introducing LP

"It was like the first day of Spring to me"

Behind the scenes in 1982

Despite what the record books say, The Style Council were actually formed in the Summer of 1982. Paul Weller had returned from a head churning holiday in Sorrento, Italy where he had made up his mind to break up The Jam, a band truly at their peak. He secretly met with Mick Talbot, formerly of the Merton Parkas, to tell him about his shock decision and future ideas.

'When I first started talking about doing the collective with Mick I got this great big box of records and gave them to him to go away and listen to. I said, 'you'll see what I am looking to do from these.' There were old soul and R&B albums in there and a bit of jazz too. It was a musical reference for him.' (Paul, official website)

Mick confirmed he was definitely interested but he had to keep this front page news to himself for fear of jeopardising his own big chance of stardom and success. From this they would secretly be working on songs, *Speak Like A Child* and *A Solid Bond In Your Heart.*

The next phase in Paul's plan was taking the unusual step of putting an advert in *Smash Hits* seeking a young female singer. Despite receiving 'hundreds' of tapes he was a bit disappointed that there weren't many more.

One of these hopefuls was 17 year old Tracie Young, currently working in Customs and Excise in Hereford. Tracie's contribution was a bedroom recording of her singing *Shoorah Shoorah* by Betty Wright into a cassette deck. A few days later Tracie got a phone call from Paul's girlfriend Gill Price to come to an audition in London. At the audition she sang *Band of Gold* and *Reach Out,* impressing enough to get the job.

'The first tape Paul ever gave me was for *A Solid Bond In Your Heart*. It was meant to be a Jam single and Paul wanted me to sing on it, to ensure me a little exposure, prior to doing anything solo. However, the next thing I knew The Jam were splitting up, *Beat Surrender* was now going to be the next (and last) single and then it was on to *Speak Like A Child*.'

Tracie made an appearance on the last Jam single *Beat Surrender*. 'Paul was very into using all opportunities to gain me exposure. The reason I was asked to sing on *Beat Surrender* was to get me seen!'

Record Mirror confirmed Paul was now a 'solo artist, signed to Polydor' but said he 'refuses to reveal any more details.' Paul allegedly accepted a £250,000 contract, the 3 year deal being for 3 singles and 1 album per year.

JANUARY 1983

'It was like the 1st day of Spring to me, like having a fresh canvas and starting again. The first 3 years were amazing, we made some great records that stand the test of time.' (Paul, *Into Tomorrow*)

After the hugely publicised break up of The Jam (see *A Beat Concerto* by Paolo Hewitt), 24 year old Paul Weller, having already decided on his next move, started to drip feed out information. Though it wasn't him who 'leaked out' a secret forthcoming appearance with the up and coming Everything But The Girl (EBTG) to a London journalist.

5th - Only 25 days had elapsed since The Jam's final gig when Paul appeared live alongside EBTG at the ICA Rock Week in London. As word of Paul's appearance had leaked out through the *London Standard* ticket touts were now shifting the £3 briefs for £10, with *Record Mirror* saying, 'the world and his brother wanted to be there.' It would be a year before EBTG would enter the charts and they welcomed the publicity that Paul would bring.

EBTG were 2nd on stage after Wah Wah Heat and before the headliner King. Paul sporting polka dot shirt, grey trousers and white socks sang on Astrud Gilberto's 1964 *The Girl From Ipanema* and Peggy Lee's *Fever*. He then played guitar on his Jam track *English Rose* and on Cole Porter's *Night and Day*. Paul told Jim Reid from *Record Mirror* it was 'something different to do. It was a good laugh. I really enjoyed it.'

10th – The company Stylist Music Limited, Clay Street, London is incorporated on this day. This was Paul's company and everything he wrote went down as Stylist Music Limited. He also invested in a recording studio in the heart of London, just around the corner from his flat. This was at Stanhope House, the old Phillips Studio building in Stanhope Place, near Marble Arch, which he bought for an estimated £200,000. He had previously produced a single for Apocalypse in 1982 at the studio and subsequently said it was always 'a dream' to own one. Dusty Springfield and The Walker Brothers had previously recorded there.

According to Dennis Munday in his *Shout To The Top* book the band were nearly named The Torch Society. However, it was The Style Council (TSC) who would reside at the studios, now named Solid Bond Studios.

Tracie Young described the studio as 'a second home, it was the nerve centre of everything. Offices, studio, it was all there, and parties too! From the fans perspective, I suppose it was their place of worship, though it's hard to see that when you're in it.'

Paul was still actively promoting Tracie for his own *Respond* label when he revealed that Mick Talbot would be his partner in crime with his new band. The Style Council would only consist of two concrete band members, 'not having a fixed line up will keep The Style Council fresh and always sounding new and different.'

'I needed someone to work off and Mick was the perfect person for that but I wanted to keep it open outside of that.' (Paul, official website)

On this day the first track was recorded - *Speak Like A Child*, the title influenced by Herbie Hancock, who had an album of the same name originally released on Blue Note in 1968.

Anyone who assisted TSC was labelled an Honorary Councillor. The track featured Tracie Young on vocals who would have a top 10 this month with *The House That Jack Built*. Also appearing was Zimbabwean born drummer Zeke Manyika (b.23/05/55) who was currently at number 8 in the charts with Polydor's Orange Juice on *Rip It Up*. Later he would play on The The's *Soul Mining* LP where he met bassist Camelle Hinds, himself shortly to be an honorary member of The Style Council.

Zeke had been playing the Glasgow live circuit with Route 66 before he joined Bob Cameron and Gary Anderson in The Zeros. Bob recalls, 'He came along to a practice session or two and then we had a gig at the *Burn's Howff* which he played at. Zeke seemed very focussed on making music his career, whilst some of us had day jobs that we would only give up if we 'made it' and Mr EMI came knocking. It was all very fluid in those days and firm commitments weren't seen as de-rigeur. Zeke had other bands on the go and went on to play with them and has done great things thereafter.'

13th - *Party Chambers* (vocal) and *A Solid Bond In Your Heart* are recorded at the studio. Within three days 2 tracks, both future singles, had been recorded. They would surprisingly be released 8 months apart.

Music press rumours indicated that Paul would debut with The Jam's *A Solid Bond In Your Heart* though all Paul would confirm on Radio 1 is that it was a straight choice between 2 tracks - *Speak Like A Child* or *A Solid Bond In Your Heart*. In the end, he decided to use the former in an attempt to try something new, different and outside the constraints of The Jam.

20th - *Headstart For Happiness* is recorded at Solid Bond Studios and would be used on the b-side of a future single.

Smash Hits had ran an article about the possibility of Paul playing live at the Drill Hall, London, in a gig which he had arranged for tonight. Sets from Bananarama alongside Tracie and The Questions reportedly did not go down well with the crowd. Bananarama may have had four top 5 hits by this time but a good percentage of the crowd were hoping Paul would put in an appearance, just like he did earlier with Everything But The Girl. Paul though never had any intention of playing.

I spoke to Gary Crowley in May 2008 and the 'Drill Hall' event cropped up, 'Those memories of the early days were great. I was talking to Paul recently and I can remember that when the band formed, he organised those, almost like under 18's discos in London! I had just joined Capital Radio at the time and there was one that we did at the Drill Hall in Covent Garden. The Questions played and Bananarama did something and it was a really, really young crowd. It wasn't just guys, there were a lot of girls there and it was a really, really lovely vibe. I thought those kind of early shows and those sort of things I don't suppose he would have been able to have done with The Jam because they were so big. It was almost like starting again really.'

FEBRUARY

It was the industry standard that you worked 6 weeks back from release date of the next single so promotional photographs were required - a trip to Boulogne, North France, was quickly arranged. Making the ferry trip from Dover to Calais and beyond with Paul and Mick would be Paolo Hewitt and photographer Peter Anderson from the *NME* who would for many years take the majority of the official photographs. Peter went on to work with Madonna, Iggy Pop and Tom Waits.

The *Speak Like A Child* promotional video was filmed on the Malvern Hills in Worcestershire, roughly 140 miles from London. Tim Pope (b.12/02/56) was the director - in 2008 he is still doing this work - recently with KT Tunstall, The Kaiser Chiefs and Fatboy Slim. Tim had decided a 5am start was required to capture the sun rising, so TSC, Tracie, Nicky Weller and a few friends stayed overnight in Great Malvern, spending the £15,000 allocated budget on the hotel, the open top Routemaster London bus and a rocking chair.

By the end of the month the next single *Money Go Round* had been recorded. 'We did the backing track first with me, Mick and Zeke just jamming between takes. This Jam lasted around 10 minutes. From there I retained the best bits and put them into versus, edited the words to fit the sequence and then arranged the sequences into patterns. Then you have a song.'

During Paul and Mick's coffee trips to Linda's Café round the corner from the studio they sometimes met George Michael from Wham, a relatively unknown singer and band at this time. From these meetings session singer Dee C Lee was discussed as Dee was currently singing with Wham and Animal Nightlife who were both on the Innervision label.

She appeared on *Love Is The Great Pretender* and *Native Boy* with Animal Nightlife before concentrating on Wham who were set to become one, if not the biggest pop band of the 80's.

'Paul rang me out of the blue. He called me at my mothers house, needed a soulful singer.' (Dee, *Into Tomorrow*)

MARCH

1st - Live interview with Richard Skinner on Radio 1 to explain what TSC and Respond Records was all about, 'the time was right to get something different going, something more youth orientated.' Paul also announced the forthcoming Brockwell Park charity event in May.

The photographs from the Boulogne trip appear in an advert for *Speak Like A Child,* the debut single. The main focus is a picture of Paul and Mick next to a wall spray painted, 'Yank Bases out.' Beside this in very small writing, 'whose continent is this? Ours or the USA?' Then 'a new record by new Europeans' translated into 6 languages. This was the first indication of TSC's soon to become obsession with Europe and its culture.

7th - Paul and Tracie appear on the Timmy Mallet show, Piccadilly Radio, Manchester, talking about their respective projects and of when Paul discovered Tracie in the street, 'Hey your just the chick I've been looking for!' This was not exactly true as it was common knowledge that Tracie sent in a tape in response to an advert in *Smash Hits*. Paul also slates the current British pop scene;

PW: 'I hate all the wimp, pop music we get over here, like Duran Duran and all these creeps.'
TM: 'Kajagoogo?'
PW: 'Same Thing'
TM: 'Eddie Grant?'
PW: 'No he's useless, though quite a good songwriter.'
TM: 'Australian bands, like Men At Work?'
PW: 'No, crap, all of them, I don't like any of them.'
TM: 'Well is there anything currently out in Britain which you like?'
PW: 'Oh, yeah! Culture Club are great, George has got a brilliant voice. Fun Boy Three are brilliant.'
TM: 'Favourite record in the chart at the moment?'
PW: 'Orange Juice with *Rip It Up*, the 12" version especially.'

Paul was not impressed with the pop world which he was trying to distance himself from, 'I think their behaviour and attitude just stink.' Though later he would say that Kool and the Gang are 'brilliant' and Animal Nightlife were 'really under-rated.'

Listeners are encouraged to send tapes to Respond but Paul issues a warning and an early indication that the guitar was out of favour. 'If it's Rock music don't bother, I just can't take those blaring guitars anymore. We have had 20 years of Rock rebellion, it's got us nowhere. We'd better sit down and start again.'

11th - The debut release *Speak Like A Child*, c/w *Party Chambers* (produced by Peter Wilson and Paul Weller) was labelled as a 'raunchy Stax sound-alike.' The big surprises were the lack of a 12" single (the norm to increase sales) and the fact there was neither mention of the song title *nor* a picture of the band on the sleeve. Just a black glossy cover with The Style Council logo.

Peter Wilson was Polydor's resident sound engineer at their studio at Stratford Place but would now be spending more time at Solid Bond over the coming years with Paul, Mick and the Respond artists.

'I thought *Speak Like A Child* was a great first single, I have some good first memories of The Style Council.' (Gary Crowley)

The sleeve introduces us to the 'Keeps on Burning' logo and the mysterious, secretive and anonymous Cappuccino Kid. He would appear throughout the bands career, 'sometimes amusing, sometimes impenetrable, often pretentious.'

'A true sparkle that will not be extinguished.' (Cappuccino Kid)

12th - Fan club information is announced requesting you to send a stamped addressed envelope for details to Sinclair Road, London. The reply offered a membership card, photos, magazine and exclusives in return for a yearly fee.

18th - Trip to BBC Manchester studios for the television debut of *Headstart For Happiness*, performed live on *Oxford Road Show* by Paul and Mick. 'We kind of fit into the electric pop duo thing, we line ourselves with the likes of Blamange, Tears For Fears, that sort of thing, that's why we wear make up.' (Paul)

20th - *Speak Like A Child* enters the chart and would peak at number 4, staying in the top 100 for 8 weeks selling over 350,000 copies and earning Tracie a silver disc from Polydor. Tracie kept this until 2007 when she kindly auctioned it as part of a charity function at the 100 Club, London. On the night she performed *Speak Like A Child* for the 1st time in 24 years.

25th - 5 foot 5 inch Tracie Young is 18 today. Born in 1965 in Derby, she lived in Chelmsford, Essex. Her favourite bands at the time were Squeeze and Spandau Ballet. The celebrations would need to wait though as TSC travel 15 miles to the Hillside Studios in Bushey. This was for Channel 4's music show *The Switch*. Stomping versions of *Speak Like A Child* and *A Solid Bond In Your Heart* were performed live. Paul didn't pick up the guitar for the former featuring Tracie on backing vocals. Chris Hunter joined the line up on Saxophone for the only time that we would hear a proper live version of *A Solid Bond In Your Heart* in the UK.

I caught up with Chris in July 2008, 'I don't remember that much about the Solid Bond Studios recording of *A Solid Bond In Your Heart*, although I somehow think Dennis Munday may have called me for it. I did a lot of recordings in that period but it all came via word of mouth, there was never any kind of agent involved. I also played with Paul on a short lived TV show *The Switch* which was a lot of fun. I currently live in NYC and have been pursuing a life in Jazz pretty much exclusively since that time.'

27th - Tracie's *The House That Jack Built* enters the chart and makes it into the top 10, a glowing early success for her hard work and for Respond as a label. The press release said, 'from the land of a thousand young hopefuls, from the influence of soul to the essence of pop, Respond Records ask you to try Tracie then decide.'

In 2008 this song is available on the UK wide pub touch screen jukeboxes, though Tracie told me she doesn't receive any royalties for it. Campaign girl, campaign!

31st - TSC debut on the BBC music show *Top of The Pops* with *Speak Like A Child*. It's interesting to note that a different version to the single was performed, and it was not sung live. Very poor miming as Paul stood near the back of the stage, Tracie a little closer to the front beside Mick. Tracie told Wholepoint of her fond memories of this day;

'This is one of those very funny memories that you retain better than others. Back then you still had to re-record tracks for *Top of The Pops* so we re-recorded *Speak Like A Child* at Nomis Studios, near Olympia in Sinclair Road, London. (This was the main postal address for all to do with TSC). Paul booked out a studio at Nomis early in the morning to rehearse the performance because it was the first time that he, Mick, and myself would do it publicly. Well, Paul thought it was really funny to encourage me to dance as wildly as possible. You noticed that I was at the front. The idea was that I would go for it and make a complete tit of myself, while he stood behind me, laughing at me. At Nomis Studios, he was getting me to do this little dance (nothing complicated, neither he or I are natural dancers) and swearing he would do it on *Top of The Pops*. I'm not a very trusting soul. I knew he was trying to set me up. So I went along with it, but when we had to do the actual taped performance, I was well aware that he'd bottle out.

At *Top of The Pops* I started off sat on Mick's organ and early in the song, I was supposed to jump down, position myself in front of Paul and we would start this gyrating in perfect sync. If you watch the tape, you can actually see him looking at me and smirking because at one point, I look like I'm going to get into it, but I knew he wouldn't so I held back. My mentor, my leader! I still, to this day, don't know if he would have done it if I had. I just knew that he wasn't going to do anything unless I started it and I didn't trust him.'

APRIL

The band head to Europe for a short TV promotional tour for *Speak Like A Child.*

First up was a memorable performance on Suburbia Hotel, Amsterdam with live vocals and backing tapes. It starts with Paul, Mick and Tracie under the covers in bed before getting up to sing and dance on top of the bed. Paul's mum Ann brought in the tea and bass player Claudia Konijin was found playing bass in the wardrobe as Paul in-between singing, couldn't stop laughing. Strange but true! Look for this memorable show on *You Tube.*

The second show in comparison was a tame affair in a TV studio in Belgium again with Claudia on bass. However, that was it with her and she was never seen nor heard from again.

The first quarterly fan club magazine *The Style Population* (TSP) is released, always a very interesting and informative read. Paul's sister Nicky would run the fan club with mum Ann assisting. The magazines were criticised for featuring Respond artists but to be fair Paul, Mick and Steve always contributed an article and there were some excellent photos included. TSP would continue for 17 issues until 1987 and as a set is very collectable to this day. Nicky estimated to me that there were around 7,000 members of The Torch Society.

9th - Tracie makes the cover of *NME*. 'Tracie: The girl star Paul Weller would build.'

15th - *Harvest For The World* was performed on *Three of A Kind*, a music show featuring 3 presenters (hence the name); Tracey Ullman, Lenny Henry and David Copperfield. This initial meeting with Lenny Henry planted the seed for further work in 1984 & 1985.

On *Harvest For The World* Paul played bongos, Mick the keyboard with Tracie and The Questions on stage. Tracie told me, 'from a personal viewpoint, not one of my better performances. I remember we only had a short time to put the track down in the studio, and although I was dissatisfied with my vocal, there wasn't time to redo it. That string vest! Why didn't I just stand still! Good song though.'

This was not performed live and a recording was put onto tape. This is the only time *Harvest For The World* was heard and it has never been released in any shape or form. Dennis Munday told me around the time of the box set that it does exist in the vaults but Paul did not want to include it.

The vault for Polydor is at the Eisenhower Centre on Goodge Street – a former World War II underground bunker with an amazing array of tunnels. It was originally equipped with 8,000 bunk beds but now houses companies video and tape archives. Paul's own archives are stored in Boreham Wood, at a wild guess the BBC Elstree Studios? Dennis Munday in his *Shout To The Top book* said, 'Paul never gave me access to his personal collection of tapes, which he has stashed away in a cupboard.' Cupboard!

Paul - If you ever want to hunt out some unreleased TSC demos and gems for a future project then you know where to find a volunteer.

16th - Paul, Mick, Tracie and The Questions model clothes from C&A and Top Man in a *Record Mirror* fashion special.

Gary Crowley who met Paul back in 1977 via his Punk fanzine commented that TSC were 'an outlet for Paul's love of clothes, films, literature, political views and 60s fashion.' Gary, at only 19 had his own radio show, *The Magic Box,* on London's *Capital Radio* on a Saturday night. He also had a residency at Bogarts in South Harrow at the *Wag Club* on a Friday. 'The British jazz funk thing was kicking off and it was wicked.'

21st - The Respond Posse are on tour until 22nd May before joining TSC on 25th for a major event. The Posse in question are A Craze, Main T Posse and Tracie Young.

24th - The Questions *Price You Pay* enters the chart and peaks at number 56.

MAY

The first outdoor live Style Council shows would take place this month.

1st - The make-shift 'band' travel to the Liverpool Empire Theatre for an event organised by the Campaign for Nuclear Disarmament (CND) in aid of the Merseyside Unemployment Centre and Liverpool 8 Law Centre. The forthcoming single *Money Go Round* was played alongside *Speak Like A Child*. Paul informed the audience that he was using backing tapes for the songs - only live vocals and keyboards were used. A live recording exists of this historic event.

Joining Paul and Mick were Albaie Johnson and Breeze James (vocals); Jo Dworniak (bass); Pete (drums); Ted (Sax); Paul Taylor (Trombone) and Spegos (Percussion).

4th – Dennis Munday was previously asked by Paul to find and arrange an audition for a jazz influenced drummer. He found 17 year old Steve White who agreed to audition at Nomis Studios on Sinclair Road. Also in the building when Steve arrived were Spandau Ballet, Culture Club, A-Ha and Duran Duran. Unknown to Steve, TSC had since had another drummer in mind so weren't too keen to hear him - when told this Steve insisted on being heard as he had travelled there especially. As it was his enthusiasm and ability won TSC over and Steve was asked to return to London tomorrow for the bands debut *Radio 1* session.

5th - A trip to the famous Maida Vale 4 BBC studios to record the first *Radio 1* session. Steve White joined TSC and was the only change to the May line-up replacing Pete. The four tracks performed live were *Mick's Up, Here's One That Got Away, Headstart For Happiness* and *The Paris Match.*

This confirms *The Paris Match* may have been recorded to tape in Paris, but it was written and performed in the UK long before the trip across the English Channel in June. It was also the first airing of the new b-sides from the forthcoming single as *Speak Like A Child* and *Money Go Round* were left out.

7th - Another free festival, this time at Brockwell Park, London for unemployment and Youth CND. Also appearing were Madness, Hazel O'Connor, The Damned, the late great John Peel and Paolo Hewitt who along with John would DJ between acts. The official 24 page festival programme was actually issue 11 of the CND magazine *Second Generation*. In it Paul spoke about *Money Go Round's* lyrics, 'They are not only about the nuclear arms race but about Capitalism as a whole.'

The 2 track set did not go down well, Paul calling it, 'disastrous.' *Speak Like A Child* and *Money Go Round* were played as thousands threw mud balls and beer cans. There were also problems with security back-stage and Paul was heckled by drunken teenage fans. He said the appearance was not intended to be a Style Council concert, 'We just wanted to show our support and try and bring attention to both issues.' This was broadcasted on radio so a quality recording exists.

10th - The BBC session recorded 5 days ago is played on the David Jensen show along with a session from The Questions.

15th - Dee C Lee gets to number 2 in the charts singing backing vocals on Wham's *Bad Boys*. She would not be on the forthcoming trip to Paris to record the French EP due to her current commitments to Wham. Their *Fantastic* LP was due out in July after the top 3 success of *Young Guns (Go For It)* in October 1982 and *Wham Rap* in January 1983. Dee though would soon leave Wham as she said they weren't interested in her voice - it was apparently mixed right down. 'It was nice when I was with them, but one has to move on.'

17th - Another appearance on The David Jensen show, Radio 1, this time to answer questions sent in from listeners. Most concerned Paul and the disbanding of The Jam.

20th - Another trip to Hillside Studios, Bushey for a superb 7 minute live *Money Go Round* on what was becoming The Style Council's own TV show *The Switch*. Live vocals and keyboards along with backing tapes identical to the recent outdoor festival performances. Dee C Lee made her TV debut with TSC.

21st - A newspaper advert appears for *Money Go Round*. Again we are furnished with French. 'Money vous amisdu continent immuables et exaltants! Penchez vous en avant ce la na vous feras pas mal pic mic.'

Translated, 'Friends of/from the unchanging and exhilarating continent, Lean forward, it won't hurt.' (thanks John Adamson)

20th - A few weeks before the UK General Election the second single *Money Go Round* (Parts 1 and 2) is released. There was no suitable 7" recording of the song so side-a was named 'part 1' and the music faded at a suitable point to meet official chart single length requirements.

The 7" included a double sided photo insert. There would be a 12" this time round with 2 bonus tracks, the classic *Headstart For Happiness* and Mr Talbot's first instrumental *Mick's Up*.

Zeke was retained on drums but Dee C Lee replaced Tracie on vocals, and Spegos (Percussion), Jo Dworniak (Bass), Annie Whitehead (Trombone) and Guy Barker (Trumpet) were added. Produced and arranged by Peter Wilson, co-produced by Paul Weller. The Royalties were donated to Youth Campaign for Nuclear Disarmament (YCND).

'The music fits the words because its got an aggressive heavy feel to it. It is based on the "merry-go-round" and the way money circulates in the same way.' (Paul)

An interesting 12" Dance Mix (7:50) of *Money Go Round* was released in Holland and Australia. This mix appeared on the UK 12" promotional copies. The sleeve is similar to the UK 12" bar the 'special 4 track EP with extra dance mix of *Money Go Round*' written on the front. In addition a 3 track 10" acetate was pressed by Tape One Studio's and named *Headstart For Happiness* as the main track.

25th - Paul's 25th Birthday ended in the 'Respond Package' night at The Paris Theatre, London. A Craze, Main T Posse and Tracie all appeared before TSC got on stage; 'Happy Birthday' the crowd sang to Paul, 'Thank you, I'm very touched by that' cried he before kicking off a 4 track acoustic set of *Headstart For Happiness*, *Here's One That Got Away*, *The Paris Match* and *Times Are Tight*. The Questions then closed the show. This was Steve White's first live gig with the band.

Times Are Tight has never been released and this was the only time it was performed. It is a cover of Jimmy Young's version released in April on Nitelife Records (Life 2). Jimmy was a disco/soul/R&B singer, born and raised in Mount Vernon, New York and this was his 1st top 20 dance hit single in the UK.

29th - *Money Go Round* enters the chart and would peak at number 11, staying in the top 100 for 7 weeks.

Susanna York gets in touch with the band about making an appearance at a concert for peace, planned for 18th December, initially titled 'The Big One.' TSC accept and would fit their UK tour around this date.

JUNE

2nd - An appearance on *Top of the Pops* to celebrate *Money Go Round* reaching number 11 on the chart. Paul (again minus the guitar), Mick and Dee mimed to the single.

9th - General Election day in the UK and time for the Councillor's on the back of the politically tinged *Money Go Round* to cast their vote.

However, by the end of the night news was not good as the Conservatives commanded 397 seats (+58) against Labour's 209 (-59). I guess Paul knew the outcome long before judgment day when he wrote the singles lyrics, 'It means the same old people stay in command.'

Paul said when discussing *Money Go Round*, 'The UK'ers made the wrong one by voting Thatcher back in, that's the reason for this.'

10th - No doubt the Election was discussed on the drive to Hillside Studios, Bushey to perform *Headstart For Happiness* live on *The Switch*. For the first time this song would have Dee C Lee on vocals.

11th - The 'Respond Package' concert from 25th May was broadcast on Radio 1. The BBC still have this show in their vaults.

12th to 16th - Paul knew he had to write a classic to firmly establish his new band as a force to be reckoned with. That inspiration came during a five day visit to the impressive 4 studio Grande Armèe studios in Palais des Congrès, Paris.

Long Hot Summer, The Paris Match, Lè Depart and a revamped *Party Chambers* were recorded, 'because we felt they all had a similar blue mood and a certain French flavour about them. All the songs are romantic and why not? We all need a bit of love now and again, but they are meant as mood sounds.'

Paul told *Watch* magazine that *The Paris Match* was, 'about a brief affair I had at the time and that thing where you want to be together but you cannot.'

A lengthy photo session took place, again in France, to guarantee the Parisian pair's appearance in every pop and teenage magazine throughout the summer months. There are 2 memorable photos from this trip. The 1st appeared on the Japanese *Introducing* mini LP, Paul & Mick in the poppy field. The 2nd was the long admired photo of Paul's shoe with the Eiffel Tower in the background.

TSC spend the remainder of June on holiday, Paul in Capri, Italy and Mick in Crete, Greece. The band then prepared for their biggest hit to date, the *à Paris* EP by shooting the promotional video on the River Cam in Cambridge.

'Everything in the video is done in a really suggestive way. The pole Mick uses for punting is used as a phallic symbol, and there's a shot of us lying down on the grass caressing each others ears. It was just a laugh, but now apparently there's going to be a cut and an uncut version of the video. I think that's ridiculous, because we didn't have any girls in it. If people get upset by me and Mick stroking each others ears what is the pop world coming to?'

The 'uncut' *Long Hot Summer* video appeared on UK TV once, *Summer-run,* before being banned, and replaced by the 'cut' version. Every official TSC video compilation has used the cut version, against the bands wishes. The uncut version sneaked out on the limited promo 6 track video in 1984 and then you had to wait 20 years for *The Style Council on Film* DVD compilation.

Around this time Paul met the 'virtually unknown' Bert Bevans. However, the history books tell us that Bert is now, 'the New York house DJ most famed for helping set up London's *Ministry of Sound* and who would became one of the forefathers of dance music.'

His job with The Style Council in 1983 was to create club mixes of *Money Go Round* and *Long Hot Summer*. I caught up with Bert in the Summer of 2008;

Q. How did you first get involved with The Style Council?
'I heard Paul had left The Jam to form The Style Council. I asked his record company for the address of his studio and I went there too meet him. I asked Paul if I could remix *Long Hot Summer* and he said yes. He had heard the mix I did of *Lies* by the Thompson Twins and liked it.' This mix had spent 2 weeks at Number 1 on the American dance chart.

Q. What was your background before then?
'I grew up in New York. I was a DJ in New York, Bonds, Pippins, Playboy Club and Studio 54. I moved to London and worked in Xenon's, Embassy & Camden Palace.'

Q. Do you recall the 12" mixes for *Long Hot Summer*, and *Money Go Round*?
'Of course. I really liked The Style Council so for me it was an honour. Music in the UK was exciting and being played all over the world.'

Q. Did you make major changes to the originals?
'Yes, loads. I got this rapper Dizzy Heights to write/do a rap on it, he later released a tribute to it called *The Gospel*. I also got Camelle Hinds from Central Line to do Bass and Steve White did some more percussion.'

Q. How much freedom were you given by Paul?
'He gave me complete freedom, the use of his studio and engineers. If he didn't like it he wouldn't release it.'

Q. Is there anything else you mixed that has yet to see release?
'No, but I think it's time we put new mixes out of *Money Go Round* & *Long Hot Summer*!'

30th - Tracie and the Main T Posse play at Dingwalls, London watched by Paul and Mick.

JULY

10th - Dee gets to number 1 in the album charts when Wham's *Fantastic* enters the chart. It would stay in the chart for an incredible 2 years, 12 weeks!

Mick agrees to assist on Respond artists A Craze's new single *Wearing Your Jumper*.

Paul was actively involved in Respond as he produced, wrote, played guitar and designed the record sleeves for many releases. In addition Steve White was assisting The Questions on *Someone's Got To Lose* then playing percussion on their LP, *Belief*.

15th - Paul drops a bombshell on the new LP, 'We were gonna put one out this year but after looking at the schedules it would have been a rush so I decided to leave it. The LP has to be right. I think we'll put it out in the New Year. January or February.' He talks about putting out a double LP, the 2nd vinyl being a cover versions album.

16th - Tracie makes her debut on the front cover of *Record Mirror*.

17th - Tracie's *Give It Some Emotion* makes it to number 24.

21st - Tracie appears on *Top of the Pops*. She cringes looking back, 'I was wearing a pair of very tight pink jeans with a very visible knicker line. That alone was bad enough but the production team then decided that the dancers should work with me. To this day, I'm still amazed at what I let myself get talked in to. Flick Colby decided she wanted two male dancers to writhe with me and I would give my right arm to go back in time and erase that moment forever. I wasn't happy about it, I can't dance and didn't want to be involved in any kind of routine, but I was intimidated very easily. It was one of my worst TV moments ever.'

Dee sings on the *Native Boy* single for Animal Nightlife, reaching number 60 in the charts. She also appears with them on lives dates and on *The* Switch.

AUGUST

4th - Tracie makes another appearance on *Top of the Pops*. 'That wasn't so bad. I remember Dave Lee Travis was presenting and kept pretending to 'flash' at me while I was doing the song. I also remember being very embarrassed while standing around on stage, just prior to doing the song, because it's so obvious to the audience right in front of you that you are holding a dummy microphone. I was having a bit of a laugh with several of the girls in the front about it.'

5th - The release of *à Paris* had Steve White (Drums) replacing Zeke, Jean-Louis Rocques (Accordion) and Rebecca Bell (Vocals) replacing Dee. The single was produced by Peter Wilson and Paul Weller.

On the same day TSC are driven to CTVC's Hillside Studios in Bushey for a stunning live vocal/keyboard version of *The Paris Match* (complete with jumper over the shoulders) on *The Switch*. Steve White made his TV debut on the 7 minute Club Mix version of *Long Hot Summer* - Paul played the bass guitar for the one and only time. Joining TSC were Terry & Desi on vocals and percussion who had written to Paul asking if they could be considered for Respond records. Paul had sent them tapes a week earlier to learn claiming it was, 'quite a simple song to do.'

6th - Newspaper adverts for the 3rd time do not entertain us in English, this one with Mick, 'et entre les heures, rien qu'un peu de tristesse.' I have received two translations for this, 'and nothing but a little sadness between the hours' or 'and between the hours, nothing but a little sadness.'

The other advert just shows Paul's waist with the scribe, 'Ils disent que lorsque Lon est amoureux le monde sarrète de tourner mais quand on a plus personne à aimer les aiguilles de la montre ne semblent plus tourner.' This translates to, 'They say that when you are in love the world stops turning but when you have no one left to love the hands on your watch don't seem to move.'

The European obsession was being stretched to the limit - the *Long Hot Summer* video, the photos sitting on accordions, the 7" UK sleeve notes and the newspaper adverts written entirely in French. Oddly, the import single for *à Paris* has a full English translation, even the lengthy Cappuccino Kid notes.

TSC continue to wind up many people. The article on the *à Paris* sleeve notes 'originally written for French chanteuse Suzanne Toblat' was a mis-understood joke, it's an anagram of Talbot. Then Paul, 'I don't see myself as British anymore. We regard ourselves as European. In fact I'm trying to apply for a world passport. This is my world and I want to belong to it wholly.'

This 4 track EP faired well for radio play as Britain sweltered in the heat. A record busting 30.8 Celsius in Belfast 1983 still stands to this day. Paul telling Paolo Hewitt's *Watch* magazine, 'I think this song has that heady summer's evening, heavy scent in the air type feeling along the lines of some of the later Isley Brother ballads like *Between The Sheets.'*

Interview with Mark Curry on *Get Set* (Children's TV)

13th - Mick and Paul travel to Studio S2 at Broadcasting House, London to perform *Le Depart* and *The Paris Match* live on Radio 1's *Saturday Live,* complete with interview.

The same day *Record Mirror* has Paul and Mick on the front cover.

14th - *Long Hot Summer* enters the chart and would peak at number 3, staying in the top 100 for 9 weeks.

It is reported that Paul and Mick appear un-announced at Gary Crowley's Friday club to do a PA for *Long Hot Summer*. I quizzed Gary about the accuracy of this unusual event, 'This is really weird as I was looking through some old photos only last week. I used to DJ at a club in Harrow, the suburbs of London, called the Tuesday Club. To cut a long story short the audience was very young, all late teens, early 20's, postmen (!), men into their music and into their clothes. Paul and Mick came out to the club a few times and they felt a real sort of connection to it.

In actual fact Paul and Mick did a PA, a personal appearance which wasn't the sort of thing they would normally do really. They kind of entered into the spirit of it and that was sort of something that Paul had never done before with the Jam, wouldn't have been able to really.

It was a general sort of loosening of everything, it was back to basics. He got ideas and sort of just did it. The Wag moved to a Friday for a while, that whole sort of early/mid 80's period I thought was a very exciting time for clubs, especially in London. Infact I also remember going up to clubs in Glasgow and Edinburgh as well with The Bluebells and Orange Juice. It was something that Paul was excited by. '

18th - The 'style boys' were in demand for TV and something unique happened on *Top of the Pops*. The *Long Hot Summer* promotional video was aired on the week of entering the chart and *The Paris Match* complete with cello on the next. This was rarely seen, a b-side strong enough to make it onto prime time TV.

In addition, on *Top of the Pops,* Paul sat at the Keyboard, Mick played the Banjo with Steve on Bongos. For the same track on Dutch TV's *Playback* Paul sat at the Bongos and Mick returned to the Keyboards and as mentioned, he played Bass on *The Switch*. 3 shows and 3 instruments. TSC even threatened a '5 year plan' to record different EP's around the world, the next in Switzerland using Alpine Horns and yodelling! with a dance theme and titled *The Postcard EP*.

The inspiration for this came from The Modern Jazz Quartet (MJQ) who used to play classical jazz through recordings in distant and different lands. *The MJQ plays Jazz classics* LP was under Paul's arm for a photo shoot and he voted their *Django* as his current favourite record. The MJQ influence would not appear until the *Confessions of A Pop Group* LP in 1988.

Huge fan Tony Pacey confirms that in the *NME* Paul said a forthcoming EP would have a Tibetan feel. He mentioned that the band had been practising Tibetan levitation and would be levitating on their forthcoming tour. He also mentioned that support would be a levitating stripper named, *Dick and his two swingers*.

20th - *Money Go Round* on the back of *Long Hot Summer* re-enters the chart for one week at number 74, three months after its original release.

25th - *The Paris Match* is performed on *Top of the Pops*.

By this time bassist Anthony Harty had joined TSC. He spoke to *Wholepoint* in 2001 about the audition. 'A friend of mine suggested I should write to Paul as I was just about to leave school and I wanted to become a professional musician. So I wrote to Paul and sent a tape of me playing along with *Speak Like A Child*. He wrote back, asking me to come down. I showed the letter to my careers officer who said I'd be better off going on a Youth Training Scheme!

Dave Liddle told me later on that someone else had exactly the same idea as me at exactly the same time, so one audition turned into a couple. My brother took me down to the audition as he lived in London and my mum didn't think a 16 year old boy should go to London on his own! Steve White and Mick Talbot were there, I think they were still in the middle of recording *Café Bleu* as Peter Wilson was in the control room. I got my bass out and Paul took one look at it and gave me his! I can't remember what songs we went through, but I obviously impressed!'

SEPTEMBER

Rumours in the press hinted that there would be a series of small UK venue gigs in October - but only 5 European countries had confirmed dates. *Trinity* in Hamburg, *The Palace* in Paris, *The Volkhaus* in Zurich, *Meervaart* in Amsterdam and *VUB University*, Brussels.

2nd - *Introducing The Style Council* turned out to be the first LP, but as with everything, there was a twist. Paul had complete control and did not want this LP to be released in the UK - no singles to date will go on a UK album. Thus, this LP was heavily imported into the UK from Holland (Paris Cover) and later Japan (Paul and Mick roaming in the poppy fields).

The track selection captured the first year perfectly with superb Bert Bevan's Club Mix 12" versions of *Long Hot Summer* and *Money Go Round*. The cassette contained 2 extra tracks, *Party Chambers* and *Lè Depart* with the running order shuffled around to make both sides an equal length. Later as the CD became the standard, the LP version was converted onto CD.

It took a while for CD players to become affordable and thus accepted by the public. As an indication on the revolution of the CD, the first one released was Abba's *The Visitors* in August 1982.

This was the Cappuccino Kid's first chance to get a lengthy message across and he touches on the formation of the band when Paul met Mick. 'Sunny Sunday morning, they cross their cappuccinos in the up west bar and put their pasts on the Formica table. They discuss acceptable sounds, clothes, better sounds and growing up with a 70's feeling for life, love and ambition.'

Further news of "The Kid" is released, 'he only appears in unexpected places. It may be a café, an art museum, a cinema, or the top of a bus. But it's always with a scrap of paper containing the pearls of wisdom we are proud to present on the covers of Council and Respond singles.'

The blazer Paul wore on the *Introducing* LP sleeve was up for auction in London at £80 - £120 with full authentication. This was 17 years before Ebay would be the normal avenue for auctions.

An interesting and extremely enjoyable comic book was released in the USA titled *Long Hot Summer*. It was a graphic novel inspired by Weller's mournful tale of love lost, set against the backdrop of California's mid-'80s mod scene. This was written by big TSC fan Eric Stephenson and the art was by Jamie McKelvie. Jamie still lives in London and went on to draw the Britpop inspired graphic novel Phonogram.

Paul sent Everything But The Girl's Tracey Thorn a tape of *The Paris Match* with the hope that she would agree to sing on a new version for the debut album.

18th - The Questions *Tear Soup* enters the chart and peaks at number 66.

23rd - This date is on the ticket only invitation to the Solid Bond crew's 13th Anniversary at Woking Football Club for the recording of the *A Solid Bond In Your Heart* promotional video. It was produced by Deborah Kermode at GLO Productions and is about, '2 suedeheads, 13 years later, who go for a re-union but no-one turns up.' Paul used to go to this club on a Thursday night and said *Everythings Tuesday* by Chairman Of The Board reminds him of those nights.

Guest stars in the video were Mick's brother, Paul's sister, Gary Crowley and the forthcoming Acid Jazz front man Eddie Piller. It is interesting to hear the stories of how both friends Gary and Eddie met Paul via their respective fanzines.

I spoke to Eddie Piller in July 2008 about his first encounter, 'I knew the pair separately, long before they were in The Style Council. I first met Paul in 1980 when I interviewed him for a fanzine. I had been following the Jam since 1978 and had run the *Extraordinary Sensations* fanzine since 1980. The interview though was for *Patriotic* modzine. Mick I knew from The Merton Parkas, who I followed around. I knew his brother Danny better, but had met Mick a lot in 1979. A couple of years later I released a Merton Parkas single, a version of *Band of Gold* that had somehow slipped through the net at Beggars Banquet. The Merton Parkas were just splitting up at the time so it was their last release. I was both surprised and pleased when Paul set up The Style Council with Mick.'

I also asked Gary Crowley the same question, 'When Punk came along we decided to hijack the school magazine and effectively turn it into a Punk fanzine with the help and encouragement of a very nice teacher Dave Meadon, our English teacher. We were right in the middle of London, the Clash signing on at the dole office, Steve and Paul from the Pistols lived round the corner from the School, we were bang right in the middle of it really. '

'Melody Maker used to do this thing, 'Band file', in 1977, basically the facts of a band, who they were signed to, who managed them, that sort of thing, a history of the band. The Jam's one had the band as managed by John Weller and it had his Woking phone number. I thought, "hold on a minute, I'm sure I read somewhere that Paul lived at home with his mum and dad." So I just called up one day from outside the school. We used to commandeer a phone box every lunchtime, ringing up people, trying to blag free tickets.

I called up and Paul's mum Ann or sister Nicky answered and I was rattling away, no it was Ann, not Nicky. She said 'calm down, calm down' as I was going 20 to the dozen. She said, "look, Paul's here why don't you have a chat with him." I then spoke to Paul and he said, "why don't you come up to Polydor Records tomorrow and we can do the interview there." That was when we first met, mid summer of 1977 as I had just seen them at Battersea Town Hall.'

'An interesting story. My club Bogart's played a bit of a part. Paul & Mick came down and said the video was going to be shot at Woking Football Club in the banqueting hall. They said we need to get some people down for the dancing for the video, so we got a lot of people who came to Bogart's to come down.

My sister was there, Eddie Piller was there. I remember my hair was quite long. I had a bit of a, well if you want to be cruel, a footballer's mullet, even though I didn't think of it as that. Ann Weller had to put it up in pins so I could get a pork pie hat on. She was like 'your hairs to long Gary,' I remember Ann putting it in a bunch to get it into the hat! It was a lovely afternoon and into the evening, just a lot of fun. The Director was a very colourful guy called Tim Pope.' (Gary Crowley)

'The filming came about because a mutual friend of mine and Pauls, Gary Crowley, was looking for people to be in the video. He called me up knowing that I had recently been going through my 'suedehead' phase - all window pane check shirts and light coloured three button suits. Gary called and asked me if i could find a few dozen suedeheads for the video. I was a bit stumped because suedehead was a kind of personal thing to me, but I did know a crew from Ealing who were into the same look. I called them and we all met up to go down to Woking, a few scooters and a coach. I followed in my Lancia Spyder with the roof down, the target of much abuse from the lads in the coach. It was a film set, we all trooped in, they took a few shots and then we all trooped out again. The atmosphere was created for the shot.' (Eddie Piller)

'I've still got the jacket of the suit that Paul wore in the video, I had the trousers. For the life of me I can't remember where the trousers have gone. The Jacket is lovely, a beautiful suit, I can just about squeeze into it now but I'd give Norman Wisdom a run for his money, it is quite tight.' (Gary Crowley)

Gary would also interview, promote or appear in promotional videos through most of Paul's career. 21 years later at the exclusive 2004 launch of Paul's massive Studio 150 LP at the Riverside Studios he would be the one introducing Paul onto the stage. It's now August 2008 and on his BBC Radio London show he still personally selects tunes like My Ever Changing Moods. Nice one Gary!

Also DJ'ing at Bogart's was Phil Jupitus who on his BBC profile said the club was, 'made up of suburbanites and Soho trendies - dancing their espradrilles off to a soundtrack of funk, rock and rap and rubbing shoulders out on the dance floor with the likes of The Style Council, Wham and Bananarama. Happy daze!'

Constant rehearsals took place with the new live band for next months debut tour. 15 songs would be played, virtually the entire catalogue to date.

29th - The Respond Posse are back on the road until 20th October on the *Love The Reason Live* tour. This would give Tracie some good experience before her support slot with TSC in Europe a week after the Respond tour ends.

Paul was interviewed on *Riverside* TV complete with an interview at Solid Bond studios. The Questions performed *Tear Soup* whilst Paul sat at the mixing desk.

OCTOBER

5th - Debut UK tour dates are announced for 6 cities in December though a Scottish date was still to be announced. A full UK tour would take place in 1984 after the debut LP is released.

Hammersmith Odeon, London (7th)
Southampton, Gaumont (8th)
Coventry, Apollo (10th)
Ipswich, Gaumont (11th)
Sheffield, City Hall (12th)
Halifax, Civic Hall (13th)

10th - Respond compilation LP *Love The Reason* is released.

5 'meetings' would take place this month in Europe with Paul keen to add more, 'I'd still like to play in Austria, I feel a bit alpine at the moment.' In order to play down the debut live event TSC decide to go on stage first, then Tracie and The Soul Squad would do a set before TSC returned for the second and final part.

24th - The Volkhaus, Zurich

26th - Le Palace Theatre, Paris

28th - V.U.B. Auditorium Q, Brussels

30th - Trinity, Hamburg

31st - Not a good day. As well as the tour coach being impounded by the police in Amsterdam, the Saxophone was stolen from the stage of the De Meervaart. Paul made a plea to the capacity audience of 750, 'has anyone in the audience seen a saxophone... bring it up on stage.... I'm not joking, this is serious business.'

The show was broadcast in a 1-hour radio special sounding rough and unpolished, with the version of *Long Hot Summer* probably their career best version. This show was to form part of the 1997 *In Concert* Live LP but unfortunately Dennis Munday was unable to locate the original recording.

15 songs were played on this tour. When broken down a remarkable 6 b-sides and 4 a-side's were played. This indicated that the quality of the b-side really mattered and was of equal importance to the band. The remaining songs were from the forthcoming LP or unrecorded tracks;

It Just Came To Pieces In My Hands, Money Go Round, Council Meeting, Here's One That Got Away, Mick's Up, Long Hot Summer, Up For Grabs[†], Le Depart, The Paris Match, Party Chambers, Speak Like A Child, Headstart For Happiness, One Nation Under A Groove[†], A Solid Bond In Your Heart, Hanging Onto A Memory[†]. [†]Unreleased.

NOVEMBER

Favourable reviews from back home, 'the newer songs are better than 80% of the music coming out of Britain at the moment.' (*NME*)

Anthony Harty recalls, 'It was an unbelievable experience. For TSC to give that opportunity to a fresh faced teen, straight out of school was incredible. The whole 2 years with TSC were probably my best. I learnt most about being in a band from that.'

Anthony didn't get asked to record on any songs, 'I just used to get calls for live work and live TV, though on a few occasions I nearly made it into the studio but Paul always ended up playing the bass parts himself, as he knew how he wanted them to go. He is a very under-rated bass player.'

On their return from Europe, *My Ever Changing Moods, Headstart For Happiness* and the unreleased *Hanging Onto A Memory* were all performed live from Tyne Tees television studios in Newcastle. The show was *The Tube* featuring presenters Jools Holland, Paula Yates and Muriel Gray. *Speak Like A Child* was performed after the show went off air and would only be shown on Italian TV a few years later.

5th - Despite rumours, *Record Mirror* confirmed the UK tour is on with 1 show at Hammersmith Odeon in support of the British Olympic Team.

7th - *A Gospel* was recorded at Solid Bond Studios, main vocalist being a certain Dizzy Hites who was introduced to Paul by Bert Bevans. Other than being on the Polydor label and having released a single in 1982, *Christmas Rapping,* not much else is known about Dizzy. This would remain the case until the debut LP was released in 1984.

10th - *My Ever Changing Moods* was recorded. Short, long, slow and fast versions.

11th - *A Solid Bond In Your Heart* adverts, 'Push it to the limit and build' and 'It hits you where it counts', promote the 7" only single (though an additional gatefold version was limited to 100,000 copies). It is backed with the haunting *It Just Came To Pieces In My Hands* described by Paul as, 'a song about the blind foolishness of conceit until one day the mat gets pulled from under your feet. Never stop caring or thinking about others, because you really can't afford too, is the message.'

Produced by Peter Wilson and Paul Weller this would be the last single without an accompanying 12". Zeke Manyika (Drums) and Chris Hunter (Saxophone) were the guests. This was an easy release as it was all recorded in January.

'A bit Northern-Souly with a bit of sax on it. A touch of the Junior Walkers.' (Paul)

'The vibes were a stab at Northern Soul. Lots of Northern Soul records had that vibe.' (Paul, *Record Collector*)

12th - Seven days after confirming the tour is on, *Record Mirror* now say it is off and spoke to Paul, 'TSC are committed to finishing their album by the end of the year and time unfortunately does not allow for both projects. It really was a choice between them and finishing the LP.'

15th - Tracie appears solo at London's Phoenix Theatre.

20th - *A Solid Bond In Your Heart* enters the chart and would peak at number 11, staying in the top 100 for 8 weeks.

24th - There was no *Top of the Pops* studio appearance for *A Solid Bond In Your Heart*, breaking the run to date, though it was performed live on *The Switch* back in March. Instead *Top of the Pops* aired the video single.

DECEMBER

6th - *Strength of Your Nature* was recorded with Dee and Peter Wilson (drum programming) at Solid Bond Studios.

All the planned tour dates have been postponed until next year so the LP could be completed. The sell out London benefit gig though was still on for the lucky ticket holders.

7th - Hammersmith Odeon, London. Postponed

8th - Gaumont, Southampton. Postponed

10th - Apollo, Coventry. Postponed

11th - Gaumont, Ipswich. Postponed

12th - City Hall, Sheffield. Postponed

13th - Civic Hall, Halifax. Postponed

18th - 'The Big One' at The Apollo in London featured musicians, actors and writers. It was organised back in May by Susanna York for various peace organisations, 'Theatrical Show For Peace' and featured TSC, U2, Elvis Costello, Ian Dury, Mari Wilson, The Alarm and Hazel O'Connor.

TSC played five songs; *Money Go Round, Headstart For Happiness, Long Hot Summer,* and two newly recorded songs - *A Gospel* featuring Dizzy Hites and *My Ever Changing Moods*, a superb one off version with Elvis Costello collaborating with Paul on vocals.

'Brilliant is all I can say, such a great atmosphere.' (Paul)

12th - *What We Did On Our Holidays* collated the four promotional video singles to date on Betamax and VHS and was released into the Christmas market. At this time the video recorder was a relatively new and exciting technology and this was a big seller for Polygram.

29th - *Top of the Pops* to perform *Long Hot* Summer (!) in a Christmas special.

31st - *Radio 1*, Saturday Live from Studio S2 to play 5 songs live to the nation. This is one of the officially unreleased classics. Twice the presenter said TSC were playing 3 tracks and in the end 5 were played absolutely live.

My Ever Changing Moods, Mick's Blessings, The Paris Match, Headstart For Happiness and *Long Hot Summer.*

This would in this day be known as an 'unplugged' session, no drums. The line up was simply Paul, Mick and Dee. They were to finish the session after the 4th song, *Headstart For Happiness* but on the last note and not pre planned Mick continued straight into *Long Hot Summer*, there seemed to be a pause, he was heard saying, "Why Not?" and off they went into a superb pianopella version. The BBC would do well to collate all TSC Radio sessions and release a CD at a special price as they are doing for Paul's solo work in November 2008. Alternatively give *Mr Cool's Dream* permission to release them with the next edition of the book!

The new song *Mick's Blessings* was said to be influenced by Billy Taylor's, *I Wish I Knew How It Would Feel to Be Free.*

Same night a pre recorded TV special, *Pop Goes Xmas* included a one-off unreleased 'live' violin version of *My Ever Changing Moods* featuring Bobby Valentino of the Hank Wangford Band on violin.

A good end to the inaugural year of the band.

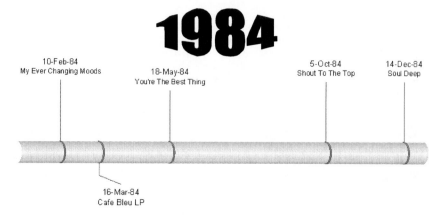

10-Feb-84
My Ever Changing Moods

18-May-84
You're The Best Thing

5-Oct-84
Shout To The Top

14-Dec-84
Soul Deep

16-Mar-84
Cafe Bleu LP

"I'm not a youth spokesman and all these crummy clichés"

JANUARY

The first UK tour is announced with new dates to replace those cancelled in December, though Coventry, Sheffield and Halifax would not get replacements. A press release stated, 'the live dates that were cancelled last year have been rescheduled and the shows will go out under the title 'Council Meeting's.' Tickets at £5.00

Southampton, Gaumont (March 13th)
London, Dominion (14th/15th)
Birmingham, Odeon (16th)
Ipswich, Gaumont (17th)
Nottingham, Sports Centre (18th)
Newcastle, City Hall (19th)
Glasgow, Apollo (20th)

Chippenham, Golddiggers (10th) was later added for a BBC TV and Radio special.

Dee C Lee has signed to CBS records and would not be partaking in this tour - her replacement would be a Jaye Williamson, a Post Office clerk who was also attending stage school in her spare time. Here she was discovered by Yvonne French, the presenter of TV show *The Switch*. Yvonne thought Jaye had a fantastic voice and encouraged her to audition for TSC. Yvonne was friends with Paul and tipped him off prior to the audition. When Paul heard Jaye sing he immediately employed her for the forthcoming World tour.

I did catch up with Jaye in 2006 but she decided not to publicly comment on her time with TSC other than saying it was not an enjoyable experience.

The debut LP, titled *Café Bleu* was still not complete and the next few weeks were crucial as deadlines were approaching for getting the LP into the shops by March.

4th - *Dropping Bombs On The Whitehouse* was recorded with Steve White's drum solo's featuring heavily in this soon to be controversial instrumental.

14th - *You're The Best Thing* was recorded with Peter Wilson doing the drum programming.

18th - *Me Ship Came In,* another jazz filled instrumental, is recorded. Paolo Hewitt said in his *Changing Man* book that Paul used the riff from a track by jazz pianist Horace Silver. In October 2007 Sony would use this tune extensively on TV for promoting its Ericsson range of mobile phones. Also worth looking out for is Austrian born Louie Austen's *One Night In Rio* which sampled the tune.

The promotional video for the next single, *My Ever Changing Moods,* was fimed as Paul and Mick sported cycling gear and took to the countryside around Woking. The focus is a bike race passing numerous 'conflict' type road signs with a few girls thrown in to make up for the lack of them in *Long Hot Summer.* Head of Polydor, AJ Morris, had raised concerns when there were no girls in the video.

FEBRUARY

Following the 'French EP' in 1983 the follow up 'Dutch EP' got as far as the sleeve being proof printed. Where the French one displayed the Eiffel Tower the "Keeps on Burning" logo was now surrounded by a windmill. The release was coded TSC 5 and detailed *Hanging Onto A Memory* as the b-side. The cover featured a very young Paul with a guitar and the slogan, 'features excerpts from two hips from Amsterdam.'

This backs up the initial reports that the b-side of the next single was to be *Hanging Onto A Memory* on the 7" and an extra track *Up For Grabs* on the 12". They and the EP did not materialise and no promotional singles were pressed. Both tracks remained unreleased for 13 years until the appearance on the *In Concert* LP in 1997. It is not known if they were studio recorded and remain in Paul's vault.

10th - The first single from the long awaited debut album, *My Ever Changing Moods* was released in two entirely different versions. A 'fast' version for the 7" and a longer, 'slower' version for the 12" (though this was not promoted on the sleeve). Mick's 3rd self-titled instrumental *Mick's Company* is on both versions with an extra track on the 12", *Spring, Summer, Autumn.* This song would also appear on Tracie Young's debut album *Far From The Hurting Kind* in June. It credited Jake Fluckery as the writer. "Jake" would also write songs for Dee C Lee's forthcoming solo LP and in the end we presumed that "Jake" was actually Paul. I don't recall anyone asking Paul about this or the reasons behind it so if you do please report back for an update in a future edition.

There was a bit of controversy surrounding the picture sleeve on the 7" and afterwards Paul apologised, saying it was 'stupid' to think smoking made him look cool - This was a full 23 years before the smoking ban in the UK.

Honorary Councillors on the single were; Steve White (Drums), Pete Wilson (Bass Synth), Barbara Snow (Trumpet) and Hilary Seabrook (Saxophone). Produced by Peter Wilson and Paul Weller.

'The sound of someone who has assimilated the Brothers Isley into his bloodstream.' (*NME*)

16th - Simon Bates and Peter Powell introduce *My Ever Changing Moods* on *Top of the Pops*. Mick wore the cycling top from the promotional video and Paul a Frank Spencer tank top. Also on tonight were Matt Bianco, Nena and Slade.

18th - *The Saturday Superstore* for 2 songs. *My Ever Changing Moods* featured horn players Barbara Snow and Hilary Seabrook with Dee C Lee leaning and tapping on the piano but not singing. *Headstart For Happiness* was also performed which Dee did sing on.

19th - *My Ever Changing Moods* enters the chart and would peak at number 5, staying in the top 100 for 7 weeks. Paul expressed disappointment that people were thinking it was a love song without actually listening to the lyrics.

20th - Respond releases keep coming with The Questions *Tuesday Sunshine*. On the b-side was *The House That Jack Built,* which Tracie had a hit with. The Questions are to play a major part in next months Council Meeting's and have a warm up gig lined up at London's Lyceum entitled *The Mad Mad Mad Rag Ball.*

A promotional trip to Holland for a *Top of the Pops* type show. Paul stirred things up by playing a v-shaped guitar, the type usually played by many hard rock bands. He also expressed his appreciation of the *NME* readers' poll on Dutch show *Countdown*. When asked what he thought of winning the award of 'Most wonderful human being' he modestly replied, 'I can see that, I go along with that.'

24th - Peter Powell interviews Paul and Mick on ORS (the new title for *The Oxford Road Show*) from BBC studios in Manchester.

27th - Dee C Lee releases her first solo single *Selina Wow Wow* on CBS Records. It did not make the top 100.

MARCH

The month of *Café Bleu*. Disappointment for many, a shock for some, 'I remember playing Rick Buckler some tracks off the album before it came out and he was stunned, "are you taking the piss?"' (Paul)

Last year Paul was raving about the debut being a double LP, 'one side romantic, slightly sad, a bit moody. 2nd side more funky, 3rd side with todays pop songs and the 4th side with remixes of the singles.' One thing he had not accounted for was Polydor's reaction, 'I should keep my gob shut sometimes, it won't be a double now as we couldn't get its price reduced to that of a single LP.' To compensate the vinyl would be released with a booklet of lyrics and photos.

Paul told *Mojo* the sleeve of *Café Bleu* was inspired by the work of Art Blakey, Coltrane and the Blue Note artists he was into at the time. The sleeve notes by Jean Paul Marat, an 18th century visionary, spoke of 'weapons rapidly developed by servile scientists will become more and more deadly until they can with a flick of the finger tear a million of you to pieces.' This was sent to Paul by a fan and they inspired him enough to include it on the album.

Café Bleu's Honorary Councillors are; Billy Chapman (Sax), Barbara Snow (Trumpet), Ben Watt (Guitar), Tracey Thorn (Vocals), Chris Bostock (Double bass),
Dizzy Hites (Rap), Hilary Seabrook (Sax), Dee C Lee (Vocals), Steve White (Drums) and Bobby Valentino (Violin). In addition Paul plays Bass, Guitar, Bass Synth, Synth and Flute sound. Mick played on the Piano, Hammond, Brass Synth, Keyboards, Brass sound and vocals.

It was a huge surprise for everyone (including AJ Morris at Polydor) when the lead singer Paul only sang on 6 of the 13 tracks; The unaccredited masterpiece, *Whole Point Of No Return,* the piano version of *My Ever Changing Moods,* a remixed *Headstart For Happiness* (now featuring Dee on vocals with a new verse), the dance floor stomper *Strength Of Your Nature* with minimum vocals, 1984's most romantic song *You're The Best Thing* and finally the popular *Here's One That Got Away,* which Paul described as 'Punk, Country and Western.'

The first four singles do not appear on *Café Bleu*, instead a re-recorded version of *The Paris Match* is sung by Tracey Thorn and rapper Dizzy Hites takes lead on *The Gospel.* There are 5 instrumentals; *Mick's Blessings, Me Ship Came In, Blue Café, Dropping Bombs On The Whitehouse* and *Council Meetin.*

Paul got truly hammered in the music press for this LP, however, 3 years later Mick was gloating when *Café Bleu* was penned a classic in 1987, 'People hated that at the time, that got panned right across the board, completely.' Continuing to tell *The Face,* 'people were asking why we didn't record another classic like *Café Bleu*!'

Paul told *Just 17,* 'I don't think Polydor were particularly happy with *Café Bleu*.'

'We didn't see ourselves as Jazz musicians, we were musicians who liked jazz.' (Paul, official website)

'Half of side one is dispensable dross, there are too many weaknesses developing unchecked alongside reassuring strengths which steer *Café Bleu* clear of being a disappointment. 3½/5' (*Sounds*)

Peter Martin for *Smash Hits,* 'Paul clearly wants to win fans not on reputation but on musical worth. Me, I never really liked The Jam but this, *c'est magnifique.*' (8½/10)

'*Café Bleu* is no bad record, it's just the Council are too full of (other people's) mood, too diverse, dilettante. Some might say that's exciting, experimental, but to me it smacks of musical tourism.' (*Record Mirror*)

'Weller and Talbot mix Latin, Salsa, Rap and Jazz around a perky, infectious beat.'

'I love a lot of *Café Bleu* but there are a few tracks that haven't really dated that well.' (Gary Crowley)

In Australia *Café Bleu* managed to stay in the charts for the remainder of 1984 even making a prime time appearance on the highly rated TV soap *Neighbours* when a very young Kylie Minogue was looking through her LP collection.

TSC appear in an advert for VOX amps, 'You have to admire TSC. Unlike 99% of bands on the circuit, their records don't rely on a bloated production sound. They rely on emotion.' TSC reply in return, 'we use VOX amps in the studio too, and the whole band will be using VOX on the tour: Mick naturally, Anthony on bass, even Stevie the drummer.' Finishing with, 'even though I've earned a bob or two I haven't changed.'

8th - Paul appears on the David Jensen Radio show to discuss *Café Bleu*. Four tracks are played from the LP, *A Gospel, Blue Café, Strength Of Your Nature* and *You're The Best Thing*.

For the forthcoming tour *Record Mirror* revealed TSC would not be appearing in the usual gig format. The Questions and Billy Bragg would play sets in-between their set. Paul explained, 'The idea is to try and create an atmosphere that you would get in a club. We will be doing two sets. We go on first and finally finish the show with a second set. Billy would also be MC for the shows.'

10th - The live line-up is presented on the first night at Golddiggers, Chippenham. This was the extra date added in order for the BBC's *Sight & Sound* to broadcast simultaneously on TV and Radio. A very nervous night for all concerned. This is the concert mentioned in Stewart Prosser's memories at the beginning of this book.

Joining Paul and Mick were; Steve White (Drums), Jaye Williamson (Vocals), Anthony Harty (Bass), Helen Turner (Keyboards), Stewart Prosser (Trumpet), Billy Chapman (Saxophone), Steve Sidelnyk (Percussion), Chris Lawrence (Trombone)

Not shown on the night but aired on future TV shows were *Long Hot Summer* and *Dropping Bombs On The Whitehouse*.

11th - The Questions *Tuesday Sunshine* peaks at number 46. This was their last visit to the top 100. The songs in their live set supporting TSC were; *Blue Line, Everything I See, The Price I Pay, The Learning Tree, Chocolate Burning, Building On A Strong Foundation, Tuesday Sunshine, Someone's Got To Lose* and *Tear Soup*.

13th - Southampton, Gaumont

14th - London, Dominion. Recorded for BBC *In Concert*

15th - London, Dominion. Recorded for BBC *In Concert*

16th - Birmingham, Odeon. Bassist Anthony Harty recalls this night, 'My whole family came to see me and halfway through Weller pulled me to the front of the stage, saying that I was a local lad, and that my folks were in the audience. He then said, "I'd just like to say we're looking after him and gradually weening him off the heroin." Apparently my mum went white.'

Café Bleu is released on LP and Cassette.

17th - Ipswich, Gaumont Theatre

18th - Nottingham, Sports Centre

19th - Newcastle, City Hall. Not a good day for the band. The tour coach was raided and Paul's box of singles and Mick's suitcase were stolen. The coach was also stopped by police on the motorway thinking they were flying pickets - highly mobile 'pickets' who were able to move rapidly to any location at short notice.

20th - Glasgow, Apollo

18 tracks were played on the tour; 4 singles, 4 LP and 4 unreleased* songs alongside 6 b-sides.

Meeting (Up) Over Yonder*, Here's One That Got Away, My Ever Changing Moods, It Just Came To Pieces In My Hands, Mick's Up, Up For Grabs*, Dropping Bombs On The Whitehouse, Long Hot Summer, Le Depart, Whole Point of No Return, The Paris Match, Party Chambers, Money Go Round, Speak Like A Child, Hanging Onto A Memory*, Me Ship Came In, One Nation Under A Groove* and Spring Summer Autumn.

One Nation Under A Groove is a cover of the Funkadelic classic; *Hanging Onto A Memory* is a cover of the original by Chairmen Of The Board and *Meeting (Up) Over Yonder* is an Impressions cover. Weller penned *Up For Grabs* which he dedicated to playwright Joe Orton. They would all remain officially unreleased until the 1997 *In Concert* LP.

Compared to the European tour in 1983 three tracks were dropped; *Council Meeting, Headstart For Happiness* and *A Solid Bond In Your Heart*.

Six were added; *Meeting (Up) Over Yonder, My Ever Changing Moods, Dropping Bombs On The Whitehouse, Whole Point of No Return, Me Ship Came In* and *Spring Summer Autumn*.

In Concert~330 was a 54 minute BBC transcription vinyl of The Dominion, London show. The following tracks were omitted from the LP; *Le Depart, Whole Point of No Return, The Paris Match, Party Chambers, Me Ship Came In, One Nation Under A Groove* and *Spring Summer Autumn*. 'Recorded at the peak of the tour, includes a selection of hits and some of the styles of The Style Council from the *Café Bleu* LP.'

Bootleg vinlys appeared on black and blue picture disc (300 of each) from the Chippenham night, captured straight from the radio broadcast so of excellent quality. It contained the unreleased *Meeting (Up) Over Yonder* and *Hanging Onto A Memory* alongside a couple from the Respond Package tour in May 1983.

The band got a weeks holiday before the 2nd European tour of Belgium, France, Germany and the Netherlands. Support this time would come from Tracie and the Soul Squad. A secret gig/end of tour party would be held at the 100 Club, London in April.

Paul appeared on the *Kid Jensen show* and when the subject of a reporter who was slagging up Respond records to simply get back at Paul was mentioned Paul burst out with, 'No, I have never seen him, but I'd like to give him a good kicking, that's what he needs.'

Quizzed on the future of Respond records Paul stated, 'the whole thing became unworkable. The music industry is geared for profit and not creativity.'

25th - Ancienne Hall, Brussels. First night of the European tour. On the same day, *Café Bleu* enters the UK chart at number 2, staying in the top 100 for a very impressive 38 weeks. The first 8 week chart placings were; 2, 7, 8, 9, 17, 21, 24 and 32. It then went back up the charts, into the top 20 with the release of a single, peaking this time at 14.

27th - Palais D'Hiver, Lyon

29th - L'Eldorado, Paris

30th - Zeche, Bochum, Germany. Same day they perform *My Ever Changing Moods* for a TV show.

31st - Shown in the UK was an earlier recorded interview where Paul was grilled by Nicky Horn on TV show *Face To Face*, 'Are you a Millionaire?' to which he replied, 'I am not a millionaire, no. What should I do, go and give everyone in the street £1?' When then asked about being a Youth spokesman Paul piped in, 'I am not a Youth spokesman and all these crummy clichés,' telling those people who think he is, 'to stop now and start speaking for yourself.'

APRIL

1st - Metropol, Berlin. Paul broke his arm whilst fooling around at a service station with Jaye. When he returned from the hospital with his arm in a sling the rest of the band thought he was playing an 'April fool' on them. Tonight's show went ahead but Paul had to leave his guitar playing to bass player Anthony Harty, not Dave Liddle as was widely reported. Dave was a member of the road crew and would remain with Paul's live entourage until he became ill and passed away in 2002.

The concert was filmed for German TV, including an interview with Paul complete with his broken arm in a sling.
3rd - Vredenburg, Utrecht, Netherlands. Recorded for radio broadcast.

4th - Paul DJ's on Piccadilly Radio, Manchester, standing in for Timmy Mallet who is on holiday. He plays TSC/Jam tracks alongside his own favourites from The Kinks, The Herd and Amen Corner. Two girls sing a jingle especially for Paul to the tune of *Long Hot Summer,* 'It don't matter what you do, Paul Weller's here for you, he's just come from the zooooo.' His love of the Hammond becomes clear when he remembers as a 10 year old using the house sofa as a Hammond Organ for the Herd's top 5 hit, *I Don't Want Our Loving To Die.*

8th - 100 Club, London. End of tour gig/party. Invited guests only.

Paul and Mick travel to France to record a unique, exclusive film for French TV, never shown elsewhere. Superb! They are setting themselves up, 3 years before JerUSAlem. Look for it on *You Tube,* albeit 25 year old footage in black and white.

Cameo Roles - Style Council short Film

TSC in France, Paul and Mick's voices are over dubbed in French so it is hard in places to work out what is being said.

Scene 1 - Mick enters *USA Record Shop* to find Paul as the record shop owner. He asks Paul many questions on TSC, thanks him and leaves without buying anything.

Scene 2 - The extended version of *You're The Best Thing* is playing as Paul and Mick peer through an underground hatch with torches, a la *Indiana Jones* style. They slowly enter the hatch and come across a group of tourists with a guide in a series of underground tunnels. They wander the tunnels ending in a wine cellar with Mick showing the camera the Talbot wine.

Scene 3 - Paul and Mick are talking to a wine expert who is offering them various vintage bottles, 'You naughty Frenchman' Paul says as they turn down bottle after bottle. Finally a 1983 bottle is shown, 'That's when we tied the knot' cries Mick, 'and we also started making records, The Style Council year' replied Paul.

Scene 4 - *My Ever Changing Moods* is playing as Paul, dressed in full waiter gear, carries a tray of food through the kitchen and into the restaurant to Mick sitting there in his white dinner jacket. The rest of the video focuses on the many French people in the bar. The song fades, the lights in the restaurant go out and the film ends. A true classic!

15th - Tracie's *Souls On Fire* only manages to get to number 73. Tracie told me that this was actually a Style Council song they were playing about with in the studio. She had heard the chorus, liked it and Paul said she could have it if she wrote the rest of it. Which she willingly did.

The rest of the month was spent in rehearsals for a short world tour of Japan and the United States of America.

30th - Koseinenkin Hall, Tokyo

MAY

Café Bleu was not released in USA, however, on Geffen Records the debut LP was re-named *My Ever Changing Moods* and contained different tracks and sleeve. The title change was because the single of the same name had reached number 29 in the USA charts. On the vinyl *A Solid Bond In Your Heart* (not on the UK release) replaced 2 tracks, *Me Ship Came In* and *Council Meetin*. The cassette, however, did contain the two tracks omitted from the vinyl. The 'fast' version of *My Ever Changing Moods* replaced the 'slower' UK version. There is also a different introduction to *You're The Best Thing*. It went into the US top 60.

'The release of *My Ever Changing Moods*, proved in retrospect to be one of the pivotal musical events of the season. The mix of diversity, dexterity and that unmistakable patina of pure pop exuberance seemed to emerge from out of nowhere and expand, all of a sudden, the way we were thinking about modern music. It was a simple question of possibilities; combining, synthesising and reinventing styles and forms in a wholly original manner, an approach that seemed so simple it was a wonder no one thought of it before. In the process, the LP elevated The Style Council to the forefront of today's most innovative and involving young artists.' (Geffen Records press release)

A very interesting USA promotional item was a Geffen Records credit card style TSC "stress meter" which measured your current mood - from stressed, through to tense, onto normal and ending at calm! This worked off of the heat from your finger. The back of the card had a lengthy piece under the title, 'How to use this card to control stress and bad habits.'

STRESS. Whenever you feel tense or the card registers black, try one (or more) of the following shortcut relaxation techniques until the card turns blue.

Clench your fists as tightly as possible and use your elbows to put Style Council's *My Ever Changing Moods* on the turntable. Position the stylus with your teeth on side one, cut one (the title track), and hold your breath for the next 14.5 minutes.

By the time you get to *Dropping Bombs On The Whitehouse* you should be feeling incredibly light headed. Exhale and let your body go limp. Get a friend to rub your back or get a cat to walk on your back.

Open up the window and scream 'I'm tense as hell and I'm not going to take it anymore.' Let all the neighbours see you dancing to *A Solid Bond In Your Heart.*

Towel off and flip the album over. Order a pizza. Charge a few mail order items on your credit card. Smile in the mirror whilst *You're The Best Thing* plays.

Imagine yourself in a fantastic place - find the *Strength of Your Nature* and ponder the meaning of life while listening to this great tune.

Stand on your head through *Here's One That Got Away.* Continue to eat pizza. Have a friend drive you to the hospital.

BAD HABITS. Many excesses (smoking, drinking, over eating, barking at strangers, showing off your collection of wax) are caused by tension and boredom. Next time, instead of reaching for your habit reach for The Style Council's *My Ever Changing Moods.* Picture some good things - tunes you can understand, an arresting set of lyrics, a beat you can snap your fingers to. Take a mental bath, remember to have a nice day and, above all, carry this card with you at all times.

2nd - Joh Hall, Osaka

'The tours were quite short as I think Weller had enough of long tours from his days with The Jam. I remember being in the centre of Tokyo with a few of the band and most of Tracie's band, just looking around and saying this is ridiculous, someone is *paying* for us to be here! The Japanese shows were a bit Beatle-esque! We were met, followed and chased at the airport by fans, a bit mad! We had a stage invasion in Osaka, but that's a long story.' (Anthony Harty). From what I hear Paul continued to sing on during the stage invasion and was surrounded by security during *My Ever Changing Moods.*

4th - SunPlaza Hall, Nakano, Tokyo. Capacity of 2,222. Filmed for a Japanese release. It would get a UK release in September titled *Far East & Far Out.*

6th - Fly onwards to USA for 4 shows, 2 each for New York and Los Angeles.

7th - Wilshire Theatre, Beverley Hills. 'The duo embarked on their first American tour to overwhelming acclaim.'

8th - Paul and Mick do a radio interview with USA radio station KIQQ explaining what the band is about and Mick answers why *Café Bleu* is renamed *My Ever Changing Moods* for the USA. 'The record company suggested it. In England singles stand on their own but in America you have to have an album with them.'

Paul confirmed Geffen Records had refused to release the LP with the title *Dropping Bombs On The Whitehouse*. However, Paul dismissed this terrorist talk by saying that 'dropping bombs' was a Jazz drumming term and Steve's surname is 'White', hence the song title. There's also a discussion on the lack of promotion from earlier USA record company Polygram, 'Not showing any interest or enthusiasm, it's just like they're throwing the records away.'

Conflicting stories surround TSC's invitation to appear on the famed US TV show *Soul Train*. Paul's was quoted as saying, 'we don't want to fly to LA just for a poxy television show' in the *Internationalists* book, but at the time said, 'we'd liked to have done it' on KIQQ as Paul explained the only reason for not doing it was the filming dates clashed with TSC flights home on Saturday. He also asked if *Soul Train* could visit and film in the UK. This would happen in 1985 for *The Lodgers*.

8th - Wilshire Theatre, Beverley Hills.

10th - The Savoy Theatre, New York. Recorded for *King Biscuit Flower Hour*.

11th - The Savoy Theatre, New York. Recorded for *King Biscuit Flower Hour*.

TSC impressively did 5 encores during one Savoy Theatre concert, they were having a great time on stage, Paul telling Radio that he was sizing up them and they were sizing up him. The capacity of the venue was only 841 so it was an extremely intimate night.

King Biscuit Flower Hour is a famous and now rare LP on similar lines to the BBC transcription discs. Featuring *The Big Boss Groove, Here's One That Got Away, You're The Best Thing, My Ever Changing Moods, Speak Like A Child* and *Headstart For Happiness*.

12th - TSC fly back to the UK, next item on the agenda is the promotion of the forthcoming single, *Groovin*. The music press advertisement promotes a double a-sided 45 with the slogan, 'Don't wait for judgement day.' The title is created from the last word in each song title *The Big Boss Groove* and *You're The Best Thing*. *Groove* + Thing = Groovin!

Promotional videos were made for both but the *Big Boss Groove* was rarely shown - until 1987 when Satellite's *Music Box* received repeated requests for it. Dennis Munday makes a one-off appearance, doing a spot of break-dancing. Read about how this came about in his *Shout To The Top* book, now on paperback. The video was directed by Mark Stokes and did not appear on any official Style Council release until the 2004 DVD compilation. *NME* released it on a postal only VHS video compilation and by the end of the year it would be donated to the Live Aid/Band Aid projects.

Video Aid (The Feed The World Compilation) was a ninety-minute, 21 track limited and numbered edition on VHS and Betamax. *Big Boss Groove* was track 16, sandwiched in-between *You Can't Hurry Love* by Phil Collins and *Cry and Be Free* by Marilyn!

A limited edition 250 promotional in-store VHS videos are sent in a special Style Council sleeve to the major record stores. It featured all singles to date.

18th - Fans eagerly await the release of 'the love song of the year.' We are told it is not pulled straight from *Café Bleu* but a newly recorded and remixed version featuring Billy Chapman from Animal Nightlife on Saxophone.

Appearances by Steve White (Drums), Kevin Miller (Bass), Stewart Prosser (Trumpet), Chris Lawrence (Trombone), Billy Chapman (Saxophone), Jaye Williamson (Vocals) and Dee C Lee (Vocals). Produced by Peter Wilson and Paul Weller.

In 2007 *You're The Best Thing* was voted at number 78 in the 100 greatest love songs of all time. I am writing this 17th July 2008 and it is playing in the Café on BBC's *Eastenders* so the royalties and publicity are as prominent as they were back in 1984.

Kevin Miller was the new bass player and he told Wholepoint about getting the job, 'It was more like the Tracie job really. I met her in a pub in North London, got chatting and she told me she was looking for a band to do a few promo gigs. I went up to Solid Bond Studios to be auditioned by Paul and I played the bass line to *Give It Some Emotion* for about four bars. "You'll do" he said! I just ended up doing the odd Style Council session simply because we were there nearly every day. Usually Paul would always play the bass parts but occasionally he just needed a different style.'

24th - Janice Long and Mike Smith introduce the promotional video on *Top of the Pops* as the band rejected a studio appearance. On the same show were Wham at number 1 and Status Quo.

26th - *Apollo Theatre*, Coventry for a CND benefit night. 'The Style Council with general public,' tickets at £5.00. Following a day of 'work for peace' marches and protests at Trident dock in Burrow-In-Furness, Paul confirmed this as, 'the best TSC gig to date.' The marchers are praised by Paul and the final song is dedicated to them, cleverly re-named *One Nation Under A Cruise* (missile) for the night.

27th - The double a-sided *Groovin* enters the chart and would peak at number 5, staying in the top 100 for 8 weeks. *The Big Boss Groove* is rarely heard on the radio as *You're The Best Thing* is favoured by the majority of stations.

A quick trip to Italy to promote *You're The Best Thing* on the *St.Vincent Estate*. There were two performances of the song, a change of wardrobe being the only difference to cleverly allow the song to be shown on consecutive weeks. Top Italian weekly paper *Basta! comments on the band*, 'two beaming faces that bring much joy and wisdom to our ears.'

A unique, extremely rare Australian 12" promo, *Le Club Rouge*, was issued in an impressive red and white sleeve with 2 dancers silhouetted on the cover. The text read, 'The Style Council present a limited edition collection of dance faves.' *Speak Like A Child, A Solid Bond In Your Heart, Big Boss Groove* and *Money Go Round* (Club Mix 7:42)

Dee's second solo single is released, the rather strangely named *Yippie-Yi-Yay* on the back of *Selina Wow Wow*. Dee will have to explain these titles!

JUNE

2nd - Gary Crowley invited TSC onto his *Earsay* TV show to perform live versions of *You're The Best Thing* and *The Big Boss Groove* with the full tour band. They were sounding very fresh and confident, a large step up from the nervy Chippenham concert in March. *Earsay* was recorded at a TV studio in Wandsworth called Ewarts on a Friday throughout the day from 10am to 7pm.

Mick lets the cat out of the bag by saying that he uses the Hammond on TV when miming even if it's not used on the song because it looks good and has The Style Council written across it.

10th - Tracie's *(I Love You) When You Sleep,* which was written by Elvis Costello, reached number 59 in the charts, a little more success than Dee's single. Tracie met Elvis Costello on a plane and he suggested that he would write a song for her - he delivered his promise with this track.

18th - *Tracie* releases her debut LP, *Far From The Hurting Kind* which only stays on the chart for 2 weeks, reaching a disappointing number 64. This ten track LP was produced by Paul and Brian Robson, sleeve designed by Paul and Simon Halfon.

Paul wrote 5 tracks, one of those co-written with Tracie. Honorary Councillor's Kevin Miller, Helen Turner and Steve Sidelnyk make up her band. Sleeve notes saying, 'not so much the girl next door but the chick at the bottom of the garden who grows tomatoes.'

Tracie's two hit singles were not on the album, explaining to Wholepoint, 'that was Paul trying to be different. It certainly wasn't my choice. It seemed like suicide to me, to be putting out an album and expecting it to sell, after only two minor hits, without including either of them. It put way too much pressure on the next singles.'

'I do think there were one or two very good tracks on it but as an overall effort, I'd say it could have been so much better, for lots of reasons. My favourite track was (and still is) *Far From The Hurting Kind*, which I always wanted to be a single. If both Paul and I could have been a little more grown up and negotiated with each other a bit better, maybe I could have got my wish and seen it released as a single. My contribution to that would have been conceding that *Nothing Happens Here Anymore* was a good choice for a single too. I didn't see it at the time, because both Paul and I plumped for one each and refused to budge, hence we released something else altogether - how very stupid! As a result, neither was ever a single. My other favourite was *Spring, Summer, Autumn.* I think it would be truthful to say that although I liked most of the songs, I don't feel particularly proud of how I sang them or of the production effort that went into some of them. No disrespect to Brian Robson, who I continued to work with, the production element was down to money, mostly.'

Clothes and shoes continue to play a big part in the band and when asked about style Mick tells *Record Mirror* he's into, 'zoot suits, smart, smooth, modernist or casual, with your own individuality thrown in, together with a dash of Noel Coward, not forgetting Bogart's Mac.' Mick continued, 'I'd love one of those Noel Coward smoking jackets, though I don't smoke. I'd wear it in the morning when I get up, my gentleman's gentleman could bring it to me.'

'the mod method is still implied in everything TSC do. Their sartorial obsession is to be smart, casual and cool.' (*The Independent*)

Liberty's in London was where the band bought there Bass Weejun Tassel Loafers, as well as at the little known John Simmons shop off Bow street, described as, 'a step further than most tourists tend to take', by Frank Mort in his book *Cultures of Consumption.*

Paul said that he, 'still sits there staring for ages at pictures of The Small Faces.' Many pictures have Weller looking uncannily like Steve Marriott though when asked what TSC and The Small Faces have in common he was honest enough to reply, 'nothing really.'

Twenty years later Paul's former best friend Paolo Hewitt along with John Hellier released the ultimate Steve Marriott book, *All Too Beautiful.* In it comparisons are made between Weller and Marriott.

Even the devoted fan was having to fork out £5.50 on a regular basis to keep up with The Style Council t-shirt collection. At least 5 have been officially produced, *Speak Like A Child, Money Go Round, Café Bleu, Council Meetings part 1*, and *à Paris* with *Shout!*, and *Council Meetings part 2* the next to be released.

JULY

7th - TSC tour coach leaves Solid Bond Studios and picks up Bronski Beat at Victoria station en route north to Liverpool for a Miners' benefit gig. There they would meet up with Madness. Bronski Beat played for 30 minutes, then TSC played 5 tracks, Madness did a set before TSC finished things off with another 5 songs. The encore was TSC/Madness on *It's Time To Stop Shopping Around* originally performed by Smokey Robinson on his *One Heartbeat* LP. £3,000 was raised on the night.

Big Boss Groove, My Ever Changing Moods, Mick's Up, Long Hot Summer, The Paris Match, It Just Came To Pieces In My Hands, Speak Like A Child, Money Go Round, Headstart For Happiness, The Whole Point Of No Return, It's Time To Stop Shopping Around.

Paul & Mick are being photographed in and around Hyde Park, London for the promotional material of the next single, due out in October.

AUGUST

The new UK tour has been announced and 10 dates have been pencilled in. Again tickets are priced at £5 and postal applications were being accepted by The Torch Society with a limit of 'two pairs per person'(!) Instead of a support band we are told a play written by Tony Marchant will be performed, *The Three Musketeers Go Wild*.

Wolverhampton, Civic Hall (4th October)
Oxford, Apollo (6th)
Bristol, Hippodrome (7th)
Cardiff, St. David's Hall (8th)
St. Austell Cornwall, Coliseum (9th)
Sheffield, City Hall (11th)
Manchester, Apollo (12th)
Edinburgh, Playhouse (14th)
Liverpool, Royal Court (15th)
Leicester, De Montfort Hall (16th)

19th - Paul sings backing vocals on the new Animal Nightlife single *Mr Solitaire*, reaching number 25 and staying on the chart for 12 weeks. This would be their highest chart single from the six that would make it into the top 100. Assisting on this single was Honorary Style Councillor's Chris Lawrence and Stewart Prosser alongside Ian Ritchie who would go on to work with Dee.

20th - *Shout To The Top* is recorded. This would be the next single and was not from *Café Bleu*. Remarkably the first 7 singles do not appear on any LP with an exact mix. This was quite an achievement and again shows the benefit of owning a recording studio, something Paul reconfirmed in June 2008 with Gary Crowley when comparing it to his current *Black Barn* Studios.

SEPTEMBER

3rd - *Far East and Far Out* video and laser discs were released in the UK. The first visual reminder of the highly successful May Japanese tour. It is, however, disappointing to discover that the full gig (an extra 35 minutes) was included only on the USA/Japanese laser disc releases. *Post Modern, The Style Council in Tokyo Night* contained the additional *Party Chambers, Me Ship Came In*, the unreleased *Up For Grabs* and the 'slow' version of *My Ever Changing Moods*. The ending credits play a *My Ever Changing Moods* (reprise).

The same day *Ghosts of Dachau* and *The Piccadilly Trail* are recorded at Solid Bond. They would go straight onto the next single, one as a bonus 12" track.

7th - A benefit gig at the Royal Festival Hall, London. TSC, Alexi Sayle, Rik Mayall, Wham, Working Week and Everything But The Girl would all show their support. The songs played are unknown.

The promotional video for the forthcoming single *Shout To The Top* was filmed at an old School hall in North London. The focal backdrop was a huge painting of miners on the wall.

22nd - *Soul Deep* was recorded. It was to be a Miners' benefit record under the banner of the *Council Collective*. The day would be spent recording the backing track.

23rd - Second and final day spent recording the vocals for *Soul Deep* with Jimmy Ruffin, Junior, Vaughn Toulouse and Dizzy Hites. The single would see release in December.

'This was for the miners' strike. Paul fully supported them and wanted to give something to them. I also volunteered my services as did everyone involved.' (Bert Bevans)

29th - TSC are interviewed by Tommy Boyd on *Saturday Starship*, classic Saturday morning children's TV.

OCTOBER

1st - Steve White's first solo project was The Mighty Eltham Funk Federation (MEFF). It was described by Steve in the Autumn '84 tour brochure as 'a casual affair, strong in belief and rich in talent and for me is something that truly justifies beating the shit out of me drum kit.' He was joined for the debut release *Never Stop (A Message)* by Alison Limerick on vocals and Gary Wallis on congas and percussion. Gary would also be a percussionist for Pink Floyd.

Steve co-wrote the song, 'check this well ard groove, the sound of the mighty drum is back with a vengeance. Seven minutes of raw percussive power, enhanced by a stunning vocal performance by Alison Limerick.'

It only made it to number 102 in the charts and although Steve hinted at future releases that was the end of MEFF.

New UK tour - The new line-up for the 'Council Meeting part 2' tour was; Paul, Mick, Steve, Dee C Lee, Anthony Harty (Bass), Helen Turner (Keyboards), Stewart Prosser (Trumpet), Chris Lawrence (Trombone), Martin Speake (Saxophone) and Gary Wallis (Percussion).

4th - Wolverhampton, Civic Hall. A benefit gig for the Miners and CND.

5th - A new music press advert reads 'make no mistake/this is all class war/fight back/SHOUT TO THE TOP.' The seventh single is backed by the haunting *Ghosts of Dachau* and the 12" includes *Piccadilly Trail*.

The single featured Steve White (Drums), Dee C Lee (Vocals), Alison Limerick (Vocals), John Mealing (String Score) and Kevin Miller (Bass). Produced solely by Paul Weller, the first single not jointly produced by Peter Wilson. John Mealing was better known for recording radio and TV jingles, his most famous being for *Bob's Full House*. He would work again with TSC in 1985. Alison Limerick who had just assisted Steve for the MEFF release would go on to have hit singles in the 90's, through until 2003. The 12" single sleeve features singer Paul Young's future wife, the model Stacey Smith.

6th - Oxford, Apollo

7th - Bristol, Hippodrome

8th - Cardiff, St.David's Hall. *Shout To The Top* is released.

9th - St. Austell, Cornwall Coliseum

11th - Sheffield, City Hall. Early shows are going well which results in *Café Bleu* climbing 12 places to number 71, making it 30 consecutive weeks in the charts.

12th - Manchester, Apollo

14th - Edinburgh, Playhouse. *Shout To The Top* enters the chart and would peak at number 7, staying in the top 100 for 8 weeks.

15th - Liverpool, Royal Court Theatre

16th - Leicester, De Montfort Hall

No support act was planned, instead there was to be a play, with a promotional poster produced naming it, 'The Three Musketeers Go Wild.' The story was about 2 ex-students trapped by the Youth Training Scheme who end up kidnapping their boss! The main actor, however, broke his leg playing football so the play could not take place. Tracie quickly came on board as support.

19 tracks were played on this tour; 7 a-sides, 5 LP tracks, 2 b-sides, 1 with Dee, 2 Steve White solo and 2 unreleased.[†]

Big Boss Groove; You're The Best Thing; A Man of Great Promise; Shout To The Top; Don't Do It Baby (Dee C Lee); *Have You Ever Had It Blue; Razor's Edge[†]; Mick's Up; Never Stop (A Message); Here's One That Got Away; Long Hot Summer; Le Depart; Whole Point of No Return; Money Go Round; Speak Like A Child; Headstart For Happiness; One Nation Under A Groove[†]; Me Ship Came In* and *Nazuri Beat.* *

* From Steve White's Mighty Eltham Funk Federation project. Steve revealed to *Mr Cool's Dream* in 1996 that Nazuri is, 'Swahili for marvellous.'

Comparing this to the debut tour in March, 9 tracks have been dropped; *Meeting (Up) Over Yonder, My Ever Changing Moods, It Just Came To Pieces In My Hands, Up For Grabs, Dropping Bombs On The Whitehouse, The Paris Match, Party Chambers, Hanging Onto A Memory* and *Spring Summer Autumn.*

In their place came 10 new live numbers; *Big Boss Groove, You're The Best Thing, A Man of Great Promise, Shout To The Top, Don't Do It Baby, Have You Ever Had It Blue, Razor's Edge, Never Stop (A Message), Headstart For Happiness* and *Nzuri Beat.*

9 songs were retained; *Mick's Up, Here's One That Got Away, Long Hot Summer, Le Depart, Whole Point of No Return, Money Go Round, Speak Like A Child, Me Ship Came In* and *One Nation Under A Groove.*

USA sports film *Vision Quest* based on a novel by Terry Davis was renamed *Crazy For You* for UK release to cash in on the Madonna hit. The film includes *Shout To The Top* using a new, exclusive version. The Soundtrack was released on The Style Council's USA record label Geffen.

18th - Another *Top of the Pops* exclusive was for the newly recorded USA mix of *Shout To The Top*. TSC all appear in sharp suits. Also on the show tonight were Alison Moyet, Kim Wilde, Paul Young and Wham.

19th - TSC are live on the legendary Channel 4 classic *The Tube* with the full tour line-up. *A Man of Great Promise, Shout To The Top, Strength Of Your Nature* and a cover of Defunkt's *Razors Edge* to end the show.
'Music was evolving and mutating, TSC had loads of influences going on, from Defunkt to Jimmy Smith, Sly and Family Stone, a mish mash of influences going on. A time of pushing the boundaries really. They didn't pull it off all the time but more often than not they did, yes definitely.' (Gary Crowley)

Onto the European tour with attendances between 500 and 5,000 each night. It has proved impossible to obtain 100% accurate European dates and venues. If anyone has a more definitive venue list then please get in touch.

22nd - Rome. This night appeared on a double bootleg LP *Altered States*.

23rd - Bologna

24th - Teatro Tenda, Milan

Unconfirmed dates in Belgium

29th - Alabamahalle, Munich. This was recorded for German TV who aired, *Big Boss Groove, My Ever Changing Moods, You're The Best Thing* and *Shout To The Top.*

Dee released her third solo single *Don't Do It Baby, which* she sang on the tour.

NOVEMBER

1st - Robert Schumann Saal, Dusseldorf, Germany

4th - Carre, Amsterdam

5th - Lindt, Austria

6th - Innsbruck, Austria

12th - Paul appeared on Piccadilly Radio with Timmy Mallet, 'Has The Style Council lived up to your expectations?' Paul confirming, 'It's more than lived up to what I expected it to do.'

25th - Bob Geldof and Midge Ure assemble 36 musicians at Sarm West Studios in Basing Street, West London to record the famous and best selling single *Do They Know It's Christmas.* This 'supergroup' was named Band Aid. Bob Geldof had previously called Nigel Sweeney, Weller's tv/radio/gig organiser, asking if he could get Paul on board as Geldof and Weller didn't exactly see eye to eye.

26th - Trever Horn who owned the studio, mixed the 12" version of the single.

Much was made of Paul arriving via tube to Ladbroke Grove, walking to the studio, umbrella in hand, whilst others turned up in Limousines. Paul was photographed with Phil Collins, James Taylor, Bono and Jon Moss. The official video, *The Making of Band Aid,* shows Paul playing the acoustic guitar with Bob Geldof and also recording his vocal part. Midge Ure in his biography said they didn't use Paul's guitar piece in the end as it didn't fit in with what they were trying to achieve.

30th - An incident in Wales would have a direct impact on the forthcoming single *Soul Deep.* Two police cars and a motorcycle outrider accompanied 35 year old Welsh Taxi driver David Wilkie who was driving David Williams, a non striking miner to work in his Ford Cortina. On route 2 striking miners, Dean Hancock and Russell Shankland dropped a concrete block 27 feet from a bridge over the road directly onto the Taxi below killing David Wilkie.

DECEMBER

1st - Benefit gig at the Winter Gardens, Margate for the organisation to protect animal rights.

2nd - Teletext states that TSC are on the brink of deleting the *Soul Deep* recording after the death of the Welsh Taxi driver David Wilkie.

3rd - Royal Albert Hall, London. The most prestigious gig to date. Special and collectable posters were handed out to anyone buying a tour programme.

4th - Royal Albert Hall, London. '99% of the gigs are very memorable. The Albert Hall shows were incredible and my Dad was there which made it even better. At one of the nights, I saw Boy George in a box, dancing.' (Anthony Harty)

Boy George talked positively of both Paul and The Style Council in the 2006 *Into Tomorrow* documentary DVD.

5th - A Polydor press release announcing the cancellation of *Soul Deep* for 'artistic reasons' was said to be a smoke screen for Paul's indecision on what to do with the proceeds after the death of taxi driver David Wilkie.

8th - However, only 3 days later the release was back on. Paul and Jimmy Ruffin, who had his first hit in 1966 when Paul was only 8, appeared on Radio 1 to discuss *Soul Deep*. Jimmy is involved because his father worked down the mines and he said he understands the suffering.

9th - Paul and Mick appear with Robbie Coltrane at The Wag Club, London. Paolo Hewitt telling me, 'I was very aware of the strike. In fact, I organised the event to raise money for Christmas presents.' He along with *NME/IPC magazines* raised over £1,000 for striking miners families. Paul and Mick were DJ's for the night.

12th - *A Man of Great Promise* was recorded. This was written as a tribute to Dave Waller, a school friend of Paul's and an early member of The Jam. He had died some time ago of a heroin overdose. The song had proved popular on the recent tour and would go onto the next album.

14th - Due to the death of David Wilkie, the sleeve notes were changed and *Soul Deep* was released featuring TSC, Junior, Jimmy Ruffin, Vaughn Toulouse and Dizzy Hites. Produced by The Council Collective and mixed by Brian Robson and Heaven 17's Martin Ware. Engineered by Jeremy Wakefield. An advance of £9,800 was received from Polydor to send to "Woman against pit closures." 'The whole record is about Solidarity, or more to the point, getting it back! If the miners lose the strike, the consequences will be felt by all of the working classes, which is why it is so important to support it.'

The b-side would feature a lengthy Paolo Hewitt interview with two striking miners Bob & Chris. I spoke to Paolo about this in March 2005 and he revealed that Paul had arranged the interview at Solid Bond Studios and he the questions. Paolo has no idea what happened to the 2 miners. We were both in agreement that it would have sounded better over an infectious beat(!) with Paolo claiming that, 'apart from the sound of my voice, this is one of my favourite ever Weller b-sides.' I left wondering what the Cappuccino Kid would make of that quote!

The same night the full length (live) version of *Soul Deep* is on *The Tube* with the complete Council Collective band.

16th - The Band Aid single *Do They Know It's Christmas* enters the chart at number 1, staying there for 5 weeks and in the top 100 for 20 weeks - remarkable when you think of a Christmas song in the charts in May! Paul got the focus on the lyrics for the absent Bono on *Top of the Pops*. The b-side of the single features a Christmas message from many artists, including Paul. Over 3,500,000 copies were sold in 1984 alone, 7 million worldwide raising £8 million for starving people in Africa. This was also Paul's only number 1 single whilst with The Style Council.

20th - *Soul Deep* is performed live on *Top of the Pops*. Paul takes over Vaughn's rapping - it is the only time you will hear and see Paul rapping. Paul also featured this week on the Band Aid single which was sitting at number 1.

23rd - *Soul Deep (Part 1)* enters the chart, climbing to number 24, staying in the top 100 for 6 weeks. It sold 100,000 copies even though some radio stations refused to play it and shops refused to stock it.

'Soul Deep seemed like a simple thing to do until all the violence occurred. I'm pleased we supported the miners, highlighted their plight because it was a crunch time.' (Mick, official site)

The fan club sent all its members a superb Christmas present. A flexi-disc containing two live tracks, *It Just Came To Pieces In My Hands* (CND Coventry) and *Speak Like A Child* (London). We are informed that they bootlegged the bootleggers to obtain the tracks.

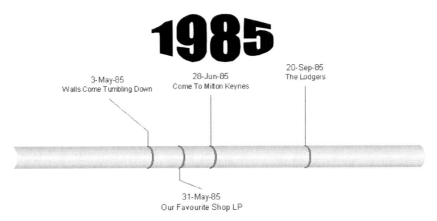

1985

3-May-85
Walls Come Tumbling Down

28-Jun-85
Come To Milton Keynes

20-Sep-85
The Lodgers

31-May-85
Our Favourite Shop LP

"The crowd loved it 'cos we were more pissed than them"

JANUARY

The Style Council are announced winners of the best debut band in the USA.

Paul rounds up 1984 in the *NME,* 'The Style Council are brilliant, you'd have to be a plank not to check 'em. We made one absolutely classic single, *You're The Best Thing*, two good ones and one interesting LP.'

1985 was declared International Youth Year (IYY) and Paul was made joint UK President alongside Julie Walters. The official release said, 'nearly one fifth of the earth's residents are young people between the ages of 15 and 24. Their numbers have already reached 922 million and are expected to pass 1 billion by 1990. Yet, until recently, youth have been among the world's most neglected groups. International Youth Year (1985) is intended to change all that.' Paul was unsure of his involvement, though stated he was more interested in the political side rather than the hiking clubs. By September he'd brand it, 'a complete wash out.'

Anthony Harty had left, 'This is a bit of an odd one, I didn't fall and I wasn't pushed. I stopped ringing and so did they. Six of one and half a dozen of the other. I think as with a lot of other members, I'd past my sell-by date! I think Paul said he wanted the line up to change on a frequent basis to keep it fresh or whatever. There was, however, one incident that changed my perspective on the whole thing. There was a little exchange of words with John (Weller) halfway through a live TV show in Germany - but we won't go into that.'

Anthony was replaced by Camelle Hinds (b.15/11/57) who had moved to London from Ipswich at the age of six. He came to Paul's attention after initial drummer Zeke Manyika had informed Paul that he knew a bassist.

Camelle spoke to me, 'I suppose my first adult interests were triggered by watching Freddie and The Dreamers, Hermans Hermits and The Beatles of course. When I witnessed and identified with the Motown era, especially the *Jackson Five* sharing affro affinity, I just had to indulge.'

'My Grandfather was a Jazz guitar tutor in Brooklyn, New York, my cousin the female singer of the *New Platters*, my mother still loves to sing Jazz and my father lived part of the *Charlie Parker/Miles Davies* era frequenting the night spots of 'Lennox Avenue' Harlem... all that organic fusion must have rubbed off in some be-bop way!'

Camelle 'came to Paul Weller's notice and then I received from him the first ever call on my newly acquired device called an answer machine, a poetic gift! Paul invited me to play on the forthcoming album *Our Favourite Shop*. I was elated! I knew of The Style Council and had met Paul once on a TV show in Holland when he was in The Jam.'

21st - *Whole Point II* and *Down In The Seine* are recorded at Solid Bond Studios. One b-side and one album track. This was the 2nd time TSC used the accordion, the last being on *Long Hot Summer*.

Down In The Seine has a clever French section which has never been translated. Wholepoint received an exact literal translation from Andrew Allen, Ottawa, Canada and printed here, hopefully Paul, as it was meant to come across.

When we have nothing left in ourselves
When we have no refuge,
When we can no longer escape
When we don't know where to run,
Black like the night
Yes, black like my soul
Black like the waters in which I sink. © Paul Weller, 1985

It is still a fans favourite on vinyl and live as a solo track when Paul plays it, minus the above French verse.

11th - *The Tube*, for a Jacuzzi based interview with Paul and long time friend Jools Holland from Squeeze, where TSC history to date is covered.

12th - Another exclusive on Lenny Henry's *Saturday Live*. Lenny joined TSC on stage to sing full live vocals and ad-lib on *You're The Best Thing*. Also performed was a much improved live version of *Speak Like A Child* with Dee doing Tracie's vocals. Paul sported a 'coal not dole' badge in further support of the miners.

26th/27th - Steve took part in a 36 hour drum marathon at Liverpool, Royal Court for the 2nd anti-heroin *Drums Over The Mersey* benefit night.

31st - *Boy Who Cried Wolf* is recorded. Tracie is asked to record the backing vocals in her last piece of work with TSC. Singer Steve Rinaldi believes he has decrypted the near impossible to make out ending, which is never listed in any of the lyrics;

'It's a funny thing that turned us round, and now it's me who's tears fall down. I played so cool when you were mine, but like a fool I froze at the time.' © Paul Weller.

FEBRUARY

5th - Photo shoot for forthcoming sleeve and promotional material. The result is the photo that was included as an insert within the LP.

The current plan is to record around 21 tracks in approximately 10 weeks. Two tracks required a studio larger than Solid Bond, for *Come To Milton Keynes* with a string section of 12 violins, 2 violas and 2 cellos alongside a harp and 2 trumpets. Also *A Stones Throw Away* with 2 violins, a viola and a cello.

An idea of what was to come on the next album could be gleamed from an earlier *Record Mirror* interview with Mick. 'Politics shouldn't be put into a little box and neatly hidden away. It is about human concerns and anyone not interested in politics is not interested in life.' He states that, 'all the best songs have human emotion in, so why shouldn't politics and music mix?'

17th - A short documentary was made for International Youth Year. It starred TSC, Madness, Strawberry Switchblade, Rik Mayall, Martin Ware, Robbie Coltrane, Julie Walters and Lenny Henry. It aimed to make young people aware of what IYY 1985 was all about. Paul played a short acoustic set, though none of it was ever shown on screen.

Steve White had just finished a 'busy day' recording *Our Favourite Shop* at Solid Bond Studios when the phone rang asking him to get to Townhouse Studios ASAP as the Redskins' drummer had unexpectedly left and the studio was costing £80 an hour. As a result, the single *(Burn It Up) Bring It Down (This Insane Thing)* was recorded in a few hours.

TSC are rumoured to be headlining at this years Glastonbury Festival in June. A 3 day advance ticket can be purchased for £16. The other main acts booked were Aswad, Boomtown Rats, Echo and The Bunnymen, Hugh Masekela, Ian Dury, James, Joe Cocker, The Men They Couldn't Hang, Microdisney, The Pogues, Roger Chapman and Working Week. As a reference point the price of a ticket for the same festival in 2008 is £155 with Shakin' Stevens putting in an appearance!

MARCH

1st - *Spin Driftin* and *Internationalists* are recorded. One future b-side and one album track.

World tour dates are released and 6 countries will be visited before the return to the UK in the autumn; Belgium, Denmark, Japan, Australia, Italy and Germany. UK dates to follow.

The Style Population hints at a song *Have You Ever Had It Blue* (performed on the October '84 tour) being included on the album. This was only partially correct as Steve White used the song's tune but penned new lyrics and renamed it *With Everything To Lose*. Paul at the time was looking for new lyrics for *Have You Ever Had It Blue*.

Steve White's visit to the House of Commons, London as part of the Youth Trade Union Rights Campaign concerning the Youth Training Scheme (YTS) had shocked him. At the time, 21 people had died on the YTS which moved Steve into putting words to paper. Steve recalls it as, 'a very proud moment for me as it seemed to shock people that the noisy sod at the back had come out and done something a bit creative in their eyes.'

The newly recorded track, *Walls Come Tumbling Down* would get the nod for the new single and would be *the* song most will associate with The Style Council.

APRIL

The proposed short film that Paul and Paolo Hewitt were scripting to promote the LP did not materialise. This had been planned since 1984 and another attempt would be made next year (in the end it would be 1987 before the film JerUSAlem would be released).

Just before the band set off for Warsaw, Poland a press release details the forthcoming UK *Internationalists '85* tour. Tickets priced at £5.50 except London at £6.50 would quickly sell out despite the LP not being released for another month.

London, Brixton Academy (June 5th)
Bournemouth, International Centre (6th). Though gig would be at The Windsor Hall.
Portsmouth, Guildhall (7th)
Brighton, Centre (8th)
Birmingham, Odeon (9th/10th)
Sheffield, City Hall (11th)
Nottingham, Royal Centre (13th)
Manchester, Apollo (14th)
Liverpool, Empire (15th)
Glasgow, Apollo (16th)

In addition, the Glastonbury Festival was on 22nd and *Live Aid* in July. The Glasgow Apollo would be the last night of the tour and last night for the famous venue as it was facing demolition immediately after.

11th - TSC with Helen Turner fly from Heathrow to Warsaw for 4 days to record the promotional video for *Walls Come Tumbling Down*. They are one of the first European bands permitted to record in Poland. Mick said that Gordon Lewis Productions were asked about recommending a band to go there and they thought of The Style Council.

12th - The day was spent filming on the trams and around the city. Mick accidentally caused a hostile situation when he bumped into a man carrying a baby, who in turn dropped it on the tram stairs. Thankfully all was well with the baby and filming could continue until the police had to be called to move on a drunk man who was deliberately blocking the filming.

13th - Today's filming was at *The Akwarium*, the only jazz club in Warsaw. The audience in the club were invited along by a local radio station and clapped politely when prompted by Tim Pope who was again the director. This scene would make up the main part of the finished video.

14th - The final scenes where Mick is seen chasing the tram were recorded before the return flight home to Heathrow.

Steve White was, 'glad to get home. A great experience and a valuable one. It made me realise what's good about living in Britain and worth valuing our health service and oil reserves.'

Helen Turner recalls, 'It didn't stop raining for the entire time we were there. We might as well have been in Birmingham.'

Paul wasn't impressed either, 'There's not actually much you can say about it without putting it down. I don't want to sound too negative, but it looked pretty much like I thought it would, drab and boring.'

17th - *Our Favourite Shop* is complete and on schedule. Steve has finished his work on the album with some percussion overdub.

Gary Crowley interviews Paul and Mick at Solid Bond Studios for inclusion on the b-side of the *Our Favourite Shop* cassette (only). Gary telling me, 'Paul sometimes, bless his cottons, could be a bit of a tinker to interview back then. I now get the impression that he is a lot more relaxed about interviews and he enjoys it now. It took him a while, but he got there! Back in the early 80's Paul was a bit begrudging of an interviewee, that is where Mick sort of complimented him. That took the sting out of Paul being interviewed on his own. When Mick came that sort of made it more fun for both of them really. They were on good form that day.'

23rd - Paul goes to see Nina Simone at Ronnie Scott's Club, London.

24th - Paul and Mick appear live on Capitol Radio, London, playing some of their favourite tracks alongside host Gary Crowley. This came over as quite a difficult and awkward interview for Gary to handle as Paul & Mick were not really answering his questions. Gary was not allowed to mention the title of the new LP to the public so when he played an exclusive 'club mix' version of *Our Favourite Shop* he had to say it had no title - even though Paul & Mick admitted the LP was finished!

Mick said the forthcoming live shows would be 'punchier', self contained and have no horn section this time. He also discussed his recent part in an Italian soap opera equivalent of *Coronation Street*.

Paul discussed International Youth Year and the *Absolute Beginners* movie which The Style Council had contributed a track too, but again he wouldn't say anymore.

I spoke to Gary in July 2008 about this show, 'They were just being a little bit awkward, maybe it was me expecting too much or something. I was a little bit peeved a little bit pissed off about it. Infact Paolo talks about this in his *Changing Man* book. I can remember I felt the interview wasn't that great, I felt they weren't really making the effort.

Paolo got it a little bit wrong by saying that Paul was a little bit pissed off with some of the bands I had interviewed on the program which wasn't true at all. What had happened was that I wasn't happy because I felt the interview with Paul & Mick could have been a lot better and felt they were both being a little bit awkward. Afterwards we were having coffee in the West End, Cappuccinos it would have been back then. Paul sort of knew I was a little bit pissed off with the interview and he was quietly fuming, then he just let rip, "If I didn't like you so much Gary I'd kick yer fuckin' head in" and then he stormed out of the café! There was Paolo, me, Simon Halfon and Eugene Manzi of London records. I was like, "what the fuck was all that about?"

'But fair play to him, he rang me up the next day and said he was out of order, apologised. '

Gary went onto say, 'They did me some great jingles back in the day, bless their cottons. They weren't doing any jingles for anyone else, I got some great ones. Mick did this great one in a Noel Coward type voice, Paul did this other one, "cool, clean, hard." That was good of them as well.'

25th - Paul appeared at the House of Commons, London in support of the Youth Trade Union Rights Campaign.

27th - Paul & Mick are interviewed on Saturday morning children's show *No.73* with the TV debut of the *Walls Come Tumbling Down* promotional video. This short lived show was based around a house in Battersea.

MAY

2nd - The music press advert for the next single shows a mosaic picture of then USA President (1981 to 1989) Ronald Reagan and the words, 'You don't have to take this crap.' Identical t-shirts were also produced en-masse. 'You don't have to take this crap, you don't have to sit back and relax' is a timeless line commenting on the 'Frankie says relax' mania which had swept the country. Youngsters everywhere were sporting Frankie Goes To Hollywood t-shirts on the back of their three number 1 singles.

3rd - The picture sleeve to *Walls Come Tumbling Down* drew a lot of attention as it featured Mick deep in make-up. This was 1 of 3 photo sessions short-listed. The UK was one of the few countries to have this picture sleeve.

The majority of releases featured the black and white, February 1985 photograph, given away as an insert in the LP.

Steve White was for the first time, a band member, listed alongside Paul and Mick, with the Honorary Councillor's being Dee C Lee (Vocals) and Helen Turner (Piano). Produced by Peter Wilson and Paul Weller.

Trip to BBC Broadcasting House for 2 appearances. The 1st was earlier on Radio 1 where Paul, Paul Hardcastle and Janice Long featured on *The Round Table* - the show where everyone rated the coming weeks single releases. Later that day there was an appearance on the popular live Friday night *Terry Wogan* show to perform *Walls Come Tumbling Down.*

5th - Back to BBC Broadcasting House and *Radio 1* with DJ Janice Long. Paul and Mick previewed the new album, track by track.

The Cappuccino Kid stated that the b-side *Bloodsports* was about 'the hypocrisy that accompanies this foul and indefensible act.' Paul added that, 'just because people have been doing it for hundreds of years it's supposed to make it okay, but it doesn't.'

The writing royalties, 'go to the Bristol Defence Fund for John Curtin and Terry Helsby currently in Bristol prison for anti bloodsport activities.' There was also an address for the Hunt Sabateurs. Paul 'did not know the two boys in the nick, but I agree with what the saboteurs do. It's hard for them to raise money because they're labeled as extremists, even though support for them is really widespread.'

A 12" promotional release in Japan contained a unique sleeve with *Walls Come Tumbling Down* and *Shout To The Top* on the a-side and tracks from Brian Ferry on the b-side. In America, Artisan Studios released two 12" one sided acetates of *Walls Come Tumbling Down* and *Internationalists.*

The same day Dizzy Hites released his version of *The Gospel* which was written by Paul and originally appeared on *Café Bleu* last year.

7th - Paul and Mick are interviewed on *Whistle Test* where outtakes from the *Walls Come Tumbling Down* promotional video alongside exclusive footage of a drunken Polish local attempting karate-style kicks at the camera.

9th - An excellent powerful (albeit mimed) appearance of *Walls Come Tumbling Down* on *Top of the Pops*. Mick sporting his striped 'Zebra' jacket which he would next wear at Glastonbury.

12th - *Walls Come Tumbling Down* enters the chart and would peak at number 6, staying in the top 100 for the now customary 8 weeks. This has been quoted by many as being the career best single. The b-side *Whole Point II* was recorded using Paul's original lyrics for the song. Strange as it may seem, if this makes sense, the version on *Café Bleu* was the newer version of the song. Honest!

A quick trip to Italy to promote *Walls Come Tumbling Down*. They would come back aboard the prestigious Orient Express train from Venice to Calais, citing the fear of flying as the excuse for such extravagance. Sara Silver telling Steve Malins, 'they nearly died in a small plane during a storm and that had affected them.'

The tide was turning in the Council's direction and all that is needed is the seal of approval on the much hyped, 'new LP containing 14 absolute new and classic tracks.' The title *Our Favourite Shop* came from a mythical place where Paul and Mick show off the items that have influenced their lives. Cheekily promoted as, 'the second and finest LP from probably the best pop group in the world.'

'The original idea was a kind of parallel between a shop where all our favourite things are jumbled up and thrown in, but in a way which worked, the same way our music has a lot of different styles but what comes out makes sense to us.' (Paul)

'If you wanted a soundtrack for politics and the way society was at that time then it is all contained in that record.' (Paul, *Into Tomorrow*)

'Paul had been a massive fan of British born actor Rupert Everett (b.29/05/59) for a while. He ended up doing the voice over for *Our Favourite Shop*. I was kind of the connection there as I had Rupert on my radio station at the time. We all loved *Another Country* and I got Rupert on the radio show. Rupert said, "Paul and Mick are fans? Wow, I think they are great as well" - so I was the intermediary. You'll notice the movie poster is prominent on the sleeve of *Our Favourite Shop*.'
(Gary Crowley)

Paul played 6 and 12 string Guitars, Bass Guitar and Synth. Mick on Hammond, Piano Forte and electronic Keyboards. Steve on Drums and Percussion.

An incredible 22 Honorary Councillor's assisted on *Our Favourite Shop*. Dee C Lee (Vocals), Lenny Henry (Vocals), Tracie Young (Vocals), Camelle Hinds (Bass), Stewart Prosser (Trumpet/Flugel Horn), David Defries (Trumpet/Flugel Horn), Mike Mower (Flute/Saxophone), Chris Lawrence (Trombone), Clark Kent (Contra Bass), Gary Wallis (Percussion)

John Mealing (Orchestration/String arrangement), Anne Stephenson (Violin), Charlie Buchanan (Violin), Jocelyn Pook (Viola), Audrey Riley (Cello), Peter Wilson (Keyboard Sequencing), Jeremy Wakefield (Keyboard Sequencing), Patrick Grundy-White (French Horn), Steve Dawson (Trumpet), Billy Chapman (Saxophone), Kevin Miller (Bass) and Helen Turner (Piano).

'The subject matter of the album is Britain today, all that we see around us. There are songs about families breaking up, to have to find work in other areas, new towns where only a facade of real community exists, the disgusting waste of life through heroin. Songs of despair, hope, total realism, luck, selfishness and love. I've never believed so positively in any record as I do in this one. I don't say we will never match it again but it will take some doing!' (*Style Population*)

Mick took lead vocals on *Homebreakers* which was a direct attack on Norman Tebbit who in 1981 said, 'I grew up in the 1930s with an unemployed father. He didn't riot. He got on his bike and looked for work, and he kept looking until he found it.'

Compared to *Café Bleu* there was only 1 instrumental, Mick explaining how *Our Favourite Shop* originated, 'This started on the last tour in the soundcheck when I had been doodling around with a Latin rhythm. Rather than call it *The Talbot Samba* we thought we'd call it *Our Favourite Shop*. I see it as the kind of theme music for the album, if we made a film of the LP it would be up there at the front.'

This comment seemed out of place when the USA release actually removed *Our Favourite Shop* and replaced it with a new mix of *Shout To The Top*. For some European releases *Shout To The Top* replaced *A Stand Up Comics Instruction*.

'Not the noise of revolution.' (*Sounds*)

'Slicker and more confident than ever.' (*Melody Maker*)

'The Council at their vibrant best.' (Chris Mugan, *The Independent*)

'The Lenny Henry track, I thought at the time it was OK, but I got sick of it quite quickly. The rest of the album has so many different colours across the whole thing, different moods. Paul and Mick's writing and musical ability is all distilled wonderfully for that album. It was The Style Council right on the button.' (Gary Crowley)

In the *Internationalists* tour program Paul spoke about the single, 'People shouldn't take it too literally. I wouldn't like, "you don't have to take this crap" to be taken as our final statement on the album as it tends to oversimplify everything we've said before. There's a brilliant quote on the sleeve from Tony Benn which says something like it's not enough to write songs and poems about liberty, you have to dedicate your whole life to it.'

For the USA, *Our Favourite Shop* was renamed *Internationalists* with a brand new sleeve and remix of *Shout To The Top* replaced the instrumental *Our Favourite Shop*. This mix appeared on the original UK CD only. Also, for the one and only time there was an exclusive USA Cappuccino Kid story, though substantially shorter than the European equivalent. 'Welcome comrade citizens! Our greetings go out to you, we hope, through the sounds and words of this - the second long playing record from Europe's very own *Stilyagi* The Style Council.'

'About as unexpected a pleasure as one finds in our retreated world, among the most politically astute, socially incisive and purely radical statements ever set to vinyl. It is an album that exceeds expectations by exploding them. It is a vital, inflammatory, savvy offering from an important new band.' (USA press release)

The LP did not make the USA charts but it is reported that over 1 million copies had sold worldwide by the end of 1985. Chart hits were scored in Australia, New Zealand, Belgium, Holland, Italy, Germany, Norway, Japan, Sweden, Iceland and Denmark. It was stated that a minimum of 100,000 LP's sold in Japan.

This success was credited to Richard Ogden, at 35 the youngest Managing Director in the UK for a record label. He was previously 'Head of International' at Polydor. Richard had co-managed Motorhead of all people and alongside trying to make TSC more internationally appealing he signed Andrew Lloyd Webber's musical *Phantom of The Opera* in 1986. He was also the major influence behind *Our Favourite Shop* being released in so many formats across Europe.

In Europe the *Internationalists* theme of *Our Favourite Shop* had to be made clear as music journalists received translations of the lyrics in their own language along with a copy of the album to review. There was no gatefold sleeve for many of the European releases and like the USA release *Shout To The Top* replaced *Our Favourite Shop*.

In 2003 *Our Favourite Shop* was voted album of the day on BBC Radio 6 and Julie Cullen said many positive things, 'It's musically all over the map incorporating soul, r'n'b, and jazz and addresses a huge range of social issues from the miners strike to apartheid with scathing criticisms of racism, unemployment and Margaret Thatcher which makes it sound a bit like a Ben Elton routine except this is good.'

21st - To promote *Our Favourite Shop* a live appearance on *The Whistle Test* took place where very powerful, raw versions of *Homebreakers* and *Walls Come Tumbling Down* were performed. The line up was Helen Turner (Piano), Camelle Hinds (Bass), Robbie Granfield (Keys), Steve Sidelnyk (Percussion), Steve White (Drums) and Dee C Lee (Vocals)

26th - Paul and Mick are live on Sunday night TV for a BBC Ecological/green issues program, *Worldwise* for an exclusive, live version of *Bloodsports* which came across really well. This is the only live appearance of the song. Paul was also interviewed by Sarah Greene, 'No one could accuse you of being a purveyor of pop pap.'

31st - *The Lodgers* was performed on *6:20 Soul Train* alongside *With Everything To Lose*, though not known at the time it will be released as a single in September. A scene from this would be used for the picture sleeve of the next single. *The Lodgers* was a new recording from scratch over a two week period and not just re-mixed.

TSC returned Lenny Henry's *Our Favourite Shop* favour by appearing on his show to mime to *Internationalists*.

JUNE

1st - Whilst tour rehearsals were underway, *(When You) Call Me* was recorded. Far too late for the LP but too good to shelf. It would make it straight onto the b-side of the next single and into the live shows starting next week.

5th - London, The Brixton Academy. 'Style Council on stage at 7.45pm.'

6th - Bournemouth, Windsor Hall

7th - Portsmouth, Guildhall

8th - Brighton, The Centre

9th - Birmingham, Odeon Theatre. Big party atmosphere on the back of the news that *Our Favourite Shop* entered the chart at number 1. It would stay in the top 100 for 22 weeks, more successful and more well known than *Café Bleu*, but four months less in the chart.

10th - Birmingham, Odeon Theatre

11th - Sheffield, City Hall

13th - Nottingham, Royal Centre

14th - Manchester, Apollo

15th - Liverpool, Empire

16th - Glasgow, Apollo Theatre

For the first time TSC did not have a brass section, 'We dropped the horn section because I think there was a danger of us getting stuck with that sound. We like to feel that we're adaptable and that we can change the line-up.' (Paul)

The line-up for the Internationalists '85 tour; Paul, Mick, Steve, Dee, Helen Turner (Keyboards) and Camelle Hinds (Bass). Vaughn Toulouse and Dizzy Hites guest for *A Gospel* and *The Stand Up Comics Instructions*.

23 tracks were played on this tour; 1 *unreleased, 1 Dee C Lee solo, 2 b-sides, 9 LP tracks and 10 singles.

The Lodgers, My Ever Changing Moods, Homebreakers, A Man of Great Promise, Come To Milton Keynes, Luck (Dee C Lee), You're The Best Thing, Big Boss Groove, It Just Came To Pieces In My Hands, Down In The Seine, With Everything To Lose, A Stones Throw Away, See The Day (Dee C Lee), A Word From Our Leaders*, Walls Come Tumbling Down, Internationalists, Long Hot Summer, (When You) Call Me, The Stand Up Comics Instructions, Money Go Round / Soul Deep / Strength of Your Nature - medley, Move On Up.

Compared to the autumn 1984 tour 18 tracks were added;

1983 - It Just Came To Pieces In My Hands.
1984 - My Ever Changing Moods, See The Day, Strength of Your Nature and Soul Deep.
New - The Lodgers, Homebreakers, Come To Milton Keynes, Luck, Down In The Seine, With Everything To Lose, A Stones Throw Away, A Word From Our Leaders, Walls Come Tumbling Down, Internationalists, (When You) Call Me, Move On Up, The Stand Up Comics Instructions.

Fourteen tracks were dropped;

1983 - Mick's Up, Le Depart, Speak Like A Child, Headstart For Happiness
1984 - Shout To The Top, Don't Do It Baby, Have You Ever Had It Blue, Razors Edge, Never Stop (A Message), Here's One That Got Away, Whole Point of No Return, One Nation Under A Groove, Me Ship Came In, Nzuri Beat.

The songs retained were; A Man of Great Promise, You're The Best Thing, Big Boss Groove, Long Hot Summer and Money Go Round.

'TSC's problem is that their competence is sufficient only for them to operate at that most useless of levels, semi fluency. Weller simply doesn't have the commanding presence and magistical ease of a soul man...he can't dance.' (*Sounds*)

21st - *Come To Milton Keynes* was the 2nd single from *Our Favourite Shop*. Steve was re-confirmed as the 3rd band member on the sleeve. Produced by Peter Wilson and Paul Weller with orchestration by John Mealing. Outside the UK, *Come To Milton Keynes* was only released in Spain (different sleeve) and Ireland, then later in Japan as part of their exclusive 7" box set.

Elsewhere, *The Boy Who Cried Wolf* was released. The 7" contained an exclusive, edited version, as the original was too long for a single. Produced by Peter Wilson and Paul Weller.

22nd - TSC's first ever outdoor festival headline took place at Glastonbury. It had been pouring rain all weekend with the potential of 50,000 mud throwers. The only remedy for the band was to drink on the bus and go on stage blitzed on Pernod.

There is actually a photo of Paul under an umbrella backstage looking the worse for wear with the aforementioned Pernod in his hand.

'I got pelted with mud, all over my white trousers. It was so bad that I had to put down my guitar. I was so drunk I couldn't even play.' (Paul)

In 1985 Paul told *Style Population,* 'I had never seen so much mud, but what a gig, brilliant. I was drunk though, I took one look at the rain and mud and decided I couldn't go on sober.' Eleven years later in *Select* magazine his memory of the event was still clear, 'Everyone of the band, even Steve White, who doesn't really drink, were slaughtered. I fell over on stage, couldn't get up. The crowd loved it cos we were more pissed than them!'

If you closely listen to the tape you hear Mick say, 'you cannot keep a good man down' at the point where Paul clambers back to his feet. Priceless.

'It was total utter mayhem, to see Paul flailing away on his guitar with his white Levis, trying to keep them clean as the mud was flying. It was brilliant.' (Steve White in Steve Malins' book)

Glastonbury was Dennis Munday's last gig with TSC as he moved onto pastures new. In his 2007 book *Shout To The Top* he talks about how Steve White invited the entire Glastonbury crowd to his leaving night at the Lamb and Flag pub in James Street, London.

Tracks - *Internationalists, Come To Milton Keynes, Homebreakers, See The Day, The Lodgers, Whole Point of No Return, Our Favourite Shop, Long Hot Summer, (When You) Call Me, Walls Come Tumbling Down, Money Go Round, Soul Deep, Strength of Your Nature, It Just Came To Pieces In My Hands, The Stand Up Comic's Instructions and The Big Boss Groove.*

In Concert~365 was a 55 minute BBC transcription disc of Glastonbury. Only 2 of the above tracks were omitted: *Come To Milton Keynes* and *The Stand Up Comics Instructions.* Engineered by Crispin Murray and produced by Pete Dauncey. This disc like most of the transcription discs is near impossible to obtain as the stations were instructed to destroy the vinyl after the broadcast.

23rd - The Redskins single which Steve helped record on 17th February, *(Burn It Up) Bring It Down (This Insane Thing),* made it to number 33 in the charts.

28th - Trip to Denmark for the Roskilde Festival, filmed for TV. Accompanying the band would be professional photographer Tom Sheehan whose photos from this would appear throughout the year.

Italian TV run a 1 hour special featuring no less than 8 interviews (dubbed), all promotional videos to date and an exclusive live performance from *The Tube* of *Speak Like A Child*, not originally shown in the UK.

30th - *Come To Milton Keynes* enters the chart and would peak at number 23, the first single not to make the top 20, staying in the top 100 for 5 weeks, the shortest to date. However, it did contain the much preferred *(When You) Call Me* on the b-side and the 12" with the adventurous *Our Favourite Shop* and *The Lodgers (Club mix)*.

TSC were also scheduled to promote the video single on children's TV show *Poparound* presented by Gary Crowley but the appearance was cancelled following concerns by the program makers over the videos content. Gary remembers, 'Dee did it with *See The Day*. It was done in Birmingham and then in Nottingham, but I don't remember the boys doing it.'

'I regret *Come To Milton Keynes* as a single choice, and not because of its low chart position.' (Paul)

I spoke to Gary Crowley about this single, 'I am always the one that gets the blame for that single. I loved that song, it is a great song. At the time I said to Paul, "that's a pop classic, this is a classic, it has got to be a single, got to be a single." When it only got to number 23 Paul told Gary, "That is the last time I ask you what record we should release."

Lyrically it was very dark, but the tune was so uplifting, an effortless pop tune, I still love it to this day, "may I walk you home tonight" (sings), it was my fault, yeh!'

Was this single the first mistake? Much had been made of the *Milton Keynes* issue which definitely affected the airplay and validity of the track as a single. Such was the outrage it would even get a headline slot on Breakfast TV News. Paul hit back saying, 'It was about urban life in general.'

The hard to make out closing lyrics of the song are, 'The songs we live by are beyond our means, but the sun never sets, and were all safe and sound, God bless you all God bless.' Words and Music © P Weller, EMI Music Publishers Ltd.

JULY

Trip to Belgium for 2 appearances in the 4 day Torhout - Werchter festival held in the towns of Torhout and Werchter.

6th - Torhout Festival, West Flanders, Belgium with The Ramones, Lloyd Cole & The Commotions and R.E.M.

8th - Werchter Festival, Rotselaar, Belgium with U2, Depeche Mode and Jo Cocker.

12th - Today we got a classic, strange, awkward interview on BBC Breakfast time to review the papers. Paul even doing impersonations. For the entire interview Paul sat down, doubled over with arms across his stomach (head nearly at his knees).

Things were not going well with the presenter as *Milton Keynes* was discussed. 'They're up in arms about it, big deal!' and on the subject of Princess Michael of Kent, 'Poor old thing, viewers please send your cheques to the Royal family' with Mick adding, 'Poor old stick.'

TSC get the front cover of *Melody Maker*, titled 'We're the best band in the world.'

That afternoon the band head to Wembley Stadium for rehearsals to prepare for the biggest live event in the history of music. Mick had to then get to BBC Radio 1 for a *Roundtable* show he was already late for. If memory serves me right he reviewed the first few singles via telephone on what must have been a very early car phone.

13th - The most successful pop concert ever, *Live Aid,* took place at Wembley Stadium and was beamed throughout the world. Live Aid tickets only cost £5 but with a donation added you ended paying £25. Doors opened at 10am.

The official 164 page £5 Wembley tour programme contained various pictures of Paul at the making of the single and also a 3 page colour TSC spread containing an all-time classic Weller statement, 'Look upon us like you would a bottle of Ribena - we stand for our children and their children's children.'

Ribena would repay the compliments in 2003 by using *You're The Best Thing* for their UK TV advertising campaign!

TSC were 2nd on stage at 12:19 after Status Quo to perform in 15 minutes, *You're The Best Thing, The Big Boss Groove, Internationalists* and *Walls Come Tumbling Down*. Paul and Mick were then interviewed back-stage by Janice Long.

With the Royal Family in the box, including Prince Charles and Lady Diana, the expected political statement from Paul did not materialise and the set past without incident.

Looking back Dee confessed to *Smash Hits*, 'I was so nervous about that. I threw up half an hour before we went on-stage. I was shaking so much I couldn't put my eye make up on so I had to go on-stage in sunglasses.' Mick was also beaming, 'atmosphere both on-stage and back-stage was terrific.' Steve was just as enthusiastic, 'The atmosphere was unbelievable and the genuine warmth of the crowd as we stepped out and grooved to *You're The Best Thing* was truly inspiring.'

Helen Turner told me, 'We were backstage, second act, waiting for Status Quo to finish. We had a peek at the auditorium and someone said, hold your arms out straight. Everyone was shaking. I gave silent thanks that in the first song I was at the back of the stage and didn't have to face the ocean of faces. But it was great.'

Camelle Hinds, 'It signified a ray of hope for more consideration regarding the vast level of cosmopolitan integration that makes up a significant proportion of our United Kingdom. Furthermore, my father began to allay his disappointment at me never reaching Wembley as a professional footballer.'

Remarkably on the same day, TSC travel to record *Come To Milton Keynes* for TV show *Kelly's Eye*. Helen Turner, 'Oddly, we went off to Kent straight after to do some local TV show. Something, I think, that had been booked some time before.'

This was a bizarre, rarely played live rendition, where TSC called in around 10 assistants, all dressed as monks to play the harp, horn, cello, trumpet, etc.

I caught up with Cello player Audrey Riley in July 2008 who was one of the "monks"; 'I was asked to play on *Our Favourite Shop* through another player I think. I turned up at the studio, there was an arranger, John Mealing, who'd done some very good arrangements. We played and recorded them, and that was it. I was then asked once more for a TV show (Kelly's Eye) where, bizarrely, we all had to dress as monks. Finally we were asked to go and play again at Wembley Arena in December, I remember enjoying it. Paul Weller seemed a really nice guy, courteous and modest.'

Everyone returned to Wembley Stadium from Kent for the grand finale. Helen Turner confirming, 'We returned to Wembley shortly before the finale and edged out onto the stage with everyone else. Not really knowing the words to *Feed The World*, Dee, Camelle, Sidelnyk and I were desperately trying to look at a lyric sheet on the piano, somewhere over Freddie Mercury's shoulder, I think.'

Summing up *Live Aid* one magazine said, 'No one could call Paul Weller a hunk but when he speaks (or sings) people take notice and he's not afraid of appearing wimpish because he has faith in his ideals.'

'Preferred to take the world by stealth, not storm in an unmemorable performance.' (Nigel Cross)

A David Bailey *Live Aid* portrait of TSC sold at Sotheby's auction for £198 and Paul's Rickenbacker guitar for £2000.

The actual *Live Aid* concert had never seen release until an official DVD was issued in November 2004 to combat growing piracy. TSC got two of their four songs included, *Internationalists* and *Walls Come Tumbling Down*. In 2005 Steve White (with The Who) & Steve Sidelnyk (with Madonna) would be the only Style Councillor's from the original show appearing in the 20 year anniversary *Live 8* concert.

A compilation album *Son of Jobs For The Boys* was released for awareness of unemployment in Merseyside. '112 jobs for 32,000 school leavers.' An exclusive TSC track was donated, *Come To Milton Keynes (Instrumental)*. Initial copies also contained a 7" EP featuring Dee C Lee as part of the Dust Choir on *Another Fly Network*.

23rd - A meeting took place at the Labour Party Headquarters in London to discuss a future project involving politicians, yet unnamed. Paul is there with Billy Bragg.

TSC had scheduled to tour North America but it was cancelled. A fan, Keith recalls one date, 'It was due to take place at a venue called the "Pine Knob Music Theatre" or "Pine Knob Amphitheater" and is located in Clarkston, Michigan. This is about an hour outside of Detroit. Tickets were sold for the gig, and I had one in hand. Needless to say, it was cancelled and I was gutted. On November 14, 1992 Weller was in the Detroit area for a show and when asked about the aborted TSC show he said that the record company pulled out, or pulled out the backing for it at the time.'

Exact USA cancelled tour dates are unknown so please forward on any details.

28th - TSC fly to the Far East for a tour of Japan, mainly in stadiums, including 2 nights in Yokohama for 27,000 people.

AUGUST

2nd - Osaka, Castle Hall for 'Rock in Japan.' TSC only play as "special guests" on a bill that included the headlining Culture Club, Go West, and The Associates.

4th - Fukuoka Kokusai, Center, Fukuoka

7th - A group of musicians hold another meeting at 104 Walworth Road, London, the Labour Party Headquarters. Paul sent his apologies as he is currently in Japan. The movement today named themselves Red Wedge, the name and logo from a 1919 poster by Russian constructivist artist *El Lissitzky*, "Beat the Whites with the Red Wedge." The logo was designed by Neville Brody a graphic designer and art director, known for his work with *The Face* magazine.

8th - Nagoya Kokusai Tenjiho, Nagoya

10th - Yokohama Stadium. Afternoon slot. It started off with a rendition of *Singing In The Rain*, led by Steve White. Camelle Hinds recalls, 'We decided to go on with umbrellas imitating Gene Kelly. It tickled me, reminiscent of my paper round days doing the same along the dimly lit streets of Limehouse, E14.'

11th - Yokohama Stadium. Afternoon Slot

12th - The Style Council Fly to Sydney, Australia for the 'Tumbling Down Under' tour. However, the unfortunate news that a plane from the same airline had just crashed 30 minutes earlier, killing over 500 people, no doubt played on their minds throughout the flight.

Apart from an appearances on the chart show *Countdown* the band have a week's holiday before the tour begins. Paul & Mick presented *Countdown* and were quite humorous in their comments of the forthcoming bands. It was the most popular music program in Australia and was shown on the nationwide ABC network every Sunday. The Style Council appeared for 2 mimed performances, *Walls Come Tumbling Down* and *The Boy Who Cried Wolf*. They were also presented with a gold disc each for sales of *Café Bleu* in Australia.

Back home, the British press report a major incident at the Regency Hotel where a girlfriend allegedly trashed the room. It said that Paul had to foot a bill of £2,600 for "ripped wallpaper, a smashed stool and burns on the carpet."

18th - Melbourne, Australia. Recorded for a one hour TV and Radio broadcast and from this came an Australian only single, *(When You) Call Me*. This came with a superb unique picture sleeve, available on a two track 7" and three track 12". Producer: Chris Boniface, Engineer: Jim Atkins. 7" imports sold at an expensive £7 on initial UK release.

Back home Tracie's last single to make the top 100, *I Can't Leave You Alone*, peaks at number 60.

19th- A surprise, impromptu gig at The Venue in Melbourne for local children's charities, in particular homeless youths.

20th - A near 600 mile train journey between Melbourne and Sydney (again to avoid flying) for another four dates was made eventful as the tour manager had Drums, Keyboard and Guitars brought on board for the band.

21st - The 3,500 capacity Hordern Pavilion, Sydney Showground sees a colourful show. Paul in a blue and white stripe t-shirt with a jersey tied round his waste, Mick with a red and white striped vest with a large cowboy style hat and Helen in a lemon 2 piece!

The local newspaper was raving about the gig with the title, "Superb performers come of age." Starting with, 'Paul Weller bounced on stage dressed to dance. It was obvious he was there to enjoy himself and the other all-dancing Council members complemented his enthusiasm.' The negative points were the feedback on the amps during Dee's solo piece and the 'unnecessary' Steve White drum solos. The review ended with, 'they left so much of their repertoire out and still gave a solid jam-packed show. It is safe to say that after only 2 years TSC have come of age.'

22nd - Second night at The Hordern Pavilion, Sydney Showground. Mick was, 'very pleased with the reaction we got there and on a personal level I found the people nothing like the stereotype image we are usually given of Australians.'

24th - TSC fly back to the UK.

A double-sided picture disc interview LP, recorded in Australia, appeared in the UK from Baktabak records. Mick on one side, Paul on the other. Promoted as containing, 'rare and spontaneous interviews with the stars. These interviews are exclusive and in many cases have been heard by no-one other than the interviewer prior to the release in this series.' Over 150 artists had been covered by the time of TSC release.

SEPTEMBER

2nd - Before the European tour Paul told *Record Mirror* he's keen to add dates, 'I would like to play Russia and China. I think it should have been TSC playing over there, not Wham!'

3rd - A few days to recover from jet lag before leaving for European shores, first stop being Italy for TV and concerts.

7th - *Our Favourite Shop* has reached 100,000 sales in the UK alone.

8th - Festa De L'Unità, Ferrara

10th - Theatre Tendra, Rome. The same night Italian TV broadcast a Style Council special with *You're The Best Thing, Internationalists* and a dubbed interview.

11th - Palasport, Firenze

12th - Modena

13th - Teatro Tenda, Milan. Back in the UK, TV show *Bliss* broadcasts clips of *Walls Come Tumbling Down* from the Roskilde Festival in June.

14th - Parco Pellerina, Torino

Back in the UK, the alternative title, *She Was Only A Shopkeeper's Daughter* was dropped for *The Lodgers* single ('a newly recorded version presented to you by public demand.') Nearly 20 minutes of live music on the 12" meant it had to be recorded at 33rpm. For the first time Dee C Lee got full band member credits, bringing the total permanent members to four.

Joining them was the largest studio entourage to date. Guy Barker, Roddy Lorimer and Luke Tunney (Trumpet), Chris Lawrence, Ashley Slater and Pete Thams (Trombone), Steve Sidelnyk (Congas) and John Mealing (Horn arrangement). Produced by Paul Weller and Brian Robson. Ashley Slater would go on to front a top 3 hit with Freakpower.

For the live b-side tracks it was just Helen Turner (Keyboards), Camelle Hinds (Bass), Steve Sidelnyk (Percussion), Vaughan Toulouse and Dizzi Hites (Rapping).

23rd - The band's best *Top of the Pops* performance was saved for *The Lodgers*. TSC looked the part with everyone sporting blazers, white jeans and loafers. Paul and Dee had obviously been rehearsing the dancing routine as they stepped in unison to the beat. A stark contrast to the story Tracie Young told about the debut *Top of the Pops* appearance in March 1983! Alleged stories came out that Paul had a slight altercation with Martin Gore of Depeche Mode whilst backstage as Gore was apparently not dressed to Paul's liking.

27th - Live on Radio 1's *Roundtable* - Paul Weller, Roger Daltry, Noddy Holder and Phil Collins. After 14 years this was to be the last ever *Roundtable*. Paul cheekily brought along Dee C Lee's forthcoming single *See The Day* to get reviewed and achieve early airplay. Surprisingly Roger, Noddy and Phil all gave it the thumbs up.

28th - *Record Mirror* front cover, titled 'roomer with a view' saying TSC have made 'some excellent music, some mistakes, some incredibly funny videos.'

29th - *The Lodgers* enters the chart and would peak at number 13, staying in the top 100 for 6 weeks.

30th - Tracie releases *Invitation* on Respond with *Record Mirror* full of praise, 'voice is so natural, clean and cutesy.' This is from Tracie's forthcoming LP.

Although not comfortable with the 'spokesman for a generation' tag Paul was increasingly being used to galvanise the youth, particularly those approaching voting age or starting college. The National Union of Students starter pack used the line, 'Stand up, declare yourself an Internationalist' within the editorial from the national President for the UK.

OCTOBER

5th - A full page *NME* advert appears listing all the singles and LP's to date with the scribe, 'for your listening pleasure from probably the best pop group in the world.'

The 2nd leg of the European tour takes in 4 nights in Germany and one in Belgium.

10th - Laeiszhalle Musikhalle, Hamburg

11th - Tempodrom, Treugast, Berlin

13th - Ludwigshafen, Pfalzbau

17th - Philipshalle, Dusseldorf

19th - Deinze Brielpoort, Brussels

26th - Over 100,000 turn up at Hyde Park, London for a benefit gig under the banner, 'Human race or nuclear race - Britain can make a difference.' Paul, Steve, Junior, Gil Scott Heron, Billy Bragg and The Communards all put in an appearance. Tracks played are not known, but as Mick was not there Paul and Steve helped out within the 'supergroup.'

28th - *See The Day* was written two years earlier but is released today by Dee C Lee. Dee has been singing this regularly at Council Meeting's so the fans were well aware of the song. No one though imagined by December this single would be sitting at number 3 in the charts.

A big pull for TSC fans in the single was a live performance of *Luck* from *Our Favourite Shop* and Dee's version of *The Paris Match*. These were performed by 'The Council Quartet.' Dee wrote the sleeve notes, 'It has been a long time since my last piece of plastic went out, and since then some of you might have realised the change in the image as well as in the music. I hope you, like me, feel it is a change for the better, and for those of you who have stuck by me over the past two years, what can I say but thanks for the letters of encouragement.' The single was produced by Brian Robson and 'thanks to my brothers, Paul, Mick and Steve.'

'Ends up drowning in the strings.' (*Record Mirror*)

'Kids will buy it for its Simon Halfon design.' (*NME*)

Dee, despite *The Lodgers* sleeve notes said, 'I am still not a member. Paul and Mick are the only people in The Style Council, but I am an Honorary Councillor.'

NOVEMBER

10th - *See The Day* entered at number 90 and Dee is not confident of it doing much due to the lack of airplay, 'I got a complete blank from the press and radio initially.'

However, it would slowly progress up the chart, sell over 60,000 copies and peak at number 3 by the time TSC play the December dates at Wembley Arena. The actual climb makes interesting reading when you are told that every Style Council release to date has peaked at week 2 in the chart.

See The Day entered at 90, moved to 51 - 38 - 18 - 4 - 3 then stayed at number 3 before dropping to number 6 when the Xmas singles came out. When Dee peaked at number 3 it was ironically her previous employers Wham who would be at number 1 with *I'm Your Man*. Whitney Houston was at number 2.

Dee travelled to Birmingham for Gary Crowley's *Runaround* spoof, *Poparound* to promote the single. She also appeared on *Top of the Pops*, telling *Smash Hits*, 'I had been on lots of times before, but it was different by myself (not with TSC or Wham). It was really funny, the band got stuck in a lift half an hour before the show and the Fire Brigade had to come to get them out!'

Paul and Mick check out Everything But The Girl at Hammersmith Palais, London and also Black Britain, support band for the forthcoming December dates.

Steve White is currently, 'writing melody or harmony on 8 or 9 tracks with Paul Barry (Questions) and Toby Chapman (Keyboards, Spandau Ballet) for a possible solo project,' although he confirmed that nothing ever came of this. Steve is also working with Tracie and rehearsing for the Red Wedge tour, describing it as a, 'very broad socialist ideology who want a Labour Government elected at the next Election.'

21st - Red Wedge was officially launched, Paul and Billy Bragg amongst others were invited by the late Robin Cook to hold a press conference at the Labour Party Headquarters in London and also announce the tour dates. Red Wedge would take to the road in January, the money going to 'youth arts projects and other job creating ventures.'

Tickets prices between £3 and £5. A warehouse party would be announced at the end of the tour. There would also be a documentary made during the tour.

Apollo, Manchester (January 25th)
Odeon, Birmingham (27th)
De Montfort, Leicester (28th)
St.Georges, Bradford (29th)
Playhouse, Edinburgh (30th)
City Hall, Newcastle (31st)

Same night Dee would play her first solo gig, a 40 minute set at the Camden Palace, London, coming on stage at 11pm. Tickets at £4.

22nd - On the success of Live Aid, *Do They Know It's Christmas* re-enters the chart a year after the original, peaking this time at number 3. Exactly the same a-side, but there is a newly recorded b-side.

DECEMBER

Before the Red Wedge tour commences in January, TSC are doing rehearsals for this and the forthcoming 7 night Christmas tour.

3rd - De Montfort Hall, Leicester

4th - Leisure Centre, Gloucester

5th - King Georges Hall, Blackburn. As Paul was the President of International Youth Year (IYY) he agreed to be interviewed before the gig by Ian H who was chairperson of the Blackburn branch and writer of the *Just 4 minutes* fanzine.

How did you find your role as president of IYY? "I found it embarrassing, really, because I don't know what people expect of me, I am not sure what there is to be done. I couldn't see it as anything, not originally, when it first started. I kept getting questions about should we play this or that function but I don't think it should manifest itself by playing loads of gigs for IYY. But what am I supposed to do? The whole thing's been a kind of washout innit? But if it's been some kind of banner or label to organise under, then that's helped.'

A lot of people feel £6.50 for tonight's gig is too much. Do you have any control over ticket prices? "Yeah, well I can't...we HAVE got control over ticket prices but er, we don't make a fantastic profit out of it because we have so many people to employ. Our costs are quite high. I'm not saying the tickets are inexpensive but I do think people have misplaced priorities sometimes because a lot of people I know think nothing of £10 down the boozer, it's inflation."

Any plans for the future? "Nothing really. Perhaps a new record in January. I feel we've done too much in some ways, too much work, cool it a bit."

In his biography on Paul Weller, Steve Malins mentions an IYY event, *Physical Chemistry* show at Queen Elizabeth Hall on London's South Bank. Paul played an acoustic set in-between a catwalk fashion show and art exhibitions.

6th - Playhouse, Edinburgh

7th - Dee gets on the front cover of *Record Mirror* titled, 'Dee shows whose boss.'

8th - Wembley. Extra date 2

9th - Wembley. Extra date 1.

10th - Wembley. Original date. Support came from Black Britain whose sound is described as, 'The Sex Pistols meet James Brown.'

'The sound quality is pretty atrocious throughout and no-one seems to be trying all that hard.' (*Smash Hits*)

The 3 nights at Wembley Arena quickly sold out and featured a 15 piece string section making this TSC's biggest ever show. It was filmed for the forthcoming *Showbiz* package and for eventual screening on BBC and ITV. This was also the first official contribution and nod to Red Wedge as 1 of the 3 shows was dedicated to the cause.

Alongside TSC were; Steve Sidelnyk (Percussion), Camelle Hinds (Bass), Robbie Granfield (Guitar and Sound Engineer), Mike Mower (Saxophone and Flute), Guy Barker (Trumpet), Stewart Prosser (Trumpet), Chris Lawrence (Trombone) and Helen Turner (Keyboards). Billy Chapman (Sax) and Junior Giscombe (Vocals) would guest for the Wembley nights. Vaughn Toulouse would DJ.

Vaughn (b.1959 d.1991), real name Cotillard had appeared on Respond releases, The Council Collective and early Council Meetings. He was a singer (Department S), dancer, DJ and Journalist.

Mike Mower who had also appeared on *Our Favourite Shop* was a member of the brass section. I caught up with him in April 2008, 'My memories of the tour and recordings aren't all favourable! We (the horn section) were very badly paid for touring, something like £220 a week when bands of similar stature at the time were paying £600+ to horn players. Their record company took forever to pay and after repeated requests to be paid by us, I was delegated to go to their office and sit in reception until the secretary responsible came down with a cheque! When asked to help us with this situation, Paul Weller's dad/manager refused to be of any assistance saying it was the record companies sole responsibility. Although never being unpleasant to hired hands such as myself, we could never understand how Paul used to preach socialism and be very tight financially with his fellow musicians, keeping all the profit for himself.

We did have some enjoyable gigs though! Regarding the recording sessions, someone recommended me and I got asked to an audition which consisted of playing to Paul Weller in the style of Stan Getz. I did some of the horn arrangements, including a track with loads of flutes.'

21 tracks were played on this tour. 9 singles, 8 from LP's, 2 b-sides, 1 Dee and 1 unreleased.*

The Lodgers; My Ever Changing Moods; Homebreakers; Luck (Dee C Lee); Big Boss Groove; With Everything To Lose; A Stones Throw Away; See The Day (Dee C Lee); A Word From Our Leaders*; Walls Come Tumbling Down; Internationalists; Long Hot Summer; (When You) Call Me; Money Go Round; Soul Deep; Strength of Your Nature; Boy Who Cried Wolf; Shout To The Top; Headstart For Happiness; Whole Point of No Return and Our Favourite Shop.

Comparing it to the June tour, 6 tracks were added to the live set, no new songs;

1983 - Headstart For Happiness
1984 - Strength of Your Nature, Shout To The Top, Whole Point of No Return
1985 - Boy Who Cried Wolf, Our Favourite Shop

7 tracks were dropped from the June tour;

1983 - It Just Came To Pieces In My Hands
1984 - A Man of Great Promise, You're The Best Thing

1985 - Come To Milton Keynes, Down In The Seine, Stand Up Comics Instructions, Move On Up

Bassist Camelle Hinds was buzzing, 'Around about this period when The Style Council epitomised their name, camaraderie was all encompassing! We were an undoubted family of sort that were carefully directed within a Solid Bond vision. The Wembley Arena dates were a semi-colon to a lengthy succession of wonderful experiences for me. In full admiration for the UK's most prolific popular all round artist amidst The Style Council carnation, I and my family were proud to be a part. TSC were acclaimed and believed we were the hottest band around globally. That's how confident we were and I was tasting it!

Nothing pleases me more than enhancing the foundation of a well crafted song. I was playing with the best of them all! We were treated as all quality artists should be with respect for our talents. Therefore, the management would always make sure comfort was a high priority. An air of camaraderie filled every occasion, our instruments were attended at all times and in a sensitive manner.'

11th - Paul, Mick, Steve and Dee appear with Timmy Mallet on Piccadilly Radio for an exclusive unplugged live version of *The Lodgers*.

12th - An excellent exclusive Capitol Radio live Session on Gary Crowley's ever popular *Red Hot Club*, according to the British Library, recorded 'somewhere near Euston.' Gary confirmed this as at studio 7 at Euston tower.

(When You) Call Me, You're The Best Thing, The Lodgers, Homebreakers, A Stones Throw Away and *Headstart For Happiness.*

'We just loved playing those songs let me tell you! I always urged Paul to put *Headstart For Happiness* in the set as I adored the melodic bass and brass accented interplay. Genius mate!' (Camelle Hinds)

15th - Steve White, Steve Sidelnyk and Camelle Hinds attend a Pearl drum clinic at Ronnie Scott's, London.

Released on Polygram before a re-issue on Channel 5 was *What We Did The Following Year* (originally titled *Only Deported After 3 Days*) was a video compilation from *My Ever Changing Moods* to *The Lodgers* with the added bonus of *The Boy Who Cried Wolf* and an *Our Favourite Shop* in-store advert. Promoted in the press as, 'the eagerly awaited sequel to *What We Did on Our Holidays.*'

It is reported that Polygram have shifted 50,000 Style Council videos to date.

'Entertaining stuff but it does start one wondering, has Paul Weller gone completely bonkers?' (*Smash Hits*)

The video's sleeve uses one of top professional photographer Tom Sheehan's sessions from the bands summer trip to Denmark. This photo captured the sharpness and coolness of TSC, white Levi's, Blazer and loafers. Paul had just told *Just Four Minutes* fanzine that his favourite item of clothing was, 'a nice pair of white Levis.'

To close the year Steve White, Billy Bragg and Pete Wilson go to Greenham Common with wood for the protesters fires. *The Common* was famous for the peaceful anti Nuclear protests in the 80's and 90's until the airbase was declared redundant in 1992.

Remarkably Dee C Lee's one hit *See The Day* had sold more than all the 1985 Style Council singles put together. *Record Mirror* issued the years biggest sellers, TSC were 64th and Dee at 61. From this placing it works out that for every 1,520 records Madonna (who was in 1st place) sold, TSC shifted 162 and Dee 168!

When asked if Dee would leave for her own career Paul told *Just 4 Minutes* fanzine, 'It's not really like that with The Style Council, there's no contractual thing. I think she's quite happy with the way things are, this very loose thing. People come and go, it's quite a good arrangement.'

Paul commented on Wham's output this year, 'If you go out and buy a Wham album with eight tracks, you've already heard five of them, so all you're left with is three new songs. I'd hardly call that prolific! It's pathetic. If I was a songwriter who only turned out eight songs a year I'd give it up and start bricklaying or something.'

An interesting story came in from Andy Davis on the relaxed door policy at Solid Bond Studios for the fans, 'The first time we went we met Ann Weller who brought us in and made us Coffee and took the piss really, calling us the `Dubliners` and spoke about everything and anything! She told us she thought Red Wedge was "rubbish" - ahead of her time eh? She then got a nice old man called Ken I think to show us around the whole studio. When we were leaving she told us that Paul would be in at 11.30 but not to tell anyone who told us! Anyway we got back to Solid Bond at 11.30 and Ann came out and brought us through to the studio kitchen. Weller came in and asked if we wanted a cup of tea, he then made a pot for us. Kenny Wheeler came in and he too asked if we wanted tea, we said 'it is ok Paul is making it,' Weller replying, 'yeah, tea boy me.' We had about a half hour of just chatting.'

A WHOLEPOINT PUBLICATION

1986

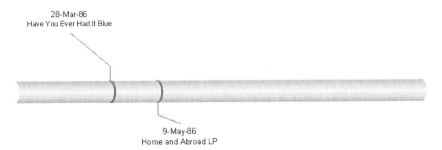

28-Mar-86
Have You Ever Had It Blue

9-May-86
Home and Abroad LP

"We want things to change and we want Thatcher's government out"

JANUARY

TSC performed well in the 1985 *NME* 'best awards' poll. Best group (3rd); Single, *Walls Come Tumbling Down* (7th); Video, *Come To Milton Keynes* (11th), LP sleeve, *Our Favourite Shop* (4th), Soul/Funk (3rd), Live (6th). Paul - Best songwriter (2nd); Male singer (3rd); Best dressed (2nd), Best haircut (2nd), Worst haircut (2nd) and most wonderful human being (7th). Dee - Best female singer (6th)

9th - Dee C Lee appears on Radio 1 to captain her side in *The Great Rock and Roll Trivia Quiz* show.

1986 was to be the year the LP of lesser known cover versions was to be recorded. However, TSC got swallowed up with Red Wedge ('our biggest mistake') a lot more than originally intended which wiped out the 1st part of the year and the covers LP.

Having said that a few 'soul' covers were completed at Solid Bond Studios but Willie Clayton's *Love Pains* and Alabama born David Sea's *Night After Night* never made it to an LP. When you listen to Clayton's original you'll hear that TSC considerably upped the tempo turning it into a very catchy and likeable pop song. One of the forgotten classics which Dennis Munday thankfully included on the *Here's Some That Got Away* compilation.

The fan club members are informed that there will be a single released from the film *Absolute Beginners*. TSC's *Have You Ever Had It Blue* would be released once David Bowies' single had left the charts. The forthcoming live LP is also discussed and would feature recordings from the last tour.

21st - Paul is live on the phone on Piccadilly Radio, Manchester with Mike Sweeney to answer, 'What do you hope to achieve with the Red Wedge Tour?'

'We want things to change and we want Thatcher's government out next time at the elections and we don't make any bones about that. The only realistic alternative at this present time is the Labour Party.'

Paul is then asked, 'Can you really understand the problems of the working classes? You're a rich man, you've never actually worked in a factory, on a building site or down the mines.'

'I know where I come from and what I've come from and the fact that I've made money now doesn't really affect the way I feel. I try to imagine myself having to live on £27 a week on the YTS.'

Paul also spoke to *Just Four Minutes* fanzine about Red Wedge, 'Basically, out of all the people involved, not the Labour Party people, but the music people, everyone's got a basic idea which adds up to the same thing. It's quite a broad left thing, that's how I see it. Eventually the idea would be that I would like to see it help certain projects such as collectives, co-operatives, unemployment centres and of course the Labour Party. I mean I've got my suspicions about Labour. I wouldn't say it's that bad (going right wing), hopefully Red Wedge could make a difference. I've had a lot of criticism but I won't sit on the fence.'

What about the other band members? 'Steve takes an interest in what we're doing, not just playing drums with us. It's kind of the whole thing, his attitude.' Are all TSC like that? 'I would say so yeah. Not like clones. It's just that we attract and are attracted to people with the same views.'

Paul appeared on TV's *Club Mix* to explain Red Wedge's aim and informed us that he was 'not on a missionary crusade' and had a dig at the presenter Baz Bamigboye, 'you yourself banned us seeing as you work for the *Daily Mail*.' Much more interesting was an exclusive live appearance with group Black Britain to sing *Funky Nassau*. This is a cover of a song by Beginning Of The End. Paul did not sing but he played guitar and Mick is briefly spotted on the Keyboards. Black Britain had been the support band for TSC's 1985 Christmas Wembley shows and their drummer, Ian Mussington, would become an Honorary Councillor in 1987. Before then he would join up with Camelle Hinds' band Hindsight.

25th - The Red Wedge tour began with Paul and Billy Bragg holding a pre-gig conference to discuss their aims, 'Red Wedge is an independent body, but we have got a channel into the Labour Party. That means we can get involved in forming arts and youth policies. The idea is to put on things that are fun, but have something behind them that people can think about. We want to make it accessible. You could ask all the people involved in Red Wedge the same question and get different answers, but we're all agreed on one thing - get rid of the Tories.'

Tonight at the Manchester Apollo were, TSC with The Jazz Defektors, Billy Bragg, Junior & Friends, Lorna Gee, The Communards, Dee C Lee, Gary Kemp of Spandau Ballet, Johnny Marr & Andy Rourke of The Smiths and Jerry Dammers of The Specials. Other acts signed to take part are Madness, Blow Monkeys, Working Week, Prefab Sprout, Tom Robinson and Lloyd Cole & The Commotions.

Not everyone would appear each night. It all went down to location and availability, though TSC and Billy Bragg were guaranteed to play on all the dates. Dee tried to appear as often as she could, 'People say you can't mix business and pleasure, but I did tonight and I'm really happy! I'd love to do the whole tour but I've got to go back to London to record my album.'

26th - St. Davids Hall, Cardiff

27th - Odeon, Birmingham

28th - De Montfort Hall, Leicester

29th - St. Georges Hall, Bradford

30th - Playhouse, Edinburgh

31st - City Hall, Newcastle. Followed by an 'end of tour party' at level 2 of the Newcastle University, entry only £1 which would go to Miners Solidarity.

A typical night on stage for the main acts - Billy Bragg (20 minutes), Style Council (20), Communards (20), Dee C Lee and TSC (10), The Smiths (20), Madness (20), finale with all bands on stage (20). Each night lasted well over 2 hours and was great value for money.

9 songs played by TSC; *Mick's Up, All Gone Away* (rarely played live), *Down In The Seine, Thank You (Fallettin Me Be Mice Elf Agin)* - a cover version of the Sly & The Family Stone classic, *A Word From Our Leaders, Back At The Chicken Shack* - a cover of Jimmy Smith's stomper, *With Everything To Lose, Homebreakers* and *Internationalists*.

TSC also play with Working Week on their most famous song *Sweet Nothings*. Jerry Dammers, Keyboard player with The Specials guested on Jimmy Smith's 1960's Blue Note song *Back At The Chicken Shack*. Paul, Mick and Steve also help out Dee on *Hey What'd Ya Say* and *See The Day*.

The Red Wedge finale 'supergroup' which included TSC performed *Don't Look Any Further, Many Rivers To Cross, Move On Up, People Get Ready* and *Stand Down Margaret*.

A futuristic moment when you think of September 2004 and Paul's single *Wishing On A Star* then read the first line of a Red Wedge review in *NME* January 1986, 'No need for Paul Weller to wish upon a star.'

The proposed Red Wedge live album did not appear and all Red Wedge performances remain unreleased. However, *Days Like These*, a 40-minute documentary about life on the road with Red Wedge (Tall Pictures) was released on video, then appeared on TV. TSC contribute on a number of occasions in various interviews and live clips, the best on a cover of *Don't Look Any Further*.

'Though the interview bits are a trifle educational it's still entertaining viewing, particularly the live music.' (*No.1*)

Mick spoke of his intention to record a solo single, which was to be produced by Mark Reilly from pop group Matt Bianco. If it was recorded then it has never seen release. Mick will be able to confirm this.

30th - There is a Red Wedge feature on *TV Eye* including an interview with Paul and the previously unseen Wembley rehearsal of *A Stone's Throw Away* with the string quartet.

FEBRUARY

Despite what the fans said about the 'open door policy' at Solid Bond Studios a glossy magazine starts up the barrage as they moan that Paul, 'has hefty doormen guarding his offices in London and even though he's a bit of a lefty, how come he's worth a packet?'

14th - Mean Fiddler, Harlesden, London. Paul, Billy Bragg and Norman Cook DJ at the opening night of the Red Wedge Club.

24th - Dee releases her LP *Shrine* hot on the heels of her massive chart smash *See The Day*. Paul co-wrote 3 of the tracks under the renowned name Jake Fluckery who first appeared in 1984 for *Spring, Summer, Autumn*.

Shrine, Hey What Do Ya Say?, That's When Something Special Starts, See The Day, He's Gone/Come Hell or Waters High, What About Me, Still The Children Cry, Just My Type, Hold On.

Fame is not without its price, 'I have just bought a really big flat in West London, but I don't give my address out because I've been a victim of obscene phone calls and burglars so I have been a bit paranoid since then.'

MARCH

2nd - Benefit gig at The Royal Albert Hall, London for GLC jobs year, titled 'Heroes' and featuring 'contemporary music for working people.' Featuring Lindisfarne and the Flying Pickets with special guests Paul Weller and Tom Robinson. No other information is available.

9th - Dee C Lee's *Come Hell or Waters High,* a cover of a song by Judie Tzuke, peaks at number 46 after entering at 76. Paul can clearly be heard on backing vocals. Limited copies come with a full poster bag. Judie Tzuke's original can be heard on her 17 track *Best of* compilation. I spoke to Judie in 2008 about the cover version, but she has never spoken to Dee C Lee or knew why she chose this particular song.

21st - Hammersmith Odeon, London as part of the GLR Farewell Festival for Red Wedge featuring Billy Bragg, The Communards, Lorna G, Junior, Paul Weller, Mick Talbot and Friends. Tickets priced at an amazing £3.50 and £2.50. 8 tracks played by TSC (as for January tour).

22nd - *NME* has an *Absolute Beginners* special with Paolo Hewitt doing the centre spread. Within the film only a few lines of the donated TSC track were used and Paul expressed his disappointment, 'God-dam awful film' considering the amount of time he put into creating it. Paul had originally offered Julian Temple the full soundtrack, but was turned down as Julian required a mixture of artists.

Paolo Hewitt covered in his *Changing Man* book the day when he and Paul watched an unfinished version of the movie at Solid Bond Studios in 'shocked silence.'

Dee was not supportive of *Absolute Beginners,* calling it a 'pile of shit' and 'tacky, a complete waste of time and money.'

'Highly stylised film suffers from two-dimensional characters and a misguided attempt to add substance by dealing with the rise of racism in England but its virtues almost outweigh its shortcomings. Don't miss that incredible opening shot!' (Leonard Maltin)

In 2008 online giant *Wikipedia* says it, 'has subsequently gained status as a cult movie, in part due to its soundtrack.'

A very interesting, humorous (and possibly best ever) one hour interview from Solid Bond Studios was shown on Satellite TV's *Music Box*. In a room smothered in disc awards Paul and Mick were relaxed and continually in fits of laughter.

'TSC is about as perfect a pop group as you can get.' (Paul). Other discussions cover the strange *Big Boss Groove* video, 'I left half way through, I had to do a radio show.' (Mick) The fear of flying, 'It's not the crashing, more about being up in the air. I miss the terra firma.' (Paul)

Then onto Paul's intention to have a vasectomy - 'Is this true?', 'Yeah, but big deal, I was gonna have me bollocks done, but changed my mind, that's life, that's showbiz' before quickly hiding behind his cup of coffee. 'Don't you like to talk about this?', 'Yeah, I don't mind talking about me bollocks. I heard what the operation entailed, it made my eyes water.'

Absolute Beginners was discussed and Paul revealed that he was actually offered the part of Dean Swift but turned it down as the filming would have taken around three weeks, 'We could make an LP in 3 weeks.'

24th - Four days before the single the *Absolute Beginners* soundtrack is released. The version of *Have You Ever Had It Blue* here is superior and does not appear on any other release. David Bedford and Gil Evans do the brass arrangement and Mick talked fondly of this collaboration to the BBC in the 2003 radio documentary *Shout To The Top*.

28th - From *Absolute Beginners* came *Have You Ever Had It Blue,* the only single of 1986. It was surprisingly written in March 1984 and then previewed on the October 1984 live dates. It sat on ice for 2 years whilst the movie was in production. The live track on the limited edition single/cassette pack was produced by Peter Wilson. The promotional video was shot in black and white to complement the two-tone images of black polo necks against white backdrops, tasselled loafers and Mick's dog tooth jacket. The dancing was by The Jazz Defektors, stars from the movie.

It would be the second single from the *Absolute Beginners* soundtrack as David Bowie's title track had to be released first. Working Week would have *Rodrigo Bay* from the film released next. The b-side was one of Mick's finest instrumentals based on the movie's character Mr Cool, titled *Mr Cool's Dream*. The single was produced by Clive Langer and Alan Winstanley, additional production work and mix by Robin Millar. The 'double' soundtrack LP is also released today.

APRIL

4th - *Have You Ever Had It Blue* was performed on the *Terry Wogan Show* complete with brass section and female vocalist (from Animal Nightlife) replacing Dee C Lee. Steve White chose to stand up to play the drums throughout and Billy Chapman returned on Saxophone.

5th - The day of the much talked about BBC *Saturday Superstore* interview with Keith Chegwin. After the *Have You Ever Had It Blue* video was shown Keith chatted with Paul and Mick about the single, film and writing songs before the previous week's competition was drawn. Then for TSC competition there was a sweatshirt, large poster, t-shirts, 'Glenda Jackson', live videos and 'two chocolates' straight from Paul's pocket. The question read out by Paul was, 'What major band was I in before joining The Style Council?'

Fellow presenter Mike Reid's biggest mistake that day was to invite Paul onto the video vote. Singles by Bronski Beat, 'a bit too poppy for me, one for the kiddies' and Simple Minds, 'that effect was used years ago with *Bohemian Rhapsody* so I won't give anything for that one.' In total Paul gave 1 point out of a possible 15 for 3 videos. Looking back Paul told *NME,* 'We just look stupid. We just don't fit into those sort of things, it's really humiliating. It can look really desperate, as if you need to sell records to kids or your career's in ruins.'

6th - *Have You Ever Had It Blue* enters the chart and would peak at number 14 staying in the top 100 for 6 weeks. It was the first single not to have 'TSC' as the catalogue number.

Record Mirror get the review of the single completely wrong, 'Weller has completely souped up the song, with completely different words and a very snazzy and sharp "big band" brass arrangement.'

Many more people believed *With Everything To Lose* (it uses the same music) was written first but this is not the case as explained in 1985.
'It allows Weller to croon and even scat-sing his way through a piece of wretchedly half-baked cool jazz.' (M*elody Maker*)

8th - Paul appears on Radio 1's *Kid Jensen* show to discuss the new single, forthcoming live album and the *Absolute Beginners* film.

13th - *The Kid Jensen Network Chart* featured an exclusive 'Mastermix' of *Have You Ever Had It Blue* and has to this day never been released or heard since. During a new instrumental burst, Paul says, 'Hello this is Paul Weller from The Style Council with *Have You Ever Had It Blue* on the *Kid Jensen Network Chart*.' It is different enough to warrant a release on a future compilation.

A short promotional trip to France did not prove worthwhile as the French never did take to TSC. There was a lot more success though when they moved onto Rome for radio and television.

MAY

9th - TSC's debut live LP *Home and Abroad* is released on all 3 formats.

18th - *Home and Abroad* enters the chart at number 8, staying in the top 100 for 8 weeks. All the tracks were taken from the 1985 'Internationalists' tour. There were no surprises just ten solid versions of popular songs, *My Ever Changing Moods, (When You) Call Me, The Big Boss Groove* and *The Whole Point of No Return* stand out. The CD contained two extra tracks and the Italian LP contained a personal message written by Paul on the back sleeve, 'We've played all over the world but some of our fondest memories are of the hot Italian nights spent last year playing to the hot Italian audiences - a big ciao! to all our Italian fans. See you soon.' Signed by Paul and Mick.

The Argentinean import of *Home and Abroad* was the most interesting. The front cover was similar to the UK release but the back print has a black and white photo with the track listing in Argentinean.

USA label Geffen released a single from *Home and Abroad,* which was heavily imported into the UK. *(When You) Call Me* and *Internationalists* used the LP's inner sleeve as the cover and outer sleeve as the back print. This was only available on 7" and was produced by Peter Wilson.

A live VHS video and CD video, *Showbiz!* was released alongside the LP and portrays TSC at their peak - smart blazers, great camera work and perfect versions of songs. Paul, Mick, Steve, Dee, Helen, Camelle, Steve Sidelnyk and the boys on the brass were regarded by many as the ultimate line up.

This 52 minute video was directed by Vaughn and Anthea. It starts with scenes cutting between the empty Wembley Arena, filling up to capacity, whilst Vaughan Toulouse spins the vinyls and the band get prepared in the dressing room - Surely influenced from the Beatles 1965 concert movie, *The Beatles At Shea Stadium*. The camera work is one of the best for a live gig, with all possible angles covered. The music itself comes over strong and powerful with some superb versions of *(When You) Call Me, Big Boss Groove, Homebreakers, Long Hot Summer* and *Soul Deep Medley* to name a few. There is a brass section throughout and a string section when required. No other TSC live video will surpass the sheer energy and passion of this performance. One disappointment was the unusually poor sleeve with mistakes like *Strengthen Your Nature* credited as a track.

Mick says, 'about ¾ of it is material that was written and released in studio versions in 1985. It's a sort of end of a second chapter for us.' (*Tracks*)

'Rather shoddy, a big disappointment.' (*Smash Hits*)

Curtis Mayfield plays to a sell out crowd in London. Paul was in the audience but declined an invitation to go up on stage with Curtis for *Move On Up*.

Dee released another single from the LP *Shrine, Hold On,* although it failed to get into the top 100. In an interview she is asked if she is dating Paul which she replies, 'that is none of your business.'

Smash Hits ask her what it is like being hounded by the big guns in Fleet Street, 'It is so pathetic. They don't want to know about the music.'

JUNE

TSC are 'locked away' in Solid Bond Studios recording a new album for release 'later this year.' Songs seemed easy to come by, around 16 tracks were recorded for the album, 9 being chosen, the others for b-sides or deemed not good enough for release. The majority of the ignored tracks would appear on the future rarities LP, *Here's Some That Got Away*.

Apart from Red Wedge and benefit gigs there will be no tour in 1986. One benefit event which Billy Bragg was headlining came under fire when the Young Socialists promote Paul Weller as playing, when he never was.

Steve hinted in fan club magazine *Style Population* that he was writing a song *Rumblin Ground* for Artists Against Apartheid (AAA) with bassist Camelle Hinds. It would feature 8 vocalists and Steve. The vocalists were Camelle, Linton Beccles, Paul Barry, Pat Wright, Paul Johnson, Tracie Young, Stephen Dante and Linda Foster. I asked Steve about this in March 2005, 'Yes, it was recorded, cost a fortune and was shit to be honest. Too much money and too little knowledge, although it wasn't a bad song.'

26th - An advertisement appears in the music press detailing three consecutive Sunday night events at the Shaw Theatre, Euston Road, London in July. All presented by 'Soul on Sunday.' A number of bands would headline each week, and a few were Style Council related. Tickets were £5 or £3 and each show commenced at 7:30pm. The host was to be Porky The Poet with 3 DJ's, Paolo 'house rocker' Hewitt, Paul 'modest pied a terre' Weller and Michael 'maisonette' Talbot all 'rocking the foundations.'

Porky The Poet, better known as Phil Jupitus, would go onto greater things and would play his final show supporting TSC at Hammersmith Odeon, London in November 1987.

28th - Artists Against Apartheid's *Freedom Festival* at Clapham Common, South London. This was organised by Jerry Dammers and was said to be the Festival which influenced the now yearly Nelson Mandela birthday party concerts, also organised by Jerry. London Police estimated the crowd at 30,000 (Paul said there were more than this backstage) and Steve estimated it as nearer 110,000. Also on the bill were Gil Scott Heron, Spandau Ballet, Sting, Sade, Princess and Elvis Costello. TSC themselves were a very late addition as they fill the gap left by The Communards, one of the headliners.

TSC performed *My Ever Changing Moods, A Stones Throw Away, Internationalists, Johannesburg* and *Move On Up*. The weather was superb and TSC sport t-shirts and checked shorts. Paul read out a personal message from Madness who were billed but could not make the event. The marchers missed the majority of TSC set as they appeared just before Jane from Loose Ends joined for a cover of Gil Scott Heron's *Johannesburg*. It was the only time TSC performed *Johannesburg,* fittingly in front of the songs creator. It was a bit of a scoop to get the Chicago born Gil (b.01/04/49) on the set. The musician, poet and author, 'became a mouthpiece for the black person in America during the Seventies and Eighties.'

A VHS video was released under the banner *Clapham Common Productions, Freedom Beat* with *Move On Up* TSC's choice. It was edited to show Paul before *Move On Up* saying, 'a big round of applause, all the marchers coming in now please,' where in actual fact this was said before *Johannesburg.*

A Sickle Cell Anaemia charity auction ball is held in London. A suited Paul sang *Harvest For The World* with David Grant and Dee sang *That's What Friends Are For* with Madeleine Bell. Short clips of Paul and Dee's performances were broadcast on the BBC 2 show *Behind The Beat*. Further support of the charity would be in the form of a benefit single to follow in July.

'It's a good cause that genuinely needs funding, that's why I got involved.' (Paul)

JULY

6th - Shaw Theatre week one of three. Tonight was billed as 'One of the UK's leading vocalists.' Dee C Lee, The Cookie Crew plus Spirit of Watts (amongst the best in young gospel). Porky The Poet was joined by the 3 DJ's, 'house rocker', 'modest pied a terre' and 'maisonette' as explained in June. They would not appear on stage but instead make short announcements from a DJ box in the back, above the audience.

8th - *The Long Hot Summer* Jezamix is mixed and will appear on a forthcoming summer compilation.

13th - Shaw Theatre week two of three. Tonight was the 'Jazz special' with the same DJ's welcoming The Jazz Defektors, Steve Williamson Quartet and The Renegades (featuring Steve White and Steve Rose). The Renegades would later become the Jazz Renegades. Steve Williamson is the brother of former TSC vocalist Jaye Williamson.

19th - The BBC TV *Annie Nightingale* show screens 30 minutes of the *Showbiz* video.

20th - Shaw Theatre week three of three. Tonight was 'Sedately Yours'. An amazing night in TSC history where Terence Trent D'arby, Hindsight (Camelle Hinds) and 2 of the DJ's would join the unknown Party Chambers Group on stage. Such was the buzz surrounding tonight's gig many A'n'R people were in the crowd and as a direct result both would be signed to major labels. I caught up with both artists in September 2008, Camelle Hinds and Sananda Maitreya, formerly known as Terence Trent D'Arby (TTD) and one of the organisers, Paolo Hewitt.

Paolo has fond memories of the night, telling me, 'Two things about Shaw Theatre. We were the first to put a certain Terence Trent D'Arby on and another week I remember Paul and I DJ'ing in the box and joking about holding a wet t-shirt contest as it would go down really well with the mainly leftie female audience. It was only later when someone came up and told us the microphones were on we realised the audience could hear every word we were saying!'

I mentioned this night to Camelle, particularly on the immergence of his new band Hindsight who would be making their debut; 'Vivid memories. Having been a freelance/session musician for some years since my band Central Line split in August '84 I had a compelling desire to express myself in a somewhat solo form. Not for the sake of solo identity, but simply because I had a lot to say. At this pertinent time, my Fathers wish for me to acknowledge world affairs was starting to play havoc on my sub conscience. Whilst travelling back from the TSC trip to Australia, lack of sleep allowed me to pen my humanitarian beliefs in one composition, namely *Small Change*.

Lets talk about distribution, a sorrowful affair, a lot of confusion, a million tons of wheat and grain, how much wheat can one man eat and there's still starvation in Africa, Africa, Africa... Lets talk about education, opportunity, devastation - each verse subsequently displaying a rap of dismay towards a chorus 'Ooohh! Small change! I persuaded a taxi driver to recite, "What the world needs now is love sweet love" in several African dialects - he happily received a £30 session fee (decent at the time). So! that became the birth of Hindsight....

Paul admirably allowed me to headline The Shaw Theatre night as a launch. How brilliant is that? I had the scary task of rehearsing the TSC and Dee C Lee set during the day and the Hindsight set in the evenings. Knackered but elated, I nervously played the intimate TSC and Dee C Lee set sitting on an unplugged stool before transforming into a funk outfit (essentially adding Henry Defoe ex-Central Line guitar and Ian Mussington on Drums) to express the mutron bass and vocal side of my character. We opened with *Let It Whip* which allowed me to sing and play some funk bass at the same time.

We were well received and somewhat immediately signed to a singles deal by Virgin/Circa. I then sensibly, but retaining rights to North America, used some favourable negotiation tactics to eventually secure separate album deals with Circa UK and Virgin America. Hindsight gained a US billboard top ten and a UK dance number 1 in a brief but highly memorable outing.

For The Shaw theatre encore, I chose *Thank You Falletin Me Be Mice Elf Agin* by Sly Stone and the stage became Hindsight, Paul Weller, I think Billy (Bragg) was there, Phil Jupitus and of course, the amazing Terence Trent Darby who opened the evening with his mouth watering vocal antics."

Terence Trent D'Arby (TTD) from Manhattan, came to the UK to play with a 9 piece Soul and Funk band The Bojangles. From March '87 as a solo artist TTD would have 9 top 40 hit singles. In 2008 he goes under the name of Sananda Maitreya and does not acknowledge his life of TTD, instead he talks of him as another person. I caught up with Sananda from his base in Milan and he was very enthusiastic and open about the event. I respect his wishes to refer to him as Sananda and his story and acclaim of Paul Weller makes interesting reading. This is unedited;

"First of all, thank you for reminding me that I once had a past! Once upon a time, living in London was like living in a dream world, in its own way like Las Vegas, a Disneyland for your hormones. There was a lifetime which went by the initials TTD, who had a dream of becoming a star, emergent from the fresh London fog, the backdrop of all the English B&W films, youth and sick days from school had exposed him to, as a young man growing up in the hinterlands of America. Far before realising the cost of a dream in the big kingdom, a song idol and his apologist, came to his aid.

As much as I would otherwise suspect whatever Paolo Hewitt said, my memories of that life are that upon arriving to live and chart my course of adventure in London, some of maestro Paul Weller's 'crew' had caught wind of whatever was stirring on TTD's behalf and through a good friend of his, the brilliant 'scrittore' Hewitt, whose writings and reputation were known to TTD from having been a fan and voracious reader of the NME (which did later turn out to be!). He knew Paolo's by-line to have accompanied a good range of music and that he were associated with the Weller 'ensemble'. In those more innocent early days, he were always eager to speak to writers, especially of music, as it were also his passion as much as the music itself.

He were also a great and long time admirer of Paul and his many permutations over the years, as well as being in the great tradition of prolific and precocious English songwriters, while possessing a keen sense of projection and style. None of those things would have been lost to him as he was putting his 'dream-head' together for his own experience. As a showcase event, an evening presentation was put together at London's fabled Shaw Theatre, whereby TTD would sing a few songs accompanied only by Piano. To my reckoning, it were a collaboration between the Weller team, Paolo Hewitt and some peripheral involvement by the NME, and KP SCHLEINETZ, then operating as management.

Naturally, it were Weller's imprimatur which drew interest from the public, as well as added important journalistic cachet to the presentation. I had actually forgotten about a lot of this until your question 'joggled' it from my old testament brain (having gone more 'new testament' since those primitive, rollicking days). It gives me relief to thank, on TTD's behalf, those stellar gentlemen for their contribution to a man's dream and its fulfilment. It ended pretty messily for sure, but was as sweet a beginning as any fairy tale could offer, and to my knowledge of that life (oh so many 'spliffs' ago), the masters Weller and Hewitt were like the good luck Angels who showed up on time, to help usher him through his karma's gates. It is with profound gratitude that we thank them both for their generosity to his spirit, because of them, he were able to have the life he dreamt, all of those many innocent and increasingly precious years ago.

Yes, shortly thereafter, TTD were signed to a major label, a great old label by the then name of CBS (and for the then lowest amount of 'dosh' permitted by law!)

It is all the more poignant in the light of his death and the fact that he will never be seen again. It is also not lost on us, the immense influence that Paul's enthusiasm has had on other British artists, and the ongoing history of your culture's contribution to music, in its more 'popular' forms. May his God bless and keep him well, and 'weller.' Please pass on to the maestro that his last batch of songs are cracking (and that we are always eager to hear his work)!

The last time I saw Paul was in '95 at a festival in Europe and being at the time at the very beginning of this new head, I didn't really know how to react, and had really forgotten the role he had played in helping the last incarnation. He was cool though, but I felt bad for a while without knowing why! That life sucked to be honest, but Paul's contribution helped it get off the runway, and into the air. I guess, if ever again I see him, I owe the maestro a pint or two!"

Back to the night and another surprise - how many people predicted that one of the unknown bands listed over the three weeks would involve TSC? If you did then a good guess would be The Party Chambers Group, with *Party Chambers* of course being the b-side to the 1st single. The Party Chambers Group was indeed a TSC secret gig and they performed some wonderful, rarely played live tracks in a semi acoustic set which included some serious Saxophone playing.

Down In The Seine, All Gone Away (rare live, only other time on Red Wedge tour), *Spin Drifting* (only time live), *The Paris Match* (Dee C Lee), *Stay With Me* (Dee C Lee), unknown Saxophone instrumental, *Homebreakers,* a new *Le Depart/Party Chambers Mix, Mick's Company, Whole Point II, A Man of Great Promise, Piccadilly Trail* (rare live) and *Have You Ever Had It Blue.* A stunning performance in I'm sure an amazing night which luckily enough was bootlegged.

Mick looked back at this gig with *The Face,* 'We played this secret gig at the Shaw Theatre. I was playing a little classical thing just before we went into a tune, and there were all these people down the front going, 'Whooargghh! Mickey! Essex! Essex!' What's all that about? Sometimes you wonder what you're up against.'

26th - A largely unknown charity venture results in many musicians attending Sarm Studios, the location of the Band Aid recording, under the banner of *People In Progress.* The purpose is to record a track *This Is My Song.* Paul and Dee would lend their support and Honorary Style Councillor Guy Barker would play trumpet.

'People In Progress is a collection of people from the world of music, show-business and sport who have come together to raise funds for charitable purposes, specifically Sickle Cell Anaemia Relief and the Canon Collins Educational Trust for Southern Africa.'

27th - Second day of recording and producing the single. Some of the other known names of that era were Aswad, Tom Bailey, Madeleine Bell, Errol Brown, Kiki Dee, David Grant, Paul Hardcastle, Lenny Henry, Imagination, Junior, Mint Juleps, Tom Robinson, Sinitta and Mark King. It was released on Polydor (POSP 829) and though I remember a picture in the *News of The World* magazine it did not get anywhere in terms of chart success or publicity. It was written by Leee John and Ashley Ingham of Imagination and the single was split into two parts to meet chart regulations, along the lines of *Money Go Round.*

Dee's final solo single whilst with TSC was released, *Hey What'd Ya Say.*

Steve White's work with Tracie Young (now signed to Polydor) sees release, two singles *We Should Be Together* and a cover of TSC classic *(When You) Call Me.* They do not get anywhere in terms of a chart position and it is decided to scrap plans to release Tracie's new LP even though it was complete and ready for issue.

AUGUST

Dizzy Hites releases a solo single *Would I Find Love*, the b-side contains a remixed version of *The Gospel* which originally appeared on *Cafè Bleu*.

Paul heads to Italy with Dee for a two-week holiday.

An Afro-Euro compilation album *A Taste of Summer* (AELP1) is released on Polydor. The most interesting thing is an exclusive *Jezamix* version of *Long Hot Summer*. There was also a 4 track promotional 12" pressed with this track on it (Taste1). This *Jezamix* remained exclusive until it was re-badged and released as the *Tom Mix* and then the *1989 Mix*. Who in Polydor/TSC thought it was OK to rename the exact mix and release it 3 times as a 'new' version? Shame on you!

After the holiday, further tracks are recorded for the next LP which is now delayed until February 1987. Paul and Mick have managed to track down the Valentine Brothers to record on a few songs.

'The bosses are dropping heavy hints that they didn't want me to produce the LP. I have had success but they're still trying to interfere with what I'm doing.' (Paul)

29th - Radio 1 DJ Gary Davies presented, 'for the very first time on television' *Angel* and *It Didn't Matter* on *Rock Around The Dock* a show filmed on the River Mersey. This was the first indication of TSC moving towards Soul music. No-one imagined that *It Didn't Matter* would be the next single. Camelle Hinds joined the four band members, not on his usual Bass, but this time on Keyboards.

'Was that on some kind of raft floating precariously upon the Mersey docks? If so, yeah! I remember it being a fond time of my life, not least for being amongst a solid professional family bond but also it is always exciting to experience Liverpudlian humour and with a large pre-portion of gorgeous babes; the female accent, some district dialects, stir me to this day.' (Camelle Hinds, Aug 08)

Paul defends covering *Angel* by telling *NME,* '*Angel* isn't a classic from 10 years ago, it's a relatively unknown song from an import album that deserves to be heard by more people. I hate all that "you've ruined a good song" nonsense.'

Angel was written for Anita Baker by Sandra Sully and Patrick Lawrence Moten who was born in Los Angeles in 1957 - He toured with Tina Turner, Harold Melvin and B.B. King and died a month before the millennium at a young age of 42.

I caught up with Beverley Hills based Sandra Sully in 2008, not long after she had read TSC had recorded this song (i.e. 20 years later). She is, at the time of writing, still without her 50% share of the writing and publishing royalties. Sandra told me, '*Angel* was written for Anita Baker in 1983 when I was a staff writer for Beverly Glen Records. Patrick gave me the track and I wrote the lyrics. When the lyrics were presented to Anita I believe she changed a few words upon recording the song but I was not in the studio with her so I don't know which words she changed and which Patrick changed.

The song was released initially with Beverly Glen receiving my share of publishing and when they went bankrupt my publishing was to have been reversed to me. This information was sent out to the record companies and BMI.

Patrick did not discuss that he had been approached by The Style Council and I only found out about the recording a little more than a year ago. I have now secured an attorney and found that Patrick signed the licensing agreement and received payments. Universal will not disclose how much and this is a matter hopefully we can come to some agreement on.'

'Our version isn't as laid back or as Jazzy as the beautiful original, but I think we've done a good job on it.' (Paul, *Style Population*)

SEPTEMBER

14th - A single *Loverboy* by Chairmen Of The Board featuring General Johnson is released on EMI. Promoted as 'remixed by Paul Weller at Solid Bond Studios and a Keyboard solo by Mick Talbot.' Engineered by Jezar who would go on to work with TSC on a future release. A limited edition double 12" was released and the single peaked at number 56. Sixteen years earlier they had their biggest hit, *Give Me Just A Little More Time.*

The music press report that Paul and Mick appeared at a charity event to play two new songs, *Waiting* and *The Cost of Loving.*

OCTOBER

Steve and his band The Jazz Renegades play for 2 weeks this month at The London Palladium for the Soho Jazz Festival.

6th - *All Year Round* is recorded. This would make it to the b-side of the next single and then be covered live by Paul on his solo tour in 1991. A live version from this tour would appear on the b-side of his *Above The Clouds* single.

21st - Steve White plays at Camden Palace with Tracie Young as part of her 10 piece band comeback.

NOVEMBER

2nd - The Jazz Renegades are at Ronnie Scott's, London, supporting Art Blakey for 7 consecutive nights. Mick is in the crowd with Dennis Munday, manager of the band at this point.

TSC record a few songs which would remain unreleased, *April's Fool, My Very Good Friend* and *I Aint Going Under.*

Paul tells *Record Mirror,* 'I've just got bored with the guitar completely and I'd just like to be able to sing more really. It does get on my tits a bit playing the guitar.'

'My way of playing wasn't progressing so I thought it was necessary to take a rest and think it over.'

DECEMBER

A new TSC single *It Didn't Matter* is released in Japan. The b-side features a cover version of the Lionel Bart song, *Who Will Buy.* A superb sleeve on the 7" had Mick and Paul kitted out in white surrounded by men in black on a windswept hill. At this point the single was unreleased in the UK.

The Japanese 12" also appeared in a unique sleeve, white with silver lettering accompanied by a small photo of TSC from the promotional video. It is said to have a different sound (e.q.) and has been recorded slower than on the forthcoming UK release.

Lionel Bart wrote the book, music and lyrics for *Oliver! The Musical* which opened on June 30th 1960. Steve Marriott starred in a production of *Oliver!* Is that the reason TSC covered *Who Will Buy* exclusively for this b-side. Paul?

A very strange, cryptic music press advert appeared one Wednesday afternoon. Sherlock Holmes was sitting in his chair smoking on his pipe as Watson stood by. "This is certainly a 5 pipe problem," I remarked putting aside my magnifying glass. "Not a word from the **Council** for months, and don't tell me **it didn't matter.**" Yet I knew the case was about to be cracked.'

A press release details the next tour, *The General Election* tour. 'Valentine's day. New material, new haircuts and new musicians supported by The Dynamic Three who will also DJ.' Tickets at £8 and £7.

Centre, Newport (14th/15th)
Royal Albert Hall, London (16th/17th/18th/19th*)
Centre, Bournemouth (20th)
Exhibition Centre, Birmingham (21st*/ 22nd)
St. George's Hall, Bradford (25th)
City Hall, Newcastle (26th/27th)
Exhibition Centre, Glasgow (28th)

* Extra dates added later.

The Sun reports that Paul and Dee have 'secretly bought a £300,000 house together. The beautiful, three-bedroom Victorian cottage, in North London's exclusive St. Johns Wood, has a 45 foot garden. Built in mid 1800's and has been restored to include all original features.'

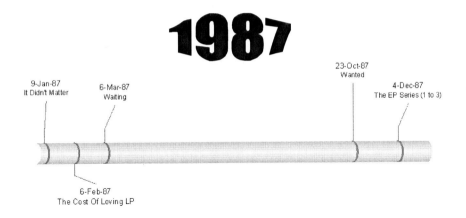

1987

23-Oct-87
Wanted

9-Jan-87
It Didn't Matter

6-Mar-87
Waiting

4-Dec-87
The EP Series (1 to 3)

6-Feb-87
The Cost Of Loving LP

"The anti-Rock forces of TSC must and did continue in our grand quest"

JANUARY

The forthcoming LP is promoted in a Polydor press release as 'two 12" discs playing at 45rpm. First record slow songs, second fast ones. The sound quality of the songs will be better this way, as each track is potentially a single and deserves its own space. There is a possibility of a late track being added to the album. Curtis Mayfield and the Valentine Brothers guest. Jerry Wakefield, the resident mixer at Solid Bond Studios also did some mixes with Matthew Casher who worked with Cameo.'

In 1986 Paul was asked if he ever thought about writing a play, book or acting? to which he replied, 'No! All that pop star turned actor bit is crap.' Interesting, as a year on the press release continues with, 'the band are alleviating the customary boredom of todays wild world of pop' and detail a debut Style Council short film, *JerUSAlem,* starring pop star turned actor, Paul Weller!

JerUSAlem was the brainchild of Paul, Mick, Paolo Hewitt and Simon Halfon. It took 3 weeks to film in Dorset, London and Aldbourne (A419 from Hungerford, Wiltshire) on a budget of just £140,000 - the majority of the money coming from a Japanese TV advert and the balance from Polydor.

Plans were in place to have the film premiered on the forthcoming 'General Election' tour then in cinemas supporting *Mona Lisa* and *Down By Law,* before making it onto *Channel 4* in the summer. Paul saw *JerUSAlem* as a 'way of getting out of doing loads of boring promotional work, the story of the new album.'

9th - *It Didn't Matter* was performed on the *Terry Wogan* show. Expensive looking casual clothes were the order of the day, but why did Paul have a picture of Radio 1 DJ Janice Long stuck to his guitar?

It was revealed that after Paul's plea for a new guitarist had appeared in *The Sun*, Janice (using a false name) pretended to be what he was looking for and was invited to an audition. At the rendezvous a surprised Paul was in good spirits and took it the right way. The *Terry Wogan* show was the perfect chance to get his own back.

It Didn't Matter, the first single for 16 months, was a major change in direction. No more punchy political songs, no more Jazz tracks, no more supporters in the music press! The b-side *All Year Round* was also slated as 'the worst song ever.' 'Weller's Soul-ed out' the nation cried as he now dabbled in Soul music.

Paul hit back, 'It is very hard sounding and quite different for us I think, a tune with a wicked bass line.'

10th - TSC get their last *NME* cover and centre spread to promote the forthcoming LP and short film, titled, 'Neat jackets in Jerusalem.'

All the promotional photographs around this period originated from the *It Didn't Matter* filming, the promotional video was from *JerUSAlem*. The sleeve notes simply state 'coming shortly, the fourth long player' next to an orange box. The colour becoming significant when the LP is released in February. No Honorary Councillor's appear on *It Didn't Matter*. Produced by Paul Weller, mixed by the Valentine Brothers.

17th - Tory (Conservative Party) Prime Minister Maggie Thatcher appeared on Saturday morning children's TV and not unexpectedly gave *It Didn't Matter* the thumbs down. 'It didn't get anywhere and I wanted to say "get on with it." Too much like a rehearsal, there is a lot to be done.'

18th - *It Didn't Matter* enters the chart and would peak at number 9, staying in the top 100 for 5 weeks. This was the first top 10 since 1985 and would be the last.

22nd - The *Top of the Pops* appearance was marred as viewers later called the BBC's *Points of View* to complain about TSC laughing throughout the song, making a mockery of the miming. There appeared to be an "in" joke in preparation for Dee's solo piece. Mick later said, 'We hate doing *Top of the Pops* but we have too if we want to have a hit record.'

Drummer magazine *Rhythm* said that what made the song 'particularly interesting is the dead stop on the 2nd beat of the 1st bar, and the rapid semiquaver bass drum figures!'

31st - 'I think what I do is worthwhile.' (Paul, *The Independent*)

AIDS Benefit at The Barbican, London with TSC, Erasure and The Communards. No recording or further details known, so if you were there then please get in touch.

JerUSAlem is premiered in a London cinema for the music press.

FEBRUARY

6th - The LP *Cost of Loving* is released and is loosely based around, 'the effects that social, economic and political issues can have on relationships.' The LP's title was taken from a line in *Heavens Above*, 'but the cost of loving has been blown sky high', and not from the most obvious choice track *The Cost of Loving*.

One political track was *Fairy Tales*, 'hard brass lifts this modern fairy tale up and into demand. Like *Jack and The Beanstalk* the monsters of reality can all be chopped down, that includes Norman Tebbit. The lyrics are quite funny on this I think.' (Paul)

The orange box graphic mystery from the *It Didn't Matter* sleeve was resolved. The LP sleeve was orange with orange writing. A similar idea to the *Speak Like A Child* single but going a step further by not even mentioning the band's name on the front or back! The packaging though was deluxe with 'initial copies' featuring dual insert sleeves in a quality gatefold. *Wikipedia* has an excellent description of the sleeve and of designer Simon Halfon's idea behind it;

'Halfon designed the international orange gatefold sleeve for the *Cost of Loving* album. The shade of orange is noted for its use in "setting things apart from their surroundings," but in the case of the Golden Gate Bridge it is also seen as a master stroke of beauty. The Style Council's sleeve was a hefty gatefold containing two solid slabs of 12" vinyl EPs and was swathed entirely in the color, opening the gatefold reveals high-contrast black and white photographs of the group, a crisp visual contrast that might have been a commentary on music as well (black and white). This was Halfon's homage to Richard Hamilton's cover art for The Beatles *White* album.

There were many tracks put onto tape with Paul confirming there were, 'still another 7 or 8 songs in the can.' Good news as he earlier told the *Music Box*, 'for 6 months of the year I am not able to write anything.'

9 appeared on the LP; *Who Will Buy* on a Japanese b-side single, *Francoise* and *All Year Round* as b-sides and the remainder would make it onto the *Here's Some That Got Away* LP, one being *My Very Good Friend*, itself scrapped from the script in *JerUSAlem*. That means there are still up to 5 songs un-accounted for and likely to be in Paul's vault.

Paul played Guitars, Synths and Drum programmes. Mick on Hammond, Piano Forte, Wurlitzer, Rhodes, Synths and Bass Synths. Dee on vocals and Steve on drums and percussion. Produced by Paul, engineered and sequenced by Jezar and Alan Leeming. Orchestrations again by John Mealing.

International Musician ran an exclusive interview from Solid Bond Studios and you get interesting information from Mick on the technical side of the album. The main studio within Solid Bond was booked out so a lot of the work was done in the back room on a Tascam Portastudio. He specifically talked about *Angel*, 'Steve's played along with it and we haven't kept anything he's played. (We) used his performance as a program for the drum machine.' Charming!

'I've got a lot of time for Weller but I get the impression he hasn't got much time for us. The *Cost* is the sound of Weller getting older, wiser and richer 3/5.' (*Melody Maker*)

'Is far too lovey dovey for these lugs.' (*NME*)

'Anaemic, slick Eighties soul as bad as anything else around.' (Chris Mugan, *The Independent*)

'The *Cost of Loving* is hit and miss.' (Gary Crowley)

Polydor's Managing Director Richard Ogden told Paolo Hewitt, 'I paid him a million quid and then he delivers this bloody album. I thought it was terrible. A terrible sleeve and an awful record.' Shortly after Ogden left Polydor to manage Paul McCartney.

'The actual musicianship on this LP is probably our best so far, certainly the most confident.' (Paul, *Style Population*)

8th - Paul appeared on *BBC Radio 1 Sunday Live* to discuss *JerUSAlem,* 'We've been trying to make a film for 3 or 4 years now. I think it's very good and makes a lot of subtle points.' In order of acting merit he places Mick at the top, Steve 2nd, himself 3rd and Dee 4th

When Paul was asked to confirm, 'If you don't like The Style Council then there must be something wrong with you?' He replied, 'I do feel that way sometimes, I must admit.'

The same day *The Cost of Loving* enters the chart at an impressive number 2, achieving instant silver status for 60,000 copies sold. It was the first TSC long player in nearly two years but it only stayed in the top 100 for 7 weeks.

For the forthcoming *General Election* tour Paul and Mick went for a complete change in personnel and introduced new musicians. Alongside Dee C Lee was Steve White's replacement Ian Mussington (Drums) from Black Britain, Steve Sidelnyk (Percussion), Steve Eyrie (Guitar), Dave Foster (Bass), Terry Devine King (Keys) and Dashiel (Flute/Sax/Keys).

Steve White told Steve Malins, 'some of the people we got in were totally wrong, some of the musicians that were playing in the band stopped me from playing well.' He would head to Tokyo with The Jazz Renegades to open a nightclub and record an LP *Tokyo Hi* which is still a much sought after vinyl in 2008. Another collaboration was with Galliano on Urban Jazz (ajazz1) titled *Six Sharp Fists*.

14th - The *General Election* tour commences in Wales at The Centre, Newport.

15th - The Centre, Newport (2nd night)

16th - The Royal Albert Hall, London

17th - The Royal Albert Hall, London

18th - The Royal Albert Hall, London. Recorded for BBC *Radio 1 In Concert*.

19th - The Royal Albert Hall, London. 4th night added after the first 3 sold out.

20th - International Centre, Bournemouth

21st - National Exhibition Centre, Birmingham

22nd - National Exhibition Centre, Birmingham

24th - The Centre, Brighton

25th - St. George's Hall, Bradford

26th - City Hall, Newcastle

27th - City Hall, Newcastle

28th - Scottish Exhibition Centre, Glasgow

Across all the nights, 20 songs were played on the tour;

It Didn't Matter; Waiting; Walking The Night; The Cost of Loving; The Piccadilly Trail; Everlasting Love (Dee C Lee); *A Woman's Song* (Dee C Lee); *Whole Point II; Mick's Company; Heavens Above; Fairy Tales; Angel; The Lodgers; My Ever Changing Moods; Homebreakers; You're The Best Thing; With Everything To Lose; Internationalists; (When You) Call Me and Money Go Round.*

When analysed you have 6 singles, 4 b-sides, 9 album tracks and 1 unreleased*

Fourteen months have past since the last tour and a massive 14 tracks have been dropped;

1983 - *Long Hot Summer, Headstart For Happiness, Whole Point of No Return*
1984 - *Big Boss Groove, Soul Deep; Strength of Your Nature, Shout To The Top*
1985 - *Luck, A Stones Throw Away, See The Day, A Word From Our Leaders, Walls Come Tumbling Down, Boy Who Cried Wolf, Our Favourite Shop.*

13 tracks were added including 8 from the latest LP with only *Right To Go* missing;

1984 - *The Piccadilly Trail, Mick's Company, You're The Best Thing*
1985 - *Whole Point II*
1987 - *It Didn't Matter, Waiting, Walking The Night, The Cost of Loving, A Woman's Song, Fairy Tales, Angel, Heavens Above*
New - *Everlasting Love*

The planned support band The Dynamic Three were ditched in place of the debut movie *JerUSAlem*. There may have been problems with them as *Right To Go* was also scrapped from the b-side of the next single. Paul would only say, 'the group who were to be supporting us didn't work out.' He did however, rate the song, 'it was up and hard with some of Steve's best drumming ever to my mind.'

This tour was slated by the music press as both reviews concentrate on Weller's white attire; 'A rather dull affair, with the performance as clinical as their white uniforms.' (*Record Mirror*); 'He'll be stepping out at Ascot next.' (*NME* or *MM*)

BBC Radio 1 broadcasted the 2nd Royal Albert Hall night and the following month the 3rd and final Style Council BBC transcription Disc appeared in *Record Collector* for a pricey £125. Today it will retain this price tag.

Jerusalem - TSC short film.

The official press release, 'A 32 minute fun-filled epic containing four brand new Style Council compositions, a variety of costume changes, and acres of perceptive and witty dialogue!' The screenplay is by author Paolo Hewitt, produced by Lucy Hooberman and directed by Richard Belfield, a known documentary maker for World in Action/Diverse Reports. Narration by Richard Coles of The Communards.

Scene 1 - The Style Council are bailed.

JerUSAlem commences in black and white with the "Daily Distraction" newspaper front page headline reading, 'Style Council out on bail.' The band have been charged with being, 'the best pop group ever' and ordered to pay '£140 to a record company of their choice.' We then witness Paul, Mick, Dee and Steve running along a corridor, down the stairs and out of the Courtroom, blanking photographers and reporters before speeding away in a car. The scene cuts to a poster with an idea stolen from a major banks advertising campaign of the time, 'TSC the band that likes to say no.'

The instrumental version of *Francoise* from the b-side of the forthcoming single accompanies the opening titles.

Scene 2 - Down by the sea (Weston-Super-Mare?)

Paul 'Welly' is sitting in his throne by the sea kicking back the waves, 'go back for my parts do freeze, thus I say go back.' Master Mick Talbot is composing a track on a mighty church organ and Steve White is drumming away on the rocks whilst listening to a pirate radio station. While up on the cliff top gazing out to sea we have Dee C Lee with a 'seagull on her shoulder' humming to the tune of *Angel*. This scene was extracted from the Cappuccino Kid's sleeve notes on *The Lodgers* single confirming the film was being planned as far back as 1985.

Scene 3 - The Beach.

A quick wardrobe change for a filmic beach rendition of *Angel*. Paul and Steve dressed in their *Showbiz!* clothes, Mick like a captain of a yachting club and Dee with white jacket/jeans/hat. Upon completion of *Angel* we are back at scene 2, Paul asking his troops, 'where to now my blessed links?' before deciding to 'be like throbbing hood and his merry men (persons) and prepare ourselves for battle.'

Scene 4 - Scooters.

After another wardrobe change TSC, 'took to the concrete' on scooters. They drive past a family camped in a field who are watching TV as the scene on their TV moves to a the music show;

Yvonne French (from *The Switch)* is the presenter interviewing a group 'The Very Tall Buildings' (TSC in disguise) Paul, Mick, Steve and Dee have their say (nonsense really) before the scene cuts to a TV studio.

Scene 5 - The TV Studio.

The scene opens with a stereotypical, hyperactive music director ensuring the scene is ready with banter and small talk. *It Didn't Matter* is performed in front of TSC TV cameras. This is the footage used for the promotion of the single. Upon completion Paul is confronted by a female fan. 'There's just one thing that bothers me - Why are you called The Style Council?' She runs off before Paul is allowed to answer. This is the common thread to the film, the question, 'Why are you called The Style Council?'

Scene 6 - The Village (Aldbourne, Wiltshire)

TSC continue on the scooters to a small village.

[This is Aldbourne in Wiltshire. A visit to Aldbourne.org.uk shows the village green and the area overlooking the square to the church, all memorable scenes from *JerUSAlem*]

'Observe if you will England's beauty...' recalls Mick before the scooters arrive to squash the peace. A black Queen Elizabeth screams 'HALT!' before reciting William Blake's 1804 poem, *Jerusalem* to a humming, clapping band. On the far side of the village, English football hooligans are being rubber stamped on the forehead, '100% Anglo-Saxon.'

The 'Queen' was an actress from TV soap *Eastenders* - She played the girlfriend of Kelvin Carpenter (thanks Tony Pacey!)

Scene 7 - The Village Church (Aldbourne, Wiltshire)

Paul, Mick, Steve and Dee, 'with dry thirst and weary bodies' head for a church to 'await the arrival of a sympathetic lawyer.' During the wait Paul gets up on the stand, 'I have been thinking, that if America were a pair of jeans England would be its back pocket.' The rest are looking bored and when Paul finishes preaching he rips off the back pocket from his jeans and says 'let's do a song.'

Scene 8 - The Windmill (Wilton Windmill)

A remix of *Heavens Above* is played with the band inside, outside and up on Wilton Windmill, switching from place to place and clothes to clothes in quite a clever shot sequence. As the song fades, we are back with the scooters in the woods.

[Wilton Windmill is the only working Windmill in Wessex and is located close to the Village of Wilton, off the A338 between Hungerford and Burbage in Wiltshire]

Scene 9 - In the (wild) wood.

A Policeman arrives on a rocking horse and Dee comments, 'trouble doth make its way', but she is told by Paul to 'Hold firm!, we may yet win the day.' The Policeman approaches and asks, 'Why are you called The Style Council?'

Paul answers, 'well actually...' but is cut off when the Police radio crackles informing the Policeman to proceed to 'Marbles Arches' the home of TSC at Solid Bond Studios.

Scene 10 - Football Hooligans.

The scene cuts further into the trees as the football hooligans from scene 6 approach TSC doing the 'conga.' Steve, trying to ease the situation, 'Oh children of this industrial wasteland...' is rewarded with a brick in the head and the now annoying question, 'Why are you called The Style Council?'

Weller, as the band leader, steps in, 'Enough is enough oh my children... away back we must go to face the music (pause) press and drippy inkies.'

Scene 11 - In the Dock.

TSC are in court, in the dock as the Judge reads out the charge, 'You have been charged with deliberately flaunting the laws of the pop land. You have lasted longer than 6 months, longer than a year even... Do you seriously believe that the people of this court or indeed the people of the land will stand for such flagrant behaviour?'

'I have no alternative but to pronounce you...**GUILTY!**'

The Judge passing the sentence was Gary Beadle, better known as Paul Trueman, again from BBC soap *Eastenders*. He first appeared in *Eastenders* on 23rd April 2001 after various TV and movie appearances. Gary was going out with the daughter of the official merchandise seller Brian when he came to Paolo's attention as an actor.

Scene 12 - The after court 'tent' Party.

It's a 'joyous' time as the band celebrate the verdict with a remix of *Fairy Tales* from *The Cost of Loving*. The crowd is a mix of friends, Aldbourne locals and the band Black Britain. The party is in full swing until Paul is taken aside by a 'drippy inky' for one final time. He pummels Paul with questions, ending the tirade with, 'Why are you called The Style Council?'

Paul - 'WELL ACTUALLY....' (THE END)

In 2005 Paolo Hewitt kindly loaned Wholepoint the master script, a 24 page document that all the actors used. Each page contained the scene number, scene overview down the left side and the main script on the right. In places the narration differed quite considerably from the final version as scenes and lines were altered or left on the cutting room floor. Over 30 scenes are detailed in the document.

The scene with Paul sitting in the throne pushing back the waves was originally meant to be 'hold back thyselves. Hold back I say for my parts freeze. Thus, hold back. Hold back.' There is plenty of previously unknown, scrapped information. After being pronounced 'guilty' the script says, 'The Council run to instruments' then scene thirty for fourth song *My Very Good Friend*. This was dropped from the final cut, more than likely because it was also dropped from the *Cost of Loving* LP.

'It's a bit of a journey, an odyssey. It's us travelling through England, a surreal England. There are comments in the film, but they're not done in a sledgehammer way. They're quite oblique.' (Paul)

'I am proud of it. I like it.' (Paul, 1995, *Boys About Town*)

'In ten years time some anthropologist will find it and start showing it at all the fringe cinemas, believe me.' (Paul, *The Face*)

'We're always being accused of being self righteous but the film is a joke at our own expense, it's self effacing.' (Paul, *NME*)

'Mad little film.' (Paul, *Into Tomorrow*)

'What the hell was that about? I've no idea.' (Dee, *Into Tomorrow*)

'But somehow it's still rather good, probably because you get the feeling all the way through that everyone knows it's going to be a touch useless and has decided to try and make it good fun anyway.' (*No.1*)

'I'm sure TSC will find this terrifically embarrassing in years to come, but for now it's a pleasantly ridiculous and jolly way to spend half an hour.' (*Smash Hits*)

'Proves that the utterly groovy Paul Weller and company are completely off their trolleys.' (*Mizz*)

'A chance for us to have a go at a lot of things we dislike.' (Paul)

Under the title "Weller blasts Britain in shock movie", *The Sun* says, 'Sick anti-British TV movie, which shows a black Queen Elizabeth mixing with football hooligans.'

JerUSAlem is a bizarre part of the bands career and despite the less than favourable reviews it is still very watchable. If you have not seen it then hunt down *The Style Council on Film DVD* compilation. Cult movie? If *Absolute Beginners* can reach this status then there is hope for the film yet.

MARCH

6th - The 2nd UK single from *The Cost of Loving* was to be the double a-sided *Angel* and *Heavens Above*. Promotional 12" records were pressed in special Style Council sleeves (code: Cost 2) alongside a 12" double-sided 'tape one studio' acetate. However, for reasons unknown, this release was scrapped and a decision was made to release the love song *Waiting*.

Waiting was mixed by the well known John Valentine and produced by Paul. This was to be the worst single in terms of chart success, only peaking at number 52, not helped by the lack of airplay before its release. *Waiting* was such a late choice that no promotional singles were pressed and record company promotional stickers were just placed on the sleeve of the standard release. The b-side was *Francoise*, the vocal version of the *JerUSAlem* theme.

At this point the song is still titled *Love Lies Waiting*. The promotional video remained unreleased until the 2004 DVD compilation and was a dull affair. One spotlight focused on a stool where Paul sat, head bowed, the other on Mick at the piano, showing no emotion. Both wore white, Mick brave enough to sport a white tie with large black polka dots.

'A haunting ballad and a song I am very proud of, especially from a musical view. Just me and Mick on this and a possible single, but it's a hard decision. This like the rest of the songs on side 2 is a love song but dealing with different kinds of love.' (Paul, *Style Population*)

Paul admitted making a mistake with some of the Honorary Councillors for the UK tour and quickly sacked them before the summer World tour. Steve White who must have been cringing at The Royal Albert Hall in February returned for this tour.

7th - Ahoy, Rotterdam. The bands Dutch popularity appeared to be on the slide as it was estimated that the 5,000 capacity arena was only 50% full.

8th - Cirque Royale, Koninklijk Circus, Brussels

10th - Dusseldorf

11th - Munster

12th - The Capital, Hannover. Broadcasted on German TV then later released as *Full House* including a 5 minute interview with the very popular English music journalist living in Germany, Alan Bangs. In 2006 an 8 track DVD was released by ARD Video and imported into the UK.

This is a worthy purchase as it is the only official footage from the 1987 tour and it contains the unreleased *Everlasting Love.*

With Everything To Lose, Walking The Night, Heaven's Above, Internationalists, Everlasting Love, Homebreakers, Money Go Round and *Shout To The Top.*

Japan again got another exclusive by releasing the full concert on CD Video, 55 more minutes of music. The extra tracks were; *My Ever Changing Moods, The Lodgers, It Didn't Matter, Angel, The Cost of Loving, The Piccadilly Trail, A Woman's Song, Down In The Seine, Mick's Company, You're The Best Thing, Fairy Tales* and *(When You) Call Me.*

13th - Freitag, Hamburg

15th - Frankfurt

Waiting enters the chart and would peak at number 52, staying in the top 100 for 3 weeks. This was the first single not to enter the top 25.

16th - Heidelberg

18th - Paris

Only three tracks were dropped from the February UK tour; *Waiting, Whole Point II* and *Money Go Round.* They were replaced by *Down In The Seine* and *Shout To The Top.*

21st - *Saturday Live* with Ben Elton to perform *Heavens Above* and *The Cost of Loving* live to an appreciative audience. The tracks chosen allowed this to come across as a powerful performance, especially Mick's screaming Hammond on *The Cost of Loving.* If these tracks were previewed last September on *Rock Around The Dock* instead of *It Didn't Matter* and *Angel,* then the early *Cost of Loving* sales may have been far greater.

TSC have a few days before the flight to Japan to record a title track and incidental music for a forthcoming British film *Business As Usual.* This was being filmed in the UK by John Thaw, Glenda Jackson and Cathy Tyson and was a politically motivated film.

In Japan, *Showbiz!* is released as a limited laser picture disc and *The Cost of Loving* is the new Japanese single, backed with *All Year Round* (b-side to *It Didn't Matter* in the UK). This single was not released in the UK.

In America, *Heavens Above* was chosen as the new single. An exclusive short mix was released as the album version was too long to be considered as a single. This single was not released in the UK, 'myself and Dee sing lead, it's good for me to trade off another vocalist and I like the two lead vocal approach, it gives the new stuff a different edge.'

APRIL

To promote the Japanese tour an exclusive box set of all the Japanese singles was released. A few copies reached the UK and sold for around £50, a decent price for 12 singles, each with exclusive sleeves and pressings.

2nd - World Kinen Hall, Kobe

3rd - Kohichan, Tokyo

4th - Kohichan, Tokyo

5th - Kohichan, Tokyo

6th - Bunka Taiikukan, Yokohama

7th - Lobe, Near Osaka

8th - Fly back to the UK for a few weeks break.

25th - Free benefit gig at Hyde Park, London held for the 1st anniversary of the Chernobyl nuclear disaster. This also incorporated The Friends of The Earth and Campaign for nuclear disarmament. An estimated 80,000 - 100,000 marchers filled the park to be entertained by TSC, Junior, Richard Coles and Billy Bragg.

Today *The Lodgers, Heavens Above, The Cost of Loving* and *Love Peace and Unity** were played amongst many technical problems. New band member, Vivienne McKone (Keyboards) debuts for the Council.

* as quoted in a music magazine. This song is unreleased if they got the title right but I have my doubts. No bootleg has yet surfaced for this gig.

MAY

Richard Ogden's replacement, David Munns joined Polydor. He would have an important part to play in the bands demise in July 1989.

Reports indicated that the Dee C Lee and Red Wedge albums would be released this month, both written by Paul and Dr Robert Howard. However, the albums never appeared though most of Dee's recordings would make it to her 90's Slam Slam LP, *Free Your Feelings*.

A trip to Europe, starting with a short Italian tour.

6th - Palasport, Firenze

7th - Palasport, Torino

8th - Palasport, Varese

Date TBC - Milan

Date TBC - San Remo

23rd - A trip to Holland at the Brabauthallen, Den Bosch for the KRO Eindexamen Festival to headline the event to around 2,500 people. For this gig TSC rely heavily on Keyboards, Synthesisers and Paul's dancing as he only picked up his guitar once for *A Woman's Song*. 'This has just guitar and electric piano with Dee singing lead. Based on an old Nursery Rhyme, but updated to tell the tale of a mother thinking out loud about the future of her child.' (Paul, *Style Population*)

An interesting point to note is that during the encore the first two rows of fans got up on stage to *Internationalists*. Most of the show was filmed for TV and recorded for radio.

Paul talks in *Style Population* about, 'writing and recording two LP's, one of our own new tunes and one of a venture, talked about for a while, of an LP of covers of some of our favourite tunes.' This covers LP never appeared, though Dennis Munday confirmed in 1998 that there is still a 'substantial' amount of material in the vaults. Despite the 90 tracks on TSC 5 CD box set and new demos on *Our Favourite Shop* deluxe, there are still many recordings amiss.

JUNE

8th - Royal Concert Hall, Nottingham for a Red Wedge night, 'Move On Up.' The line up was; TSC, The Blow Monkeys, Billy Bragg, Lorna Gee, Porky The Poet, Rhoda Dakar, Dave Wakeling/Saxa of The Beat, Junior, Everything But The Girl plus Glenys Kinnock leading the audience into a chorus of *The Red Flag*. The songs TSC performed is unknown and I am not aware of a recording of this gig.

27th - Philips take out another full page TSC advert in the music press, 'It might seem a little surprising to learn that you can pick up TSC on compact disc. Perhaps even a little more surprising that you get extra tracks on *Our Favourite Shop* and *Home and Abroad*.' The original advert appeared in December 1986.

JULY

5th - An unknown group, Boogie Box High, make it to number 7 with a cover of the Bee Gees June 1975 top 5 hit *Jive Talkin*. All sorts of rumours were circulating, mainly on the vocalist who was allegedly George Michael. George denied this as it was not released on his record label. Further reports also suggested that Paul played guitar but these were squashed and then more or less confirmed the appearance of Mick Talbot and Nick Heyward.

Top teenage magazine *Smash Hits* did try and get to the bottom of the mystery. 'George Michael helped record this with his cousin Andros Georgiou and pop chums Mick Talbot and Nick Heyward, the ex-singer of Haircut 100.... there was no mention at all of George on the sleeve, let alone Mick Talbot or Nick Heyward.' Not ones to avoid controversy *Smash Hits* followed this up with, 'If George Michael is in such demand, what on earth possessed him to join forces with The Style Council's Mick Talbot? or Nick Heyward? aren't they a bit of a letdown after Aretha (Franklin)?'

The record label were, 'unable to confirm' who recorded it though a future *Boogie Box High* LP does have Mick Talbot listed as a member. TSC sleeve designer Simon Halfon co-produced it and also designed sleeves for George so the possibility is there. The August 1989 release of the *Nervous* cassette single would suspiciously have the code TSCBK1. Co-incidence? Over to you Simon ...

19th - TSC play the 4,300 capacity Brixton Academy, London to celebrate the 8th anniversary of the Nicaraguan revolution and the Nicaragua solidarity campaign. Tickets at £6.50 and £5.50. This is the 3rd UK benefit gig in as many months. Supporting were the Jazz Defektors and Zinica. Also on the line-up were poet Carlos Rigby and compere, the late Andy De La Tour (brother of Frances De La Tour aka Miss Jones in *Rising Damp*). Andy was ideal as in 1983 on Channel 4 he compered *An Evening for Nicaragua, a* benefit concert at the Shaftesbury Theatre.

The biggest event of the year was the Saturday wedding of Paul and Dee, reported as at a 'London registry office', which actually turned out to be in Basingstoke. It was also the best-kept secret of the bands career. No photos were ever released or leaked to the papers. As news filtered through, the papers amongst other things claimed Paolo Hewitt was the head pageboy and Mick the best man.

There were only 10 guests at the wedding who were 'handed a key to the suite of a local hotel. When they arrived, they were confronted by the most sumptuous buffet and the newly-weds had hopped on a plane to start their honeymoon.'

A photo of Dee in her wedding dress was shown on the *Into Tomorrow* DVD.

AUGUST

The Jazz Defektors, a ten piece outfit and stars of *Absolute Beginners* and the *Have You Ever Had It Blue* video, release their debut LP. One track *Ooh! This Feeling* was recorded at Solid Bond Studios and four of the six were mixed by Paul and Mick. Very collectable today and a worthwhile LP to own.

A press release explains that TSC have, 'deliberately chosen smaller capacity venues to break away from the arena circuit their popularity has forced them into.' This was not the case in Scotland where both dates would be axed due to 'unforeseen circumstances' (poor ticket sales). Compare this to 2005 and 2008 when Paul admitted to playing some of his career topping gigs at sell out nights at Dundee's Caird Hall, the venue of one of the abandoned TSC gig.

UK *Renaissance* tour dates are announced for October;

Barrowlands, Glasgow (15th)
Caird Hall, Dundee (16th)
Apollo, Manchester (17th)
Conference Centre, Harrogate (18th)
City Hall, Sheffield (22nd)
De Montfort Hall, Leicester (23rd)
Leisure Centre, Crawley (24th)
Winter Gardens, Margate (25th)

Then 2 nights in November;

Hammersmith Odeon, London (24th, 25th) Tickets at £8 and £9.

SEPTEMBER

TSC return to Italy for 2 arena gigs only a few months after the last shows.

4th - Festa De L'Unità, Reggio Emilia, Italy

7th - Palatrussardi, Milan, Italy

Another remix of *Loverboy* by Chairman of The Board is released. This time on the Syncopate label and Mick gets the applause for a 'keyboard solo.'

OCTOBER

The Curtis Mayfield show, *Curtis Live* (recorded at Ronnie Scott's), was released on video and appeared on TV. Unknown to many is that Paul interviewed Curtis and this was shown between the live tracks. No mention of this interview was made on any of the promotional material. Paul & Gary Crowley discussed this memorable event on Gary's Radio London special in July 2008.

The first hint of a new single appeared with a music press advert which probably only a few picked up on; 'Waiter, there's some soup in my flies/TSC14 new next week.' The only clue here is the single code TSC14! Seven days later an updated advert appeared quoting Radio 1 DJ Simon Bates, 'very commercial, very new, very now, very them.'

The *Wanted* promotional video was shot at Solid Bond Studios and featured a new recruit Paul Powell (bass) alongside the suited TSC four. It was a totally different sound to what appeared on *The Cost of Loving* only 8 months earlier.

The Renaissance tour did not start as planned as the first two nights, both in Scotland, are cancelled due to poor ticket sales.

15th - Barrowlands, Glasgow. *Cancelled*

16th - Caird Hall, Dundee. *Cancelled*

17th - Apollo, Manchester. Now the opening night of a 6 night tour

18th - Conference Centre, Harrogate

22nd - City Hall, Sheffield

23rd - De Montfort Hall, Leicester

24th - Leisure Centre, Crawley

25th - Winter Gardens, Margate

Across all the nights, 18 songs were played on the tour. 3 from *Café Bleu*, 5 from *Our Favourite Shop*, 3 from *The Cost of Loving*, 2 from the forthcoming album[†], 2 singles not on LP's, 2 b-sides and 1 unreleased*.

*The Lodgers, My Ever Changing Moods, Homebreakers, You're The Best Thing, Down In The Seine, With Everything To Lose, Internationalists, (When You) Call Me, Money Go Round, Cost of Loving, Whole Point II, Fairy Tales, Angel, Confessions 1,2,3[†], Wanted, Cover Me With Love** (Dee C Lee), *It's A Very Deep Sea*[†] and *Mick's Up.*

8 songs were dropped from the February tour, 5 from *The Cost of Loving* LP;

1984 - *The Piccadilly Trail, Mick's Company*
1987 - *It Didn't Matter, Waiting, Walking The Night, A Woman's Song, Heavens Above.*
unreleased - *Everlasting Love*

The following 6 replaced them;

1983 - *Mick's Up*
1985 - *Down In The Seine,*
1987 - *Wanted*
New - *Cover Me With Love, Confessions 1,2,3* and *It's A Very Deep Sea.*

Steve White returned alongside new bass player Paul Powell. As far as Steve remembers a female vibes player, Annie Hogan, played for only 2 gigs. Frank Ricotti played percussion, Mark Edwards on keyboards and additional guitarist Simon Eyre.

Sounds hold no punches, 'TSC 1987 are pretty sad. Weller's voice has never got any better and one should only aspire to soul power, grace and sensation for so long before admitting defeat. Worra lorra naff! Bring back Tracie.'

Number 1 magazine, guests at the De Montfort show, focus on Mr Talbot. 'Mick's solos are accompanied by a series of faces which suggest someone is hidden under his keyboard removing his toenails with pliers!'

26th - *Wanted (or Waiter There's Some Soup In My Flies)* is released, produced by Paul and Mick. The b-side is a new, re-recorded version of *The Cost of Loving*, renamed *The Cost*. In fact, it is remarkable that this is the same song. The LP version was fast with screaming Hammond, wailing guitar and drums. Now, we have bare vocals, minimal guitar, with very low piano and percussion. This is a similar idea to *My Ever Changing Moods* in 1984, which also worked well in two entirely different versions.

'I would rather listen to this than T'Pau.' (*Melody Maker*)

The sleeve notes introduce us to Jedemiah Hampden, 'a new recruit to the talented forces of The Style Council', but other than that we get no indication of what he does and never hear from him again. *Wanted* would follow tradition and not appear on the next LP. By this time the CD era was upon us and for the first time a Style Council single would be available in four formats 7", 12", CD and Cassette.

The Cost was used as the theme tune to the British film *Business As Usual* featuring 3 well known British faces, Glenda Jackson, Cathy Tyson and John Thaw. It was a story of sexual harassment on a clothes shop manager and the subsequent involvement of the Trade Unions, right up TSC's street at that time.

The Cambridge Film Festival 1987 reviewed it, '*Business As Usual* is a notable debut feature, shot with a gritty realism and distinguished by excellent performances from Glenda Jackson and Cathy Tyson, this is an honest and thought-provoking work of great promise.'

'One of the angry anti - Thatcher films of the late 80's written by first-time feature director Barrett. Excellent performances help a one-sided script.' (Leonard Maltin)

TSC had first refusal on the film soundtrack, however, due to time restrictions noted back in March, they were unable to compose a full soundtrack LP. Mick confirms, 'we only had a few days between the European tour and the Japanese tour to work on it, but I thought it went very well.'

As a result, only a few snippets of incidental music appeared and no soundtrack LP was released. The cinema poster details The Style Council's involvement as does the book of the film.

27th - An excellent, confident appearance on the new ITV show *The Roxy* with a happy smiling Paul, Mick and Dee.

29th - Appearance on *Top of the Pops* with Steve Wright ('love them to death') did the song no harm.

NOVEMBER

1st - *Wanted* enters the chart and would peak at number 20, staying in the top 100 for 4 weeks. The catchy and instantly likeable pop-tune performed well after the backlash from the music press since *The Cost of Loving*.

Another promotional trip to Italy to perform Wanted on the TV show *Festival Bar*.

The daily press announce that Dee is pregnant and she is 'telling anyone who'll listen of the impending arrival.' However, Paul is 'refusing to confirm' the story. *The Sun* tells of Paul splashing out £10,000 on a new Jeep for Dee who has just passed her driving test.

A Polydor press release states that on December 7th 'The Style Council are releasing a special series of EP's. Each will sell for the same price as a normal single and will be released in batches of three every six months - featuring classic Style Council material.'

24th - Hammersmith Odeon, London. A month gap between the last UK dates and exactly the same live set and line-up as for the October dates. The support act was Porky The Poet, a left-wing punk performance poet, doing his final 2 shows. Porky is actually the very well known Phil Jupitus, who in 2003 would narrate the *Shout To The Top* BBC Radio 2 documentary. He had originally been a DJ at Red Wedge back in 1986, allegedly just for the chance to work with Paul Weller.

25th - Hammersmith Odeon, London. The 2nd and final night. *Record Mirror* rave about this gig, 'Here's to 19 more soul scorched years. Dig it. You'll find TSC at an absolute peak.'

DECEMBER

7th - The inaugural Style Council EP series is released. *Café Bleu, The Birds and the Bees* and *Agent '88*.

Café Bleu EP was simply 4 tracks lifted from the album and was produced by Peter Wilson and Paul Weller. The lengthy sleeve notes were by a new name Harry Monk, the so-called engineer for the 4 tracks. *The Birds and The Bees* EP was a clever title for a collection of 4 b-side songs and finally *Agent '88* EP was a collection of Mick's instrumentals, the only one to break the charts, reaching number 100, produced by Peter Wilson and Paul Weller. The lengthy sleeve notes were titled 'The fifth man or how I caught the Spyscratcher'. 'The only documented evidence we have of Britain's most regarded special agent. The phone burst into life, abrupt and stinging, Mick Talbot awoke, a hangover in one eye, a trilby on the other...'

Despite the promise of 3 EP's every 6 months only the first set was released on 7" and CD. Today they are most collectable as a set of 6 complete with the custom orange record shop display stand that neatly held them all in.

Paul's review of 1987 for the *NME,* 'The nation's pop press (and others) were perfectly beastly towards TSC. Our much-acclaimed LP *The Cost of Loving* was greeted with howls of protest. But no! The anti-Rock forces of TSC must and did continue in our grand quest. Forgive them Lord, for they know not what they've got.'

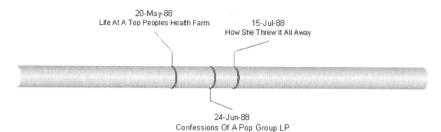

20-May-88
Life At A Top Peoples Health Farm

15-Jul-88
How She Threw It All Away

24-Jun-88
Confessions Of A Pop Group LP

"Perhaps we think we are funny and we're not"

Paul reveals his high points of 1987 were 'Red Wedge at Nottingham and TSC at Brixton (Nicaragua gig)' and low points, 'the February/March tour which resulted in a few band member sackings.'

By this time, the political and soul influences have been shelved as Paul is now immersed in The Modern Jazz Quartet (MJQ), The Swingle Singers and Debussy. The MJQ LP *Place De Vendome* was of particular interest to him, within it was a partnership he wanted to replicate with TSC.

The MJQ had followed up a December 1965 meeting with Ward Swingle in New York with a week in Paris recording harmonies with the Swingles in September 1966, 'What makes this a very special record is not so much the fact that two of the most astonishing phenomena of postwar jazz have come together, but they have blended so completely, each influencing the other, that something new and exciting has emerged.'

Paul contacted Alabama born Ward Swingle (b.21/09/27) to set up a collaboration for the forthcoming LP. The result was a *Story of Someone's Shoe,* one of the finest songs from his entire career. The original Swingles had 8 members, made up of 2 sopranos, 2 altos, 2 tenors and 2 basses, a sound retained for this recording.

FEBRUARY

14th - Paul, Billy Bragg and Norman Cook DJ at a Red Wedge club night in London, the final Red Wedge event that Paul would attend as he focused on the new LP and getting TSC to a wider audience. 'We would like to be successful in USA because we don't know where else to take it now. We are selling 70,000 - 100,000 copies of each LP there. The record company never decided to break us. I don't know why.' TSC are reasonably well known in New York, Los Angeles, San Francisco, Chicago and Philadelphia.

MARCH

6th - Hackney Empire, London with Sinead O' Connor and comedian Ben Elton for another benefit gig, this time in support of the *Fight Alton's Bill* campaign. This was an attempt by MP David Alton to reduce the abortion time limit to 18 weeks. No details are known on what tracks were played.

In *Straight No Chaser* (Issue 2) Paul again digs the Modern Jazz Quartet and their clothes, 'Sharp blue Blazers, white shirts, striped ties and on the breast pocket: a badge bearing the initials of the group, MJQ - Now compare this to the kit TSC wore on the *Showbiz* video (identical). The MJQ's blend of style, subtlety and sophistication, with increasing dashes of imagination and vision, has bestowed upon us a brilliant catalogue of music.'

APRIL

TSC had now considerably reduced the amount of press they were doing due to the increased and direct personal criticism of Paul. It got to a stage where the albums are not even mentioned in the review. Paul explains to *The Face*, 'It is about making records. The rest is all crap. I spend my life trying to make records, trying to better myself and the band through the songs I write and the records I make.' Going onto say, 'When I read the article afterwards I think, why did I bother doing that?'

To get around this problem a decision was made by Polydor to release a promotional Interview LP (TSC-IN1) The music press in turn generally ignore it as I do not recall many quotes being directly pulled from the LP. The interesting and worthwhile interview was conducted by the respected Yugoslavian journalist Sasha Stojanovic, who for 30 years before his death in 2005 interviewed many leading artists. It is quoted in the *Record Collector 2008 Rare Record Guide* as the 2nd most valuable official Style Council item at £40

Paul and Mick give the reason for producing *Confessions of A Pop Group* themselves, 'We don't have to argue with the producer, what usually happens'. They also detail the new songs, forthcoming plans and the next Red Wedge tour. Spookily enough a year before the axing of *Modernism: A New Decade,* Paul voiced concerns on Polydor's reaction to the LP, 'Now is the most pressurised time. We've spent a long time doing it and trying to perfect it as much as we can. Now we are waiting to see what the record company will do with it. They hold the whole balance of it in their hands. If they don't get behind it, it could go down the drier, that's quite a daunting thought really.'

This 'daunting thought' became reality 12 months later and with the help of David Munns, it would ultimately kill off the band.

There was an unofficial 7" interview released on blue vinyl, picture disc, black vinyl and clear vinyl. The latter also available in a special double pack with a one sided white label 7" available exclusively from record store Adrian's. The black vinyl was a test press limited to 25 copies. All formats contained an interview with the band, no music, so it could be released without Polydor's permission.

19th - Steve White had officially left TSC to pursue a career in The Jazz Renegades with saxophonist Alan Barnes. Today he was at *Rooster 11 studios* in London to produce and mix the forthcoming LP with the help of Julie Ann Jones. Joining Steve and Alan were Alec Dankwoth on bass, Paul Lacey on trumpet, David Newton on piano and Harbans Srih on percussion.

MAY

A bizarre Polydor press release titled "Life with the Lions" appeared; 'I hate you! I hate you!' screamed Mick Talbot, Hammond Organ under one arm, Piano Forte under t'other. You could have cut the silence with a knife. 'Well you've really done it this time Weller', Dee C Lee remarked, closing the door. In the half-light of the studio Paul Weller could see what she meant. After 5 years, 14 singles (all of which, bar 2, making the top 15), two No.1 albums, and the thousands they'd played to, they were being written off!!

Even the girls in press had no belief; their A 'n' R man wanted to bring in Norman Cook and Arthur Baker; things were that bad!

But hope sprang forth from Weller, never one to wallow in his own depressions, or greatness come to that. With this in mind he did pen 10 classic new songs to tickle people's minds and educate their aunties, elevate the customary boredom of today's wild world of pop and so getting the team back together, The Style Council embarked on a new course of treatment for the world.'

The enthusiastic press release detailed 15 bullet points, mainly on the new single but also propaganda like, 'one of the finest musical forces to come from this continent', 'you will not be able to ignore them any longer', 'you will learn to love it' and 'original cast, now in its fifth spectacular year. Europe's finest on LP, Cassette and CD.' It finally confirmed the release of a 33 minute studio concert on VHS and 8" laser disc.

Then an advert in *NME* appeared for the new single. It was a full page spread with Paul wearing NHS 80's style specs held together with Elastoplasts, hair slicked back, sports jacket and polka dot tie. You have to look twice (or more) to convince yourself that it is him.

Due to the reduction in interviews it was a surprise to get an excellent TV interview on *Wired,* including exclusive videos of new songs, *Changing The Guard* and *Life At A Top Peoples Health Farm.* In an open interview which covered the new single, 'It's the angriest I've heard you for a long time!' Paul replying, 'It is my age I think, my final birth before I turn 30, mellow out and move to Los Angeles.' However, it gets really awkward when Stock Market shares are discussed, 'She's got a new film out' (Paul) 'and a new record' (Mick), totally avoiding the shares subject by trying to link the question to the singer Cher. *Wired* keep pushing, 'It seems to be a minor obsession...do you have any?', 'No, I haven't got any shares.' (Mick), 'I haven't either, I don't think, mine's all in the bank.' (Paul)

'Any chance of a bloody revolution?'

'No, I can't see it happening, it is supposed to come from the middle classes...I can't see it.' (Mick). Paul had different thoughts, 'I tend to disagree, I think it will happen but it will be the wrong kind, totally confused and without any real leadership and real cause. It will just be people saying, "where's my chunk of the rock?"'

20th - *Life At A Top Peoples Health Farm* is released as a new single. It was the first single from the forthcoming *Confessions of A Pop Group* LP. Produced by Paul and Mick, possibly not the best choice for airplay success.

Paul described it as a modern version of Bob Dylan's *Subterranean Home Sick Blues* where he tried to cram as many of the tacky and distasteful things over the last few years into 1 song. It contains an avalanche of information, from flushing toilets to dog tracks to lettuce to Jeffery Archer, even a tongue in cheek, 'thank you Margaret Thatcher, may you never come to harm.'

The promotional video featured many costume changes and impersonations by Mick and Paul with his famous *Wham* guitar, which last appeared with the Jam (it would be shelved again for 8 years until August 1996 and *Peacock Suit*). Gary Crowley makes a guest appearance, 'I played the smarmy TV presenter. It was directed by Pedro Romhanyi and was recorded in Clapham or Battersea in London.'

The sleeve notes threw down a challenge, 'We're throwing down the gauntlet! Are you person enough to pick it up? If your weekdays are Sundays and your weekends Mondays, listen out for the forthcoming TSC long player. Like a phoenix rising from the ashes our enemies made, we're back, bad and beautiful. Make your confessions this June.'

New York, Gstaad, Tokyo, Marble Arch was to be the new band banner. Marble Arch is the home of Solid Bond Studios but the link to the other 3 locations is unclear. Over to Simon Halfon.

29th - *Life At A Top Peoples Health Farm* enters the chart and would peak at number 28, staying in the top 100 for 3 weeks.

Interesting and rare 10" and 12" acetates appear in a special Abbey Road sleeve with *Sweet Loving Ways* on the b-side. There was also a promotional DJ 12" issued as *Spank*! a remixed version of the single.

Mick on the eve of the new LP reminisces to the *Sunday Mail, 'The Cost of Loving* lacked a sense of humour, but *Café Bleu* was potentially quite a funny album. Perhaps we think we are funny and we're not. There are a lot of elements of humour which affect what we do. We'd like everyone to see the joke, but you can't force them. It's no big deal because we are not trying to make a living as stand-up comedians.'

JUNE

2nd - *Top of the Pops* would not allow a studio appearance and cut short the video clip due to the 'piss off somewhere else' lyric.

23rd - An unknown artist Dan Davies had his paintings launched with the new LP at a cheese and wine event in Hamilton's Gallery, a top London art venue since 1977, not too far from Solid Bond Studios in Carlos Place. *'Don't you think you are heading for trouble?' Rock of Europe* enquired, 'Yes, but that's all part of the fun' replied Paul. 'We're really pleased with them, Dan's done a wonderful job' prompts Mick. Later claiming that Dan did well financially from the paintings, probably making more money than the LP did.

24th - *Confessions Of A Pop Group* is released. Paul played Guitars, Synthesisers and Drum programs. Mick on Piano Forte, Hammond, Clavinet and Synthesisers. Dee on vocals and Steve White joined the following as an Honorary Councillor; The Swingle Singers (Vocals), John Mealing (Arrangements), Jezar (Sequencing and Drum machines), Paul Morgan (Contra Bass), Frank Ricottim (Vibraphone), Rupert Parker (Harp), Camelle Hinds (Bass), Nick Brown (Drums), Dick Morrissey (Flute), Little Jo Ruocco (Percussion) and Chris Lawrence (Trombone).

The new Simon Halfon created banner/logo *'Feriae Pecuniae Sunt Omnia'* is revealed, translated to 'Festivals, Holidays, Peace, Rest, Money, Property all together.' A proper Latin translation I am reliably informed is, 'Holidays and money are everything.'

Paul tells *The Face,* 'It is worthwhile us continuing if only to show people that there are other sides to pop music. We're still firmly in the middle ground between the two polarised areas of pop, the teenyboppers on one side and the serious artists and all that crap on the other. We're not either, never have been. We're the in-betweens.'

Paul explained to *Just 17* that Polydor were, 'bewildered by this album' saying 'this is going to be difficult, it's going to be trouble.'

Not much different than his worries over *Café Bleu* four years ago or *The Cost of Loving* in 1987.

It didn't help the band versus company relations when Paul said that he didn't want a photo of the band on the sleeve. This didn't go down well with Polydor so soon after the slated *Cost of Loving* sleeve and in this Paul backed down. It was also said that a time limit was initially set in the contract by Polydor to complete the LP, a money penalty of 'so many hundred pounds' (Paul) would be levied for each day the LP was late. John Weller's management or bargaining skills managed to get this clause removed.

The short-lived *Cover* magazine said, 'Weller reputedly banked a million pound advance from Polydor to deliver the album. When he eventually did, it apparently arrived on a C90 cassette with a suitably defiled mug shot of Polydor's A 'n' R chief attached. Relations chilled.'

Confessions of A Pop Group was the first studio album in 18 months and reached a disappointing number 15, the first not to enter the top 10. The disappointment following last years *Cost of Loving* and the largest gap in the band's history between releases probably accounted for the low sales. It stayed in the top 100 for only 3 weeks. Today it is widely acknowledged as being the 2nd best LP after *Our Favourite Shop*. The playing time exceeded 57 minutes and was by far the longest long-player to date. The track length record was set as *The Gardener of Eden* clocked in at 10 minutes 29 seconds. We are told, 'You may have to increase the audio level as running time (of the side) is over 30 minutes.' The sleeve notes did not indicate who the songwriters were for any of the tracks - an oversight? The answer came with the release of the *IMP music book*.

All words and music were by Paul apart from *The Little Boy In A Castle* and *A Dove Flew Down From The Elephant* which were credited to Mick. Somewhat surprising was that Paul wrote the classical music for *The Gardener of Eden* (part one and three). At a reasonable guess you probably would have credited these totally instrumental classical pieces to Mick.

'In *The Gardener of Eden*, the Harp/strings definitely comes under classical. I'm treading on dodgy ground by saying that, but I think it's credible enough to label it as that.' (Paul). Mick wasn't so sure, 'It has got classical elements I guess, but I feel more comfortable liking it to film soundtracks. The piano piece is a bit filmic.'

Confessions of A Pop Group was split into 2 distinct sides, *The Piano Paintings* featuring, 'Jazz tinged ballads and classical influenced pieces' and the second *Confessions of A Pop Group,* 'closer to pop.'

'Side one is for the pensioners and side two's for the kids. I'm now writing for people my age and with my outlook. There's definitely a sense of humour there, but I don't suppose we'll get any credit for it.' (Paul)

Both singles came from side 2. Of the 11 tracks, *It's A Very Deep Sea* (previewed on tour last autumn), *The Story of Someone's Shoe, Changing of The Guard, Confessions 1,2,3* (previewed on tour last autumn) and *Confessions Of A Pop Group* are masterpieces.

The packaging was also substantial with a large foldout lyric insert with Dan Davis' paintings complimenting each song. One of those, *Life At A Top Peoples Health Farm* is an excellent example of the work put into them. TSC originally wanted 12" colour inserts for each painting but due to the high printing costs had to settle for a much smaller reproduction above the lyrics.

Polydor released many interesting promotional items, the most impressive being the *Confessions* briefcase which contained; a 29 minute, 4 track sampler CD - *Life At A Top Peoples Health Farm, Why I Went Missing, The Gardener of Eden (A Three Piece Suite)* and *Confessions Of A Pop Group* [CPGCD1]. A 4 track sampler cassette, *It's A Very Deep Sea, Iwasadoledadstoyboy, Why I Went Missing* and *Gardener of Eden* [CPGMC1]. 13½ minute selections video [no reference code], orange towel with '*The Style Council, Confessions Of A Pop Group*' embroidered on it. The inside lid detailed all the release formats, prices and dates. An additional 12" black box contained the cassette and the Video neatly held by slots. All individual items are in special white TSC sleeves.

The USA release came with a 'why you should buy me' sticker. 'A fascinating new album from The Style Council heralding a return to great pop music by one of Britain's premier bands - their most important release since their debut *My Ever Changing Moods*.'

The official music book treated us to previously unavailable pictures from the *It's A Very Deep Sea* video as well as a promotional piece of text not available anywhere else. Reproduced here in its entirety as it was included to increase sales and explain what Polydor wanted to get across.

"One of The Style Council's early songs, *My Ever Changing Moods*, stated the intention: the band have continued to change with each and every album. But, it is very unlikely that any of us could have expected what is waiting for our ears on their fourth studio album, *Confessions Of A Pop Group* .

The first side of the album contains the surprises, the second being more in the band's conventional vein, without ever being a repetition of any kind. There were instrumentals on the band's previous LP's but nothing like *Castle*, almost a pure classical piece, although Mick Talbot prefers to liken it to a snippet of a film soundtrack.

Paul Weller, as the main songwriter, is on par with his own composition *The Gardener of Eden*, especially its intro of harp and string quartet.

TSC have always been into changes. A move forward, never standing still for a single recording session. Perhaps there had been more freedom available to them as the current album was produced by the two some.

'That's what we set out to do in the first place.' Paul explains. 'We don't like to repeat ourselves, we believe that progression is the most important thing.'

Some might see some similarities with their debut disc *Café Bleu* but the diversity of songs is rather like their second platter, *Our Favourite Shop*. There was hardly anything on the preceding album *The Cost of Loving* to prepare us for this delightful experience. There can hardly be a more refreshing album.

The first single culled from the album is *Life At A Top Peoples Health Farm*, the lyrics are hard hitting, the tunes to be moved by and songs to think about. *I was a doledadstoyboy* or *Why I Went Missing*, explains this somewhat conceptual album, in many an aspect but not old-fashioned.

Paul Weller has always been very aware of his environment, society and the social changes within the songs map the changes in the British society as well. There are lighter touches on *Confessions Of A Pop Group* , such as the opening cut, *It's A Very Deep Sea*, which Paul sees as a 'modern surf song Brian Wilson would be proud of, although he would have done it differently'. The album closes with a little homage to The Beach Boys, in the shape of a surfing sing along. The band became a trio due to the departure of Steve White, who played on the record. There are guests on the album, the return appearance being a bass man, Camelle Hinds. Dee C Lee is still present in this musically ever a changing combo.

As their only live album to date *Home and Abroad*, TSC have played live far and wide and, as soon as they sort out the touring personnel, will be embarking on another set of world stages and dates. It shan't be just another concert tour, they would like to make it more of an event, something to be remembered for."

Disappointingly, this live 'event' never happened. There would be no tour, just a VHS and laser disc of the *Confessions* studio concert.

'It's what we've come to expect from TSC really, some rather pious, mannered 'soul' style music, a good deal of (tongue-in-cheek) pretentious bits and of course the odd classic song 6½/10.' (*Smash Hits*).

Paul told the ultimate 90's fanzine, *Boys About Town*, 'The first side was good, but the second really patchy. The lyrics on the LP were clever, but in a kind of mechanical way. I was pleased myself with the lyrics, there was a lot of ego wound up in them'.

He went on to tell *Fresh Air*, 'the 2nd side, I think, in retrospect is flawed. I only like *Confessions 1,2,3* and *Why I Went Missing*. I didn't like either of the singles. I hate it!' (*Life At A Top Peoples Health Farm*).

'It really is an exceptional piece of pop music for the times we inhabit. Leave your prejudices at the door and step into the confessional. You'll feel better for it.' (*Record Mirror*)

NME were as kind as ever, 'It's the best LP the Council have ever made (9/10) and it's still retarded.' (2/10)

'Weller's lack of inspiration could not be disguised by sugary layers of orchestration, flute and harp. The band disappeared up its own fundament on a couple of jazzy "suites." (Chris Mugan, *The Independent*)

'*Confessions* I liked a lot of. That is an album I go back and listen to every now and then.' (Gary Crowley, 2008)

Following an alleged *Melody Maker* review of *Confessions Of A Pop Group* when the LP was not even mentioned, an angry fan wrote in, 'What it is you all have against Paul Weller?' to get the reply, 'If we reviewed Paul Weller's music and not the man himself there'd be even less to write about.' Another article appeared with the new TSC album titled *It's Meant To Be Crap*.

JULY

4th - The music press advert for the next single, *How She Threw it All Away* appeared, 'The record you've been asking for! Special EP rush release. Four wonderful titles, including the evergreen *Long Hot Summer* and a sultry ballad *Love The First Time*.'

11th - Steve White's band The Jazz Renegades release *A Summer To Remember* on label Re-elect The President. The press release claimed, 'the chaps at Re-elect The President follow up their success with the James Taylor Quartet by signing the Jazz Renegades. Alan Barnes (fresh from the Tommy Chase Band and one of the most stunning saxophonists in the country) and Steve White (from The Style Council and regarded as the hottest young Jazz drummer of the moment) team up to produce their second album (the first only available as a Japanese import) of HARD BE-BOP JAZZ for the 80's.'

15th - *How She Threw It All Away* is released, produced by Paul and Mick. Further rare pressings appear from the Abbey Road Studios, a one-sided 10" and a 3 track 12" acetate.

24th - *How She Threw It All Away* enters the chart and would peak at number 41, staying in the top 100 for 2 weeks. 'The record you've been asking for! Special EP rush release' didn't seem to speak much truth now. It also meant plans for a 3rd single were ditched, no more singles would be released from the *Confessions Of A Pop Group* . Instead to meet contractual commitments of 3 singles per year, a new song would be released in the autumn.

Q magazine reported that Paul had to cancel a Monday interview as Dee was going into labour. Their first child, Nathaniel (8lb, 7oz) was born. Mick spoke of the news, 'I know the signs but I can't see any change in Paul. Basically you just get less sleep.'

The Red Wedge tour was also shelved although a few token club nights carried on, namely at the Riverside and the Mean Fiddler.

In 2008, Nat Weller is 21, in a band and increasingly being photographed at fashion launches and events so expect to see more of him in the future. As well as accompanying Paul to collect his *Mojo* award in June 2008 Paul got him on stage to play guitar at Hammersmith and later talked of his son's goth image, 'Nat's the smartest end of goth. He's more of a moth, Marilyn Manson is his man.'

However, in September 2008 after picking up another award for Paul who was in Australia, Nat told *The Daily Star*, 'I might as well turn into Callum Best now - get fat, sleep with loads of girls.'

Back to 1988. Although Paul and the earlier press releases stated that TSC were heading to Europe, USA, Japan and back to the UK for Xmas no tour had or was now going to be arranged - totally unheard of when an LP is released by any artist. As it turned out, there would only be one further gig in the UK, next July in London.

'Rumours have suggested a split within the band itself, though reasons have varied from the sublime to the ridiculous. Reports from the Record Company sources are that Mick has a virus, which could keep him out of action for two years. The autumn 1988 tour has accordingly been scrapped.'

The Sun reports, 'Paul Weller has killed off his band because he wants to spend more time with his family.' A friend told them, 'Paul and Dee want a complete break so they can be real parents to their baby.'

Talk of a split was premature and a frustrated Paul hit back, 'When we all decide there is nowhere to go then it might be time to move onto something different, but not before.' Instead some solo projects were talked about, Paul was keen to do some producing, Mick had some ideas for solo material and Dee C Lee was to record her 2nd solo album.

SEPTEMBER

The premier edition of *The Cover* featured a Weller front page and centre spread with an exclusive interview. This saught after magazine survived for a few issues.

TSC are still in favour with girls' magazine *Just 17*, 'magic moguls and dead hip.'

Steve White's Jazz Renegades release a single written by Rogers/Hart, *Do It The Hard Way,* featuring Sarah Jane Morris (most famous for her number 1 hit with the Communards, *Don't Leave Me This Way*). The track is from the forthcoming album *Freedom Samba* which would be produced by Steve and Alan Barnes.

10th - At 10:25 after *Match Of The Day* the *Confessions Of A Pop Group* video concert is shown in its entirety.

Paul and Paolo Hewitt were frequenting Norman Jay's London Club, *High on Hope* where garage house was being played. Paul told *NME* that he believed, 'garage house was the new mod.' Having said that, Paul wasn't too keen on House music telling *The Face,* 'As for House music most of it sounds like *Stars on 45* to me, this incessant disco beat. I don't know much about it but I think it sounds like boring Seventies disco music.'

Ending with his much used quote, 'Acid House, nah. If we made a House record, we could call it a Council House. That would be nice.'
Paul's friend Marco Nelson of up and coming band The Young Disciples introduced Paul to a Joe Smooth song that had been released in Germany in 1988 on BCM records, *Promised Land.* So impressed was Paul that *Promised Land* would be recorded and would become the next Style Council single.

NOVEMBER

18th - *Promised Land* is recorded at Town House Studios, Goldhawk Road, London, W12.

Around this time Steve White has frozen The Jazz Renegades and joined The James Taylor Quartet (JTQ) for the foreseeable future. He did not appear on their latest *Wait a Minute* LP but is to take part in live dates for the remainder of 1988 and into the summer of 1989. This is no easy task as JTQ have over 100 gigs planned.

The Style Council are publicly quiet for the remainder of the year but are busy in the studio recording one of the most diverse albums you are ever likely to hear. One that would kill them off, but for Paul Weller, it was the opportunity during this en-forced break to musically re-discover himself.

Outside of this album, detailed in 1989, two songs were recorded in 1988; *Waiting On A Connection* and *I am Leaving* which both remained unreleased until the 90's.

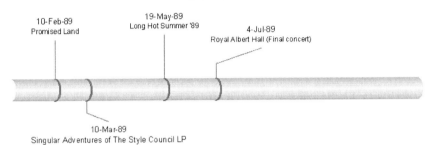

1989

10-Feb-89
Promised Land

19-May-89
Long Hot Summer '89

4-Jul-89
Royal Albert Hall (Final concert)

10-Mar-89
Singular Adventures of The Style Council LP

"garage house was the new mod"

JANUARY

From mid 1988 and into 1989 Paul became obsessed with the raw sound of American garage house which was much more lyrical and soulful than acid house. He had more or less given up on the guitar and was continually drawn to drum machines and sequencers.

It was time to plan the next single, *Promised Land,* recorded in November 1988 and initially to be from the forthcoming album. Songwriter Joe Smooth (real name Joe Welbon), does not sing on *Promised Land* as this is left to an Anthony Thomas. Joe visited Britain, 'direct from Chicago, USA' for a club tour. One was Sweatbox 3 in Dundee, an 11 hour show of 'House, Soul, Hip Hop and Italio' from 4pm and featuring the kind of music that Paul was currently obsessed with - Marshall Jefferson, Blaze and Phase 2.

Paul revealed details of the recording in *Fresh Air* magazine, 'I just thought it was a good song and it was a bit under-developed the way the original sound was. I could hear something else in there. It always sounded like a gospel song to me, the chords and the voices were. We didn't change it that much really, we just made it more inspirational, more up. The original release is more of a serious sombre sound.'

As a result very few people linked *Promised Land* with The Style Council so good news for record sales as it was unrecognisable as TSC.

'How did Joe Smooth take it?', 'I spoke to Joe Smooth, I don't think he was too bothered at all actually. From a royalty point of view he was probably quite pleased because his own version was happening at the same time as ours. I'm sure he was very pleased.' (Paul)

The hard to track down Joe Smooth spoke to me in June 2008 about his music and how the legendary anthem *Promised Land* came about;

JS: 'I was born and raised in Chicago, Illinois. It always fascinated me how people could make music, so at the age of 12 I taught myself how to play the piano. I currently reside in Chicago and am working on various musical projects consistently; Production, remixing, writing, consulting, mentoring, engineering, scoring and mixing.'

Where and when did you write *Promised Land* and where was it originally released? Was it a hit all over Europe? How did it do in the USA?

JS: 'I came up with the idea for *Promised Land* while on one of the 1st house music tours. It was released world wide. It was a hit in Europe and more of an underground hit in the USA.

Did you feel something was happening at this time in the UK?

JS: 'Yes, it was a very musically unifying moment.'

Promised Land is still attractive for inclusion on new compilations, well over 60 to date, impressive for a song now 20 years old. Did you know at the time you had something special?

JS: 'It was an inspired work. I was so amazed at the time about writing *Promised Land,* how people all around the world were touched by music and would come together regardless of ethnic background and race to appreciate the feeling and passion behind our music whether they understood the words or not. It is like music unifies the human spirit and inspires the soul to do special things.'

Anthony Thomas is the vocalist, any specific reason for choosing Anthony?

JS: 'We clicked right away and his voice along with Dohn Connley and mine worked extremely well together.'

Had you heard of The Style Council before they wanted to cover the track?

JS: Yes, I have been DJ'ing since I was in high school and have always been into alternative music.

Did you rate The Style Council's various mixes?

JS: I didn't really rate them. It was just Paul Weller's vision of *Promised Land.* What was important to me was that him covering *Promised Land* meant that it would reach a more diverse audience.

Promised Land was sent to you by Polydor in order to release a limited 12", the *Joe Smooth Alternative Mix* at 125¾ - 126-0bpm. When it was returned Paul said he 'wasn't mad about it.' Did you try to keep The Style Council sound or move more towards your version?

JS: 'I tried to stay towards their direction but make it sound a little less live.'

Did you meet Paul and Mick or were the conversations all by phone? Do you still get royalties from TSC release?

JS: No, that was all handled by the record company. I collect royalties, but I don't know the specifics of their origin. *Promised Land* is probably one of the most covered house songs and on many compilations so I really don't know.

FEBRUARY

Steve White was now playing live most nights with the James Taylor Quartet and seemed to be at his best as he excelled in some amazing drum solos. He is also recording on their new LP *Get Organised* and has already appeared in the *Starsky and Hutch* promotional video.

The *Promised Land* promotional video was filmed in a church and one noticeable difference was that Mick sported a beard. The *Chart* Show told us this was because he was to play the part of George Bernard Shaw. True?

10th - The first cover version single, *Promised Land* was released, an excellent, fast remake which set the club charts alight, rushing straight into the club top 10. Honorary Councillors on the single are Mary, Benita and Derek (backing vocals), produced by The Style Council and mixed by Juan Atkins. Engineered by Brendan Lynch and assistant engineer and sequencing by Jatin Savaria. The b-side *Can You Still Love Me* (119¾-0bpm) was worthy of a place on the forthcoming house album.

The *Promised Land* 12" contained a unique mix not available elsewhere and an exclusive version, *Latin Orchestral Workout, appeared* on the DMC 12", remixed by Brothers in Rhythm. Another interesting mix was by *Juan Atkins* at 125¾-0bpm. Juan, from Detroit (b.09/12/62), was the possible originator of techno music. He started off playing bass then keyboards and synthesisers and was working solo in a band, Model 500, when he came to Britain for the 1st time in 1989. He DJ'd at open air raves and would do remixes for TSC, Seal and The Fine Young Cannibals whilst in the UK.

It was noted that Paul commented on how boring S-Express were in *The Face,* then went on and recruited the singer from their top chart hit *Superfly Guy* to sing on *Promised Land.*

16th - For the first time since *Long Hot Summer* in 1983 Paul appeared on *Top of the Pops* sitting at a piano, with Mick at another piano, a unique moment. Dee and a dancer were sandwiched in the middle. This would be the last Style Council *Top of the Pops* appearance.

18th - This would turn out to be the final UK TV appearance, just a few weeks short of the 6 year *Speak Like A Child* anniversary. A new line up which included a bass player and *Confessions of A Pop Group* drummer Nick Brown took to the stage for *Promised Land* on the live Saturday morning children's show *Motormouth*. As a bonus, *Can You Still Love Me?* closed the show. There was also a short interview with Dee. TSC bow out with a great positive performance on an unknown, short lived Saturday morning show.

19th - *Promised Land* enters the chart and would peak at number 27, staying in the top 100 for 5 weeks.

'Horribly drum heavy and is the kind of fake-soul/pseudo gospel that 80's people dance to in order to get off with each other in sordid night clubs to the aroma of lager and Blue Stratos. I'm sorry but I hate it.' (*MM or NME*)

'It's a career move that may just work, simply because they've been rendered unrecognisable. The best TSC single ever, by default.' (*Record Mirror*)

MARCH

10th - The latest Polydor press release asks us to look out for, 'The greatest hits long player from Britain's most successful girl group' and a 30 second *Singular Adventures* TV advert was shown. *The Singular Adventures of The Style Council, Volume 1* was a neat title bringing together nearly all the singles since *Speak Like A Child*.

However, it did seem to be rushed together with very poor packaging, well in comparison to the quality of the past 6 years. A colour variation from *The Cost of Loving* CD, no release information, chart details, discography or band history were included. The tracks themselves were compiled in a random order. The cassette and CD contained two extra tracks, *How She Threw It All Away* and *Waiting*. None of the formats contained *Come To Milton Keynes*. A bright point was the CD replacing the 7" versions with alternate mixes for some songs. More thought with the documentation would have made the release a far greater and interesting reference guide.

Greatest Hits LP's are accompanied with a video selection. However, the content of the 60 minute *Video Adventures of The Style Council* was very disappointing. Again, no discography and randomly placed (*You're The Best Thing* onto *Have You Ever Had It Blue* and then back to *Money Go Round*). Ten of the tracks appeared previously on the *Video Singles* and a version of *It Didn't Matter* was released on *JerUSAlem*. This left only 3 new titles to tempt Council fans, *Wanted, Life At A Top Peoples Health Farm* and *Promised Land*.

There was no place for the best TSC video singles, *Come To Milton Keynes* and *Boy Who Cried Wolf* or the unreleased *Big Boss Groove, Waiting, How She Threw It All Away* and *Long Hot Summer '89 mix*. The inclusion of the above 25 minutes footage would have guaranteed a bigger sale. These tracks were said to be held back for *Greatest Hits Voume 2,* which would never happen.

19th - *The Singular Adventures of The Style Council, Greatest Hits Volume 1* entered the chart at number 3, staying in the top 100 for 15 weeks, selling as well as expected for a compilation. It stayed in the top 10 for 5 consecutive weeks, something no other album reached.

'Some of the strangest and most wonderful singles the radio has ever been blessed with.' (*Melody Maker*)

'The list is endless and completely brilliant. It shows just how good the often under-rated Councillors really are 10/10.' (*Just 17*)

'Universally pleasant, innocuous, harmless stuff, 2½/5.' (*Sounds*)

'I have no desire to own any TSC LP apart from this, buy a copy! You'll love it! There won't be another one like it! 9/10.' (David Quantick*, NME*)

'I'd love to know what the teenage Weller of the late seventies would have done if he'd seen into the future and heard this record. Would he have chosen a stylish beret and headed for Paris, or sold his guitar and settled for life on the dole.' (*Record Collector*)

TSC dropped 31 places to number 164 in *Record Collector's* 'Top 500 collectable artists.' There would be a further drop to 243 (down 79) in 1990 and to 412 (down 169) in 1991. In comparison The Jam dropped 23 places to number 62 in 1989, went up 22 to number 40 in 1990 and then down 36 to number 76 in 1991.

APRIL

A small tour of Japan was arranged for June as was 1 night in London at the Royal Albert Hall in July for Capitol Radio. More UK dates were to follow.

When asked in *Fresh Air* magazine why he hasn't played live since 1987 Paul commented, 'We were a bit disillusioned with playing live. We had some really lousy band members, some were really naff, so that put me off.'

Currently doing the business in the nightclubs was a future single for the Acid Jazz label by an unknown band, King Truman. The song was titled *Like A Gun*. One of the vocalists most definitely sounded like Dee C Lee and it was rumoured that The Style Council were heavily involved. However, due to Paul's contract with Polydor this was strongly denied, but then the single was withdrawn 3 days before its official release date so something was amiss.

TSC involvement would be confirmed in July when it was included in The Royal Albert Hall live set. Paul also confirmed it in 2001 for *Mojo*, 'Yeah, that was me, Mick, Dee, a drum machine and a sax player. The track had a p-funk vibe, with my vocal repeating a phrase and the sax blowing over the top.'

Up until now that was the only information that was known. However, in July 2008 Eddie Piller agreed to speak to me about the entire project;

'I knew that Paul and Mick weren't happy with the way The Style Council project had been going at the record label. Both of them were around on the proto-acid Jazz scene. I suppose it was rare groove mixed with jazz dance which appealed to them both. Paul especially was a regular at our Talkin Loud gig at Dingwalls.

The pair offered to make a single for my new label, which I'd just started with Radio 1 DJ Gilles Peterson as a side project. Mick and Paul took pseudonyms Truman King and Elliott Arnold. We'd only just set up the label which had been brilliantly received at the press and I think they both thought it was a good idea. I had recently bumped into Mick in Ibiza and we had talked the idea through to the point that when we got home we would set it up.

I remember a meeting at Paul's rehearsal studios where we decided on the name King Truman. They wanted to make a P-Funk/GoGo type track and needed a sax player to play the lead. We chose Ed Jones, an up and coming be-bop player who had already recorded an EP for the label. Contractually, we only ever signed Mick as the artist while Paul was booked as a session musician. This was to avoid any future legal problems with The Style Council's label, Polydor. If only I'd thought it through!'

Q. Was it an easy thing to accept into Acid Jazz?

'The label was new and happening, the coolest thing. It had come from nowhere and Galliano described the scene as, 'a loose mixture of mods and casuals, the mods through Eddie and the casuals through Gilles.' It was perfect for Paul and Mick. Mod had gained a new lease of life, albeit with a new look and musically, Mick was at home with the Hammond stuff and Paul with the look. It made perfect sense to make a record with them.'

Q. Did you believe that no-one would find out it was The Style Council?

'Well actually, it wasn't The Style Council. It was legally Mick, although from memory, aside of Ed Jones, the rest were Steve White, Dee C Lee, Carleen Anderson, Paul and Mick. I can't remember who played bass, but I do know that it was the first record produced by Brendan Lynch, who went on to be a major producer and did most of Paul's early solo material. To an outsider, I suppose you could say it was The Style Council, but to us, it was just a little one-off.'

Q. There was talk of someone in Acid Jazz being pinned against the wall and being forced to pull the release or face the courts?

'I worked as a consultant at Polydor at the time, for their black music imprint, Urban. I also managed the James Taylor Quartet, who had been signed there before the Acid Jazz thing exploded. The story is actually true! What happened was that I had sent some promotional copies of the King Truman single out. Unfortunately one went to a magazine called *Soul Underground*. The problem with this was that I had just had a major argument with the editor about a few bad reviews he'd published, particularly for A Man Called Adam. It was quite an influential specialist black music paper.

I was quite rude to him and so, for some type of revenge, he phoned Polydor and told them that I was releasing a Style Council record right under their noses. Unknown to me, the contractual position between Polydor and TSC had reached a critical point. The overall boss of the label had seen me in a routine A'n'R meeting and called me out of it. He completely lost it with me and bawled me out about interfering in Polydor's business. I feigned ignorance but that just made him cross and he threw me up against the wall!

I had to agree to withdraw the single and I never got much more work from Polydor, but the James Taylor Quartet thrived there so they couldn't really keep me out. The chap went on to be one of the most powerful men in the music industry.'

Q. Roughly how many copies got out?

'Three days before the release date Polydor made us pull the release. About 100 copies had already made it into the shops, 50 were given to our DJ list, 20 to press and maybe 30 white labels were made. It is the rarest release on the label by far. The rest were destroyed.'

Q. Were the rest actually destroyed or are they in someone's shed? Bearing in mind the £200+ price tag still attached to it!

'The rest were impounded and destroyed. I once saw a copy for sale in small ads in *Mojo* for £350. I don't know if it sold though, if you are lucky you can get it for £50, more likely £100. We have never made, or found any more copies to add to the general pool. For 10 years we never thought about it and then in the late 90's people started to e-mail the label asking if we had any copies for sale. I didn't really know why but then I realised that it was probably the rarest record Paul had released. I wish I had sneaked a box out but I didn't.'

Q. The recent release of *Like A Gun* on the compilation *Totally Wired and Illicit Grooves, The Birth of a Scene 1987-1990*. After nearly 20 years how did this come about?

'We were intending to make a 12" box set of the rarest 12" singles released on Acid Jazz and I asked Paul if we could include King Truman. He said yes, BUT the collection got put back to 2009 and the CD version, released by Ace has already come out. We will be releasing a vinyl box set of six 12" in 2009 in the original livery. It will be limited to 250 copies, so if anyone wants the Truman record on vinyl, they'll have to wait for that. The original vinyl is still the one to have though. I only have one myself, a proud moment in Acid Jazz history.'

As Eddie has just confirmed 19 years later, the extremely rare King Truman 12" sells for over £100, a lot of money for four tracks. *12", Safe Sax Mix, Dub Version* and *Radio Edit*. Ironically, to this day, *Like A Gun* is the most collectable and sought after TSC single that never was. There are only 200 out there. Maximum!

MAY

Back at Polydor all promotional singles pressed around this time named *Everybody's On The Run* as the primary track which backed up the story that this was to be the next single. Polydor were said to have forced the hand with releasing *Long Hot Summer '89* on the a-side as *Everybody's On The Run* is not from the greatest hits album. Paul more or less confirmed this, 'I didn't put it out. The record company did.'

Paul's argument was that it was promoting the forthcoming LP and would have potentially been a hit single from it. Though unknown to anyone outside Polydor, this LP was already facing the axe.

19th - The last single released to promote *The Singular Adventures Of The Style Council* LP was *Long Hot Summer '89*, a brand new mix or so we are told. It is if you track them down, actually identical to the 1986 *Jezamix* and 1988 *Tom Mix* versions previously released. It was produced by Peter Wilson and Paul Weller. The b-side with *Everybody's On The Run* was written by Paul and Dee, produced by The Style Council and mixes by Freddie Bastone and Norman Jay.

Freddie (b.1963) is a respected producer, actor (Sopranos) and DJ from the Bronx, New York. He is known to have worked with Queen, Jennifer Lopez and Missy Elliot amongst many others. I caught up with him in August 2008;

'It was my 2nd time in my favourite country (kissing ass), this time not just for DJ'ing and mixing but also to support my new LP *The Corporation of One*. I am at the hotel running late for my gig at *Heaven* when the phone rings, I pick up and it is a voice saying he's Paul Weller and he would like me to come down to the studio.

I say "Gary I'm fuckin late" and hang up (thinking it's my friend Gary playing with me, knowing I am a huge Weller fan). One minute later I get another call, same voice saying, 'I hope I am not bothering you but I would like you to come down to Solid Bond Studios to listen to *Everybody's On The Run* and *Promised Land*. Well I knew my friend didn't know about Solid Bond so my mouth dropped and I made arrangements to go and visit one of my idols the next day. Needless to say there was no hanky panky that night as we know you have to be well groomed to visit Paul Weller.' (Freddie Bastone)

Norman Jay spoke to Steve Malins, 'I didn't want to do it. I had never remixed anything before so I didn't know what I was doing. Now it's a big collectable 12". I went to Japan to do some DJ-ing and people over there were asking me about the Weller remix.'

Everybody's On The Run was another TSC house tune that made an impact on the club charts and not even the most die-hard fan would have recognised this as a Style Council track! It was another first for a b-side as Brian J Powell took lead vocals, leaving Paul and Dee to back him up. TSC met Brian through Dee's sister after he had appeared in a Gospel Musical on TV in 1988.

'I just felt his voice was right for it and mine wasn't really.' (Paul, *Fresh Air*)

28th - *Long Hot Summer '89* enters the chart and would peak at number 48, staying in the top 100 for 2 weeks. Would *Everybody's On The Run* have faired any better? By this time many fans had jumped ship and in addition the fun and jokes were lost on the music press and they simply no longer had anything positive to say about the band.

'TSC was loads of fun for me, maybe too much fun, I think that's what other people didn't like about it.' (Paul)

JUNE

The next single was confirmed as being a new song *Sure Is Sure* (TSC 18), due in July. Written by Paul and long time bassist Camelle Hinds.

TSC fly to Japan for three arranged shows under the 'Revue' banner.

7th - Arena, Yokohama

8th - Joh Hall, Osaka

9th - Shiodome, Tokyo

One of these 'Revue' nights was recorded for Japanese Radio, packed full of unreleased tracks. It has to be said though that this broadcast only made it to the UK long after the final gig at the Royal Albert Hall in July. Broadcasted were, 7 new songs, 3 from *Confessions*, 2 from *The Cost of Loving* and 1 from *Café Bleu*.

New - *Sure Is Sure, Tender Love, I Cant Deny Myself* (Camelle Hinds), *Now You're Gone* (Dr Robert), *Waiting On A Connection, Like A Gun, Saxophone Instrumental.*

1984 - *Mick's Company*

1987 - *The Cost of Loving*

1988 - *It's A Very Deep Sea, Little Boy In A Castle, A Woman's Song* (with Paul Weller vocals) and *Changing Of The Guard.*

Back home *Going Back To My Roots* by 17 year old Lisa M (b.16/01/72) was released on Zomba Records. The interesting point is that it was produced by Paul and Mick then engineered by Brendan Lynch at Solid Bond Studios. A few years later on *Radio 1* Paul would admit to not liking this particular event.

Lisa told *Just 17* about working with Paul and Mick, 'there were all these really great people like the Beatmasters and Coldcut, but I wanted someone a bit different, someone who would make people sit up and say, 'oh, look who's producing that'. We approached them, and they agreed. They were brilliant and so talented.'

It was revealed in the *Fresh Air* interview that the Red Wedge LP is still under construction and for this TSC contributed a Hip-House track with the JB's on horns and a girl duo of Trouble and Bass on vocals.

'They did some horns on this track, it hasn't got a title at the moment. It's a cool groove really. It's not particularly jazzy, it's a bit of both - It's jazz-funk I suppose, it's clubby, garage, hip-house, swing beat, baleric. It's a good track. Probably be on our next album.'

Marco Nelson from The Young Disciples had put Paul in touch with the JB's, Maceo Parker, Pee Wee Ellis and Fred Wesley. They were all in the UK assisting the James Taylor Quartet on their renowned version of *Starsky and Hutch.*

The writing credits went to Weller/Talbot/Lee and Marco Nelson. When it did get a title it was not the unheard *A New Decade, Hope* (influenced by Norman Jay's club) or *The World Must Come Together.* It was the jazz funk spectacular of *That Spiritual Feeling.* This would later released by Paul as a b-side solo single.

JULY

At this time there was still only one UK date confirmed, the sell out at The Royal Albert Hall on 4th. After being unable to obtain a ticket in April I was assured by the box office that more dates would be confirmed. This did not happen and no one turning up at the gig had any idea that this would be the final, much ridiculed, but most important of concerts in the career mapping of Paul Weller.

3rd - Paul DJ's at Dingwalls nightclub, London, run by DJ Gilles Peterson, also of London's Jazz FM and heavily involved in the Acid Jazz label phenomenon with Eddie Piller.

4th – The Royal Albert Hall, London. As part of the *Capital Radio* music festival, TSC would perform their first live UK show in 20 months. Fans eagerly awaited a greatest hits show after the recent release and success of the *Singular Adventures of The Style Council* album. Not to be!

TSC trot on stage, Mick immediately looking out of place in a white t-shirt tucked inside higher than waist height (!) long bright white shorts and Paul in a black t-shirt, basketball boots and a pair of the much talked about Bermuda shorts! See the back cover of 2006 release of *Mr Cool's Dream* for this infamous photo.

From the opening bars of *Can You Still Love Me?* to the closing of *That Spiritual Feeling* only a couple of reasonably well known TSC songs were aired to the dismay of many thousands of fans. Paul took a break from vocals on many occasions as Dee C Lee, Dr Robert, Camelle Hinds and Brian Powell all sang lead, not to forget Mick and his 3 instrumentals. Drummer for the night was the unknown Richie Stephens.

As the anonymous set progressed the crowd booed and some even tore up the (excellent) tour programme. A bizarre night. The band allegedly went onto London nightclub *Stringfellows*, someone saying Mick did not like the gig but Paul appeared quite happy with it.

The Wholepoint was the 1st magazine to release the full listing and clarify the events in *Record Collector* in response to an inaccurate email on the night.

Can You Still Love Me?, Move (Dance All Night), Promised Land, Sure Is Sure, Everybody's On The Run (Brian Powell), *Tender Love, Its A Very Deep Sea, I Can't Deny Myself* (Camelle Hinds), *Little Boy In A Castle, Mick's Blessings, A Woman's Song, Now You're Gone* (Dr Robert), *Mick's Company, Cost of Loving, Waiting On A Connection, Depth Charge, Like A Gun, Changing of The Guard; You'll Find Love* and *That Spiritual Feeling.*

The last ever gig, unreleased tracks from the soon to be rejected LP and many others which surfaced on post TSC projects. Of the 20 tracks played there was only one single, the most recent, *Promised Land,* unbelievable when this night was on the back of a top 3 *Greatest Hits* album! Was this on purpose Paul? We got three b-sides, three from *Confessions of A Pop Group,* one from *Café Bleu,* two from *The Cost of Loving* and the quickly deleted King Truman track.

Four songs would see release on Dee's forthcoming Slam Slam project and *That Spiritual Feeling* was used on the Paul Weller Movement dates. The remainder were performed by Honorary Councillors Dr Robert and Camelle Hinds.

'A sad medley of anonymous house orientated Soul, layered with the occasional ballad. Weller should be ashamed of himself. He refuses point blank to play his guitar until it was unavoidable. The Royal Albert Hall was a sad mixture of disbelief and boos.'

The Style Councillor's all spoke on the 2007 *Into Tomorrow* documentary about it; 'They hadn't heard it and house music. It was a kind of shock to everyone.' (Paul); 'It wasn't very good.' (Dee); 'We were booed and abused!' (Mick)

I spoke to Camelle Hinds in July 2008 about the unreleased track, *I Can't Deny Myself* where he took the lead vocal, 'Yes, it was a self penned, rubbish, half dance/housey composition. My Memories of a disastrous vocal performance and I wished the floor would swallow me up for agreeing to do it. Way out of context and unnecessary as far as I was concerned, but hey I have so many wonderful memories that it doesn't really matter. I should have had the balls to sing one of Paul's songs, namely a ballad called *Funny* - a fine soul jazz ballad, I'm hoping one day he will give his blessing for me to sing a version of it.'

It is easy to forget and rubbish this gig but the Royal Albert Hall is a major landmark in where Paul finds himself today. Although a huge risk that back fired at the time, it forced Paul to take time-out to 'find' himself and begin the long path to where he is today.... 50 years old and musically on fire.

AUGUST

An interesting release by Tears For Fears is within their Top 5 single, *Sowing The Seeds of Love*. In a verse Written by Orazabal/Smith there are 2 interesting points, 'So without love and a Promised Land, we're fools to the rules of a Government plan. Kick out The Style, bring back The Jam.' [© Orazabal/Smith]

Promised Land being the most recent TSC single and the line about kicking out The Style (Council) and in their place, bringing back The Jam.

The sleeve of the new single *Sure Is Sure* had gone to print 6 weeks ago and the Town House acetates were pressed but a release date for the single failed to materialise. This no show guaranteed the value of the acetates for years to come. *Sure is Sure* 8:22 and *Love of The World (Free Love mix)* 10:21 would sell for around £200 at auction in 1995, a good mark-up from the initial £18 asking fee in *Record Collector* in 1989. Equally a now impossible to get 7" bootleg, *Rare 4 Trax EP* used *Sure Is Sure* from this acetate.

Music press rumours indicate that TSC were calling it a day though nothing officially was forthcoming from Solid Bond Studios. Nothing. A few weeks later an unofficial statement was issued stating that the next LP had been rejected by Polydor as it was to housey for them, and as a result the band felt that they could no longer go on working with the label. The *Sure Is Sure* single has been scrapped and the LP *Modernism: A New Decade* would not be released.

It was over... 74 months since *Speak Like a Child*.

David Munns at Polydor was the man who rejected the album, telling Paolo Hewitt, 'They made an album, I didn't think it was good enough. I think it would have prolonged the agony if it was released at that time.'

He also spoke to Steve Malins in his Weller biography, 'Paul got very upset because I told him I didn't think it was acceptable. It was much more their choice to sever all ties then and decide, right we can't deal with Polydor, they don't believe in us anymore.'

'To say I didn't like it wasn't enough to reject the record', as he revealed that on the contract an album could only be released if it had 2 singles on it and David thought it only had one with the potential to chart. John Weller didn't take too kindly to this, even refusing to speak about David Munns years later in the *Highlights and Hang Ups* documentary.

David Munns said, 'John particularly took great umbrage at this ....I thought it was pretty sad that he couldn't take it on the chin, but I understand it too.'

'I have only listened to it a couple of times as I'd lost interest by that time. I felt what they were trying to do, I just didn't connect with it, I also didn't go to The Royal Albert Hall. Then there was a lengthy break and I remember hearing *Into Tomorrow* and being blown away by that.' (Gary Crowley)

Melody Maker had a laugh, 'There was open weeping in the streets, a minutes silence on national TV and radio and black flags fluttering at half mast above every Town Hall in the country as the news broke that The Style Council had split.'

Paul wrote in his first solo tour programme, 'We were never going to get the kind of recognition we felt we deserved because of The Jam's legacy. It overshadowed everything. We could have made the greatest bit of work ever and it wouldn't have made any difference. I think that got to us after a while because what could we do?'

Paolo Hewitt backed this up in his *Watch* magazine in 2003, 'Where The Jam had their roots in Britain, The Style Council favoured Europe. Where The Jam wore suits and shopped in Carnaby Street, The Style Council wore jumpers from Rome and loafers without socks.'

Paul told *Boys About Town* in 1991, 'I was pleased with TSC. Obviously there were a lot of Jam fans who never got into it, there were others who stuck with it and there were the new people as well. I think TSC is a really important group and in that sense, time will tell. I also think that there are a lot of recordings over-looked in the shadow of my past. In five or ten years time people will see more worth in what we did and in what we were getting at.'

Paolo Hewitt also summed up TSC piss take superbly in his sleeve notes for the 20th anniversary compilation in 2003, 'Adverts showing just the waist of a Modernist wearing a green cord shirt and white Levis. Press releases that spoke of summers in monasteries and musicians feeling Alpine. A debut album where the chief songwriter doesn't sing until the fourth or fifth track.'

Again Paolo in 2003 on *Radio 2* confirming that the music press were upset because, 'the Café had replaced the pub.'

Right from the offset in 1983, Paul promised something unique each time and this was delivered - From the Jazz tinged *Café Bleu*, to hard hitting social and political rants (*Our Favourite Shop*), to soul (*Cost of Loving*), through to classical (*Confessions of A Pop Group*) and ended up at house music (*Modernism*)! Where else and who else in the history of music has tried so many diverse projects album after album? TSC in that respect are unique.

'It was a special time, it was a good time, Paul was smiling a lot with TSC, he was enjoying it I guess. I think he felt he done what he wanted to do.' (Gary Crowley)

The talk of regretting not ending it after *Confessions of A Pop Group* has been said numerous times but in a way the rejection of *Modernism: A New Decade* made it intriguing enough to wonder what might have been. Would the band's or Paul's profile have remained so high if the album was released and flopped in 1989? The honest answer is no. The elusive search for the bootleg of the final gig, arguing over the track listing now dull in peoples minds and the hope that subscribing to *Record Collector* in order to receive it 4 days before general release would result in the *Sure Is Sure* acetate or the King Truman single being secured. Bliss!

Q magazine summed it up under their review of the 5 CD TSC box set, 'In the end simple tiredness finished off The Style Council. The label was bored, the press were bored, the fans were bored and the group were bored. Perhaps even the Cappuccino Kid was bored.'

Over the years there was no indication that the 'lost LP' would ever be released, Paul owned the publishing rights, it was entirely up to him. However, after reading the September 1996 issue of *Select* magazine things looked much healthier, 'It's just about picking the right time or even doing a mail order thing - fans only. Yeah, it should come out. I liked that tune *High On Hope*.'

Coincidentally enough, a few months after the original *Mr Cool's Dream* appeared I was alerted to the existence of a tape from USA. A few emails confirmed its authenticity and a review cassette dropped through the letterbox. This did not do the bootleg circuit in the UK.

This was years before TSC box set was put into production and Dennis Munday seemed very surprised that I had a copy when he was compiling the box set believing it hadn't been heard outside the close circle of Weller acquaintances. So the question has been who had a copy of it and why was it released into the 'wild'?

Paul spoke to Q about its eventual release in 1998, 'It put a big smile on my face. It sounds alright to me. I wish it had come out at the time, even though it would have been slated, cause it was just made for that moment.'

1990 and beyond

TSC had still not officially "split up" but there was no indication of anything happening and rumours of signing to Talkin Loud didn't materialize. Years later Paul told *Mojo* that he met, 'their head Dave Bates, through Gilles Peterson, the A'n'R man.' It fell through, Paul put it down to him wandering off for the toilet just after he stuck the demo on!

1990

11th February - Steve Malins' book records that TSC perform *Whole Point II* and *Down In The Seine* at the Dominion Theatre, London for a benefit show for Ambulance workers.

31st March - *Record Mirror* print the final press release, 'the group feel they have done all they can together and Paul Weller and Mick Talbot will be working on individual projects. They are both planning tours for later this year. The split is long overdue really, it is something we should have done 2 or 3 years ago but we have created some great music in our time.'

After this announcement it went quiet for around 7 months as only Steve White continued working on solo projects on Polydor's *Urban* label. Then Paul, Mick and Steve appeared on one track, *As We Come (To Be)* on The Young Disciples *Road To Freedom* LP. Carleen Anderson, lead singer, would from this recording form a strong working bond with Paul, most recently at the September 2004 recording at The Riverside Studios in London for *Studio 150.*

The Style Council re-union - The Final TV appearance

The Style Council had officially split in March so money must surely have been the only reason for the following re-union so quickly. Two songs on a little known Satellite channel only available in Japan and across Europe but not in the UK. Much was made about when this was recorded but the Japanese version *Fujisankei* gave a 1990 date and mentioned it was to be the last Style Council show as Paul was to commence on a solo project later in the year.

This Super Channel show *Hit Studio International* was presented by Bruno Brookes and the late Paula Yates and featured the *Whole Point Of No Return* live with just Paul on guitar and Steve White on bongos. Mick and Camelle Hinds joined Paul & Steve for a mimed version of *Sure Is Sure,* the only TV performance of this song. It was filmed at Limehouse Studios in London.

Paul Weller Movement -> Paul Weller solo

Whispers of Paul getting back on the road were realised with The Paul Weller Movement. Even though Paul has said he hated these dates and just needed to get back out playing live the initial dates were a superb, albeit very strange, low-key experience. None of us were sure of what to expect and only 300 die-hard fans bothered to turn up to the half empty University halls. The rest would wait a few years before appearing at the *Wild Wood* and remaining through to *22 Dreams*.

What we witnessed on those cold, cold (winter) moments in 1990 was something special - Paul Weller, a changing man. He delighted the fans with new renditions of *My Ever Changing Moods, Down In The Seine, Homebreakers, Speak Like A Child, A Man of Great Promise* and *The Piccadilly Trail* alongside Jam tracks *Precious, Pity Poor Alfie* and *That's Entertainment*. New material was still sparse but *Kosmos, Just Like Yesterdays, Round and Round* and *Bitterness Rising* stood up really well.

It got better and better and in future tours he performed *It's A Very Deep Sea, Whole Point II, It Just Came To Pieces In My Hands* and even *How She Threw It All Away,* a song he did not play live with TSC. Further details on the solo years can be found in the unofficial books by John Reed and Steve Malins. An official biography has never appeared with Paolo Hewitt the undoubtedly best person to do one. However, for reasons well known, this is now unlikely to happen.

Paul's incredible solo achievements and playing The Style Council live ensures new fans will explore his back catalogue and discover the many gems that are out there. The more recent releases of The Style Council *Box Set* and DVD collections ensure the entire back catalogue is easily accessible and affordable.

Into Tomorrow in 1991 featured *That Spiritual Feeling,* written by Paul, Mick Talbot, Dee C Lee and Marco Nelson, first heard at The Style Council's final concert at The Royal Albert Hall in 1989. Paul thought that with JB's and Fred Wesley helping out it was too good to stay unreleased, 'We were still on the cusp of The Style Council. Whether you love it or loathe it I was into that whole house, garage thing' he told *Record Collector. Above The Clouds*, 1992 featured a live track *All Year Round* which was a revamped version of a TSC b-side from 1987. Style Councillor's Steve White, Helen Turner, Camelle Hinds, Zeke Manyika and Dee C Lee appear on this CD.

Sunflower, 1993 featured a new mix of *That Spiritual Feeling* which appeared on *Into Tomorrow.* This was a mix of *That Spiritual Thing* on the *Modernism* LP.

In 2007 his promoter for the New York dates of the USA tour claimed Paul would play 3 theme nights devoted to The Jam, TSC and solo music. They kept their promise and 8 TSC tracks were played; *Its A Very Deep Sea, Headstart For Happiness, Speak Like A Child, Down In The Seine, A Man of Great Promise, My Ever Changing Moods, Long Hot Summer* and *Shout To The Top.*

It is now September 2008, a 50 year old Weller, on the back of his number 1 album *22 Dreams,* is currently mid way through a World Tour. Many, many, events, collaborations, tours and releases have taken place since 1990 and we need a *Mr Cool's Dream* type book dedicated to his solo career. Yes, there are still many chapters to add to his sparkling 30 year career.

Keeping on Burning ......

www.paulweller.com

Post Style Council releases

10th July 1993 - *Here's Some That Got Away* enters the chart at number 39, staying in the top 100 for 1 week. It featured many unreleased tracks, most from 1986, before *The Cost of Loving* was penned. There are genuinely a few classic tracks on this LP and it should be in any fans collection.

23rd February 1996 - The well thought out *Style Council Collection* enters the chart at number 60, staying in the top 100 for 1 week. Dickon, guitarist from group Orlando, describes himself as a 'Style Council obsessive.' He delighted many with his review in *Melody Maker,* describing *Long Hot Summer* as a, 'timeless pop classic', *You're The Best Thing* as a 'blissful soul ballad brimming with feeling and dizzy infatuation...essential to your life RIGHT NOW.' He also describes 3 tracks from *Confessions of A Pop Group* as being 'criminally underrated.'

13th Feb 1998 - Dennis Munday is contracted by Polydor to work on a TSC box set, due later in the year. His letter to me on this day said, 'Polydor are currently negotiating the rights to licence *Modernism: A New Decade* from the Weller's, so it is not definite at the moment.' At this point the track listing for CD 5 was to be remixes, demos and unreleased songs. This would have included, *Have You Ever Had It Blue* (Steve's lyrics), *Long Hot Summer* (Generator, mixed in New York), *Long Hot Summer* (Sweat It Out), *Right To Go* (Promo) and *Boy Who Cried Wolf* (12" instrumental).

14th February 1998 - An excellent live compilation *In Concert* featured live tracks spanning their entire career. Dennis Munday was the lucky one tasked with going through the hundreds of live tapes. With the help of others and myself, he chose a fine selection of songs, including many of the unreleased 1984 rarities. The track list I received from Dennis on 7th May 1997 had *Money Go Round* medley from 1985 included, but this was removed from the final release as the running time exceeded the permitted maximum CD length.

October 19th 1998 - Originally scheduled for August 24th *The Complete Style Council* is brought together in this superb 5 CD box set. It has 90 digitally remastered tracks, including the previously unreleased album *Modernism: A New Decade* and six tracks on CD for the first time.

With a 112 page colour book featuring discography, gig list and rare photos alongside a lyric booklet, this is the definitive Style Council collection. Not to forget the exclusive "FREE Style Council book with every box set purchased at HMV." A rare, early release of what you are now holding in your hands!

'Too good to be captured on a single *Best of* album, but stretched too thinly over 5 CD's.' (*Q*)

21st Aug 2000 - Polydor release the majority of the back catalogue under the remastered series, *Café Bleu, Greatest Hits, Our Favourite Shop* and *The Cost Of Loving*.

2nd September 2000 - *Greatest Hits* enters the chart at number 28, staying in the top 100 for 5 weeks.

2003 was a good year - Amongst the many compilations, a beacon of light was *The Sound of The Style Council*, an official Polydor 21 track compilation to celebrate 20 years. This avoided the usual tracks and focused on classics like *Headstart For Happiness, Ghosts of Dachau* and *Spin Drifting*. It also had enough official weight to get Paolo Hewitt and Paul involved in the sleeve notes, 'for me this was a great pivotal period in my life.'

9th and 16th August 2003. A *Shout To The Top Radio 2* documentary was a, 'heady mix of soul, pop and Jazz. Phil Jupitus narrates this two part tale of one of music's most enigmatic bands.' I was approached by Dave Barber, the producer of the two-hour show, for information on the band and to put him in touch with Tracie, Camelle and Anthony. This turned out to be a truly excellent biography and is the definitive spoken word on the band. The only downside, like so many other reviews, is the lack of information from 1987 - 1989. Disappointingly, the chance to air *Like A Gun* was ignored. Amongst all the regular tracks it features 16 interviews with all the main players plus contributions from, Paolo Hewitt, Dennis Munday, producer Peter Wilson, designer Simon Halfon, Anthony Harty, Tracie Young, Guy Barker, Helen Turner, Steve Sidelnyk, Camelle Hinds, Billy Bragg and Bob Geldof. Some rare footage was aired from the Radio 1 sessions including *The Paris Match* and *My Ever Changing Moods* piano version. It will probably never see release and is no longer archived on the BBC website.

24th Nov 2003 - *Excerpts From The Style Council On Film* is a 41 minute DVD featuring tracks from *Showbiz, Confessions, JerUSAlem* and 4 promotional videos. Another promotional release for the DVD was included within *The Jigsaw Man* movie starring Michael Caine and Laurence Oliver. It contains, 'exclusive live footage, promo and video from forthcoming DVD release.' There was also a full episode of *Men Behaving Badly*. This was given away free with the magazine *DVD Monthly*.

The long awaited DVD compilation *The Style Council On Film*, was perfect apart from the omission of 1984's *Far East And Far* Out. *Showbiz*! is still an excellent concert to watch and the inclusion of all the promotional videos is welcomed after the disappointment of the *Video Adventures* compilation back in 1989. Interested people should note that there is a secret 'Easter egg' track on the DVD. It is on Disc 1 in the extras menu, you have to highlight then select a small blue square at the top of the screen. Complete here what you find _____ ___ ____ _____!

Paul's live LP *Days of Speed* resulted in an excellent promo CD being released, a TSC delight, as both *Headstart For Happiness* and *Down In The Seine* were live gems.

A few bands have dared to cover two of the finest singles. Fire Island released *Shout To The Top* in April 1998 which reached number 23. In 1999 boy band 911 included *You're The Best Thing* on their top 10 LP *Their It Is*.

In 2003, *You're The Best Thing* featured on a Ribena television advert. Ribena is a 'healthy' soft drink aimed primarily at children.

According to the essential Guinness World Records *British Hit Singles and Albums 2004*, TSC singles spent 103 weeks in the chart and the albums spent 100 weeks. This puts them at 324th place overall. The Jam are 110th and Weller solo 209th

29th July 2007 - At the 100 Club in London Tracie Young got up on the stage for the 1st time since 1983 to join 17 Black and sing *Speak Like A Child* live in what was a memorable and much appreciated performance. Tracie who had just cycled from Land's End to John O Groats for charity also donated her treasured Silver disc from *Speak Like A Child* to the charity.

In January 2008 during a BBC series *Pop On Trial* Miranda Sawyer said she would have chosen TSC as one of the best acts of the 80's but felt she'd be shot down by the judges for doing so. This series also featured Eddie Piller ('I liked the Style Council') and Paolo Hewitt.

19th February 2008 - Tracie Young appeared on Hayes FM, Middlesex to discuss her career and sing live. She revealed that she was initially to be the 3rd member of The Style Council but was, 'edged out unfortunately.' She also brought with her the original version of *The House That Jack Built*, an 'un-speeded up version, no horrible robotic drum machine in the middle.' Finally she sang *Nothing Happens Here But You*. So that's 2 live appearances by Tracie in just over 7 months after a gap of over 22 years. Keep an eye on her myspace page and read Tracie's view on her 'lost' 2nd LP later in this book. I'm sure one day it will come out.

What's next? Well I said this on the *Live* LP sleeve notes and *Mr Cool's Dream* has helped to maintain interest as **The Style Council have yet to be discovered**. Many people who have discovered Paul Weller's music since 1990 are still to explore his exciting and wonderful back catalogue from 1983 to 1989.

Council Meeting, Part 1, The Style Council on tour, 1984 (Anthony Harty)

Mick Talbot, backstage 1984 (Anthony Harty)

Home of The Style Council, Solid Bond Studio's, London 1985 (Andy Davis)

Mick Talbot and John Weller, New York, 1984 (Anthony Harty)

Paul Weller backstage, 1984 (Anthony Harty)

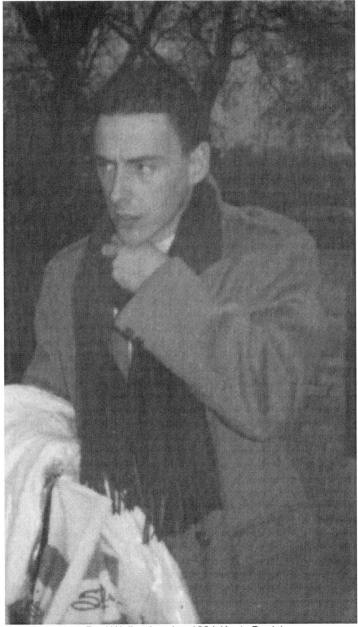

Paul Weller, London 1984 (Andy Davis)

Mick Talbot, Germany 1987
(Rene De Hey)

Paul Weller, Royal Albert Hall,
4th July 1989 (Mel O Toole)

Only a few photos exist from this
fateful night - those Hawaii shorts,
high socks and baseball boots.

Paul Weller, Solid Bond Studios, London 1984 (Andy Davis)

Steve White, 1984 (Andy Davis)

Steve White and Steve Sidelnyk, 1984 (Anthony Harty)

Mick Talbot, & Paul Weller Solid Bond Studios, 1985 (Andy Davis)

Paul Weller, Solid Bond Studios, 1985 (Andy Davis)

Paul Weller and Camelle Hinds, 1991 (Paula Cuccurullo)

"As is now" - Mick Talbot, 2007 (Simon Ayre)

"As is now"

Tracie Young sings *Speak Like A Child* for the first time in 24 years at a charity gig at the 100 Club, London, July 2007.
(Iain Munn)

"As is now"

Paul Weller,
Caird Hall, Dundee,
May 2008
(Iain Munn)

THE STYLE COUNCIL

AVAILABILITY - COMPLETE A TO Z

This A to Z allows you to quickly reference each song and determine on what formats it was released, if it appeared on Video/DVD, if it was performed on TV or on a specific tour. If the graphic is not shown under the song name then it is not available in that category. Only the official Polydor releases are documented.

Categories are; Single or Album, Official VHS/DVD release; TV show and Tour.

All times quoted are approximate.

Single		Songwriter(s)	< name >
Album		Recorded	<Year TSC recorded song>
7" 12" CD LP MC		<Released as a single, LP, both or neither> <u>\<x:xx></u> < Length of version> < Where it is available> <u>x:xx</u> < Title/length of any alternative version> < Where it is available>	
		<Released on Video or DVD> ✓ <Title of release>	
		<Stage appearance on TV show> ✓ <Title of TV show>	
		<Played on Tour> ✓ <Tour details>	

A Casual Affair

Single	X	Songwriter(s)	Paul Weller
Album	Y	Recorded	1985

3:24
- ✓ Here's Some That Got Away
- ✓ Our Favourite Shop (Deluxe Edition only)

A Gospel

Single	X	Songwriter(s)	Paul Weller
Album	Y	Recorded	1984

4:44
- ✓ Café Bleu
- ✓ Complete Adventures of The Style Council (5 CD Box Set)

- ✓ Internationalists '85 (Summer tour)
- ✓ Benefit/Festival (off tour)

A Man of Great Promise

Single	X	Songwriter(s)	Paul Weller
Album	Y	Recorded	1984

2:32
- ✓ Our Favourite Shop
- ✓ Complete Adventures of The Style Council (5 CD Box Set)

2:24
- ✓ In Concert

- ✓ The Tube, 1984 (Live)

- ✓ Council Meetings Part 2 (October 1984)
- ✓ Benefit/Festival (off tour)
- ✓ Paul Weller solo

A Miners Point

Single	Y	Songwriter(s)	Paul Weller, Mick Talbot
Album	X	Recorded	1984

✓ b-side Single. Paolo Hewitt interviews striking Miners (no music)

A New Decade

Single	X	Songwriter(s)	Paul Weller
Album	Y	Recorded	1989

3:24
✓ Modernism: A New Decade
✓ Complete Adventures of The Style Council (5 CD Box Set)

A Solid Bond In Your Heart

Single	Y	Songwriter(s)	Paul Weller
Album	Y	Recorded	1983

3:18
✓ a-side Single
✓ Singular Adventures of The Style Council
✓ Complete Adventures of The Style Council (5 CD Box Set)

3:18
✓ b-side single (Instrumental)

✓ What We Did On Our Holidays
✓ Video Adventures (Greatest Hits Volume 1)
✓ The Style Council on Film (DVD)

✓ Switch, 1983 (Live)

✓ European Tour (October 1983)
✓ Benefit/Festival (off tour)

A Stones Throw Away

Single	X	Songwriter(s)	Paul Weller
Album	Y	Recorded	1985

2:17
- ✓ Our Favourite Shop
- ✓ Complete Adventures of The Style Council (5 CD Box Set)

1:50 (Demo)
- ✓ Here's Some That Got Away
- ✓ Our Favourite Shop (Deluxe Edition only)

1:57
- ✓ In Concert

- ✓ TV Eye (Live)

- ✓ Showbiz
- ✓ The Style Council on Film (DVD)

- ✓ Internationalists '85 (Summer tour)
- ✓ Internationalists '85 (Winter tour)
- ✓ Benefit/Festival (off tour)

A Woman's Song

Single	X	Songwriter(s)	Paul Weller
Album	Y	Recorded	1987

3:02 (DC Lee on vocals)
- ✓ The Cost of Loving
- ✓ Complete Adventures of The Style Council (5 CD Box Set)

2:31 (Paul Weller on vocals)
- ✓ Here's Some That Got Away

- ✓ Cost of Loving Tour (February 1987)
- ✓ Royal Albert Hall (July 1989)

A Word From Our Leaders

Single	X	Songwriter(s)	Steve White/TBC
Album	X	Recorded	1985

✓ Internationalists '85 (Summer tour)
✓ Internationalists '85 (Winter tour)
✓ Red Wedge - Tour 2 (March 1986)

All Gone Away

Single	X	Songwriter(s)	Paul Weller
Album	Y	Recorded	1985

2:16
✓ Our Favourite Shop
✓ Complete Adventures of The Style Council (5 CD Box Set)

✓ Red Wedge - Tour 1 (January 1986)
✓ Red Wedge - Tour 2 (March 1986)

All Year Round

Single	Y	Songwriter(s)	Paul Weller
Album	Y	Recorded	1987

2:16
✓ b-side Single
✓ Complete Adventures of The Style Council (5 CD Box Set)

5:02
✓ Paul Weller (solo) b-side

✓ Paul Weller solo

Angel

Single	X	Songwriter(s)	Morton/Sulley/Griffen
Album	Y	Recorded	1986

	4:32
	✓ The Cost of Loving ✓ Complete Adventures of The Style Council (5 CD Box Set)
	✓ JerUSAlem ✓ The Style Council on Film (DVD)
	✓ Rock Around the Dock, 1986 (Mimed) ✓ Italian TV (Mimed)
	✓ Cost of Loving Tour (February 1987) ✓ Renaissance Tour (October 1987)

April's Fool

Single	X	Songwriter(s)	Paul Weller, Mick Talbot
Album	Y	Recorded	1986

	3:01
	✓ Here's Some That Got Away

Back At The Chicken Shack

Single	X	Songwriter(s)	Jimmy Smith
Album	X	Recorded	N/A Live only

	✓ Red Wedge Tour 1, 1986

Big Boss Groove

Single	Y	Songwriter(s)	Paul Weller, Mick Talbot
Album	Y	Recorded	1984

4:09 (Live Version)
- ✓ b-side single
- ✓ Our Favourite Shop (Deluxe only)

3:34 (7" version)
- ✓ a-side single - 7" Version

4:40 Extended Version
- ✓ a-side single
- ✓ Complete Adventures of The Style Council (5 CD Box Set)
- ✓ Here's Some That Got Away

4:57
- ✓ Home and Abroad

- ✓ Far East & Far Out
- ✓ Showbiz
- ✓ The Style Council on Film (DVD)

- ✓ Earsay (Live)
- ✓ Live Aid (Live)

- ✓ Council Meetings Part 2 (October 1984)
- ✓ Internationalists '85 (Summer tour)
- ✓ Benefit/Festival (off tour)

Bloodsports

Single	Y	Songwriter(s)	Paul Weller
Album	Y	Recorded	1985

3:34
- ✓ b-side single
- ✓ Here's Some That Got Away
- ✓ Complete Adventures of The Style Council (5 CD Box Set)
- ✓ Our Favourite Shop (Deluxe Edition only)

- ✓ Saturday Superstore (Live)

Blue Café

Single	X	Songwriter(s)	Paul Weller
Album	Y	Recorded	1984

2:16
- ✓ Café Bleu
- ✓ Complete Adventures of The Style Council (5 CD Box Set)

Boy Who Cried Wolf

Single	X	Songwriter(s)	Paul Weller
Album	Y	Recorded	1985

<u>5:15</u>
- ✓ Our Favourite Shop
- ✓ Complete Adventures of The Style Council (5 CD Box Set)

<u>3:34</u>
- ✓ European release (Single)

<u>4:12</u>
- ✓ In Concert

- ✓ What We Did The Following Year
- ✓ The Style Council on Film (DVD)

- ✓ Countdown - Australia (Mimed)

- ✓ Internationalists '85 (Winter tour)

Can You Still Love Me?

Single	Y	Songwriter(s)	Paul Weller, Mick Talbot, DC Lee
Album	Y	Recorded	1989

4:18 (Dub)
  ✓ b-side single

4:18 (Vocal)
  ✓ b-side single
  ✓ Complete Adventures of The Style Council (5 CD Box Set)

8:25 (Club Vocal)
  ✓ b-side single

4:35 (12 O' Clock Dub)
  ✓ b-side single

5:02
  ✓ Modernism: A New Decade
  ✓ Complete Adventures of The Style Council (5 CD Box Set)

✓ Motormouth (Mimed)

✓ Royal Albert Hall (July 1989)

Changing of The Guard

Single	X	Songwriter(s)	Paul Weller
Album	Y	Recorded	1988

	2:49 ✓ Confessions of A Pop Group ✓ Complete Adventures of The Style Council (5 CD Box Set)
	✓ Confessions of A Pop Group ✓ The Style Council on Film (DVD)
	✓ Royal Albert Hall (July 1989)

Come To Milton Keynes

Single	Y	Songwriter(s)	Paul Weller
Album	Y	Recorded	1985

	3:04 ✓ a-side single ✓ Our Favourite Shop ✓ Complete Adventures of The Style Council (5 CD Box Set) **3:01** Instrumental ✓ Son of Jobs For The Boys
	✓ What We Did The Following Year ✓ The Style Council on Film (DVD)
	✓ Kelly's Eye, 1985 (Live)
	✓ Internationalists '85 (Summer tour)

Confessions 1,2 & 3

Single	X	Songwriter(s)	Paul Weller
Album	Y	Recorded	1987

4:43
- ✓ Confessions of A Pop Group
- ✓ Complete Adventures of The Style Council (5 CD Box Set)

- ✓ Renaissance Tour (October 1987)

Confessions of a Pop Group

Single	X	Songwriter(s)	Paul Weller
Album	Y	Recorded	1988

9:29
- ✓ Confessions of A Pop Group
- ✓ Complete Adventures of The Style Council (5 CD Box Set)

- ✓ Confessions of a Pop Group
- ✓ The Style Council on Film (DVD)

Cost of Loving

Single	Y	Songwriter(s)	Paul Weller
Album	Y	Recorded	1987

3:48 (slow vocal)
- ✓ b-side to *Wanted* single (Titled *The Cost*)

3:48 (instrumental)
- ✓ b-side to *Wanted* single (Titled *The Cost*)

4:19
- ✓ The Cost of Loving
- ✓ Complete Adventures of The Style Council (5 CD Box Set)

- ✓ Saturday Live, 1987 (Live)
- ✓ Italian TV (Mimed)

- ✓ Cost of Loving Tour (February 1987)
- ✓ Renaissance Tour (October 1987)
- ✓ Royal Albert Hall (July 1989)
- ✓ Renaissance Tour (October 1987)

Council Meetin'

Single	X	Songwriter(s)	Paul Weller, Mick Talbot
Album	Y	Recorded	1983

2:35
- ✓ Café Bleu
- ✓ Complete Adventures of The Style Council (5 CD Box Set)

- ✓ European Tour (October 1983)

Cover Me With Love

Single	X	Songwriter(s)	Paul Weller/TBC
Album	X	Recorded	1987

- ✓ Renaissance Tour (October 1987)

Depth Charge

Single	X	Songwriter(s)	Robert Howard
Album	X	Recorded	1989

NON TSC	Released on Dee C Lee's Slam Slam LP *Free Your Feelings*
🚌	✓ Royal Albert Hall (July 1989)

Don't Do It Baby

Single	X	Songwriter(s)	
Album	X	Recorded	1984

NON TSC	Released on Dee C Lee's LP *Shrine*
🚌	✓ Council Meetings Part 2 (October 1984)

Down In The Seine

Single	X	Songwriter(s)	Paul Weller
Album	Y	Recorded	1985

	2:44
CD LP MC	✓ Our Favourite Shop
	✓ Complete Adventures of The Style Council (5 CD Box Set)
	2:52
	✓ In Concert
🚌	✓ Internationalists '85 (Summer tour)
	✓ Red Wedge - Tour 1 (January 1986)
	✓ Red Wedge - Tour 2 (March 1986)
	✓ Renaissance Tour (October 1987)
	✓ Paul Weller (Solo)

Dropping Bombs On The Whitehouse

Single	X	Songwriter(s)	Paul Weller, Mick Talbot
Album	Y	Recorded	1984

	3:14
	✓ Café Bleu
	✓ Complete Adventures of The Style Council (5 CD Box Set)
	✓ Far East and Far Out
	✓ BBC Sight & Sound, 1984 (Live)
	✓ European Tour (October 1983)

Everlasting Love

Single	X	Songwriter(s)	Paul Weller/TBC
Album	X	Recorded	1987

	✓ Full House (DVD)
	✓ Cost of Loving Tour (February 1987)

Everybody's On The Run

Single	Y	Songwriter(s)	Paul Weller, Dee C Lee
Album	Y	Recorded	1988

	4:22 (Version one Edit)
	✓ b-side single
	8:02 (Version one)
	✓ b-side single
	✓ Complete Adventures of The Style Council (5 CD Box Set)
	6:02 (Version two)
	✓ b-side single
	5.40
	✓ Modernism: A New Decade
	✓ Complete Adventures of The Style Council (5 CD Box Set)
	✓ Royal Albert Hall (July 1989)

Fairy Tales

Single	X	Songwriter(s)	Paul Weller
Album	Y	Recorded	1987

4:11
- ✓ The Cost of Loving
- ✓ Complete Adventures of The Style Council (5 CD Box Set)

- ✓ JerUSAlem
- ✓ The Style Council on Film (DVD)

- ✓ Cost of Loving Tour (February 1987)
- ✓ Renaissance Tour (October 1987)

Francoise

Single	Y	Songwriter(s)	Paul Weller
Album	Y	Recorded	1987

2:41 (Vocal)
- ✓ b-side single
- ✓ Complete Adventures of The Style Council (5 CD Box Set)

2:41 (Theme from Jerusalem)
- ✓ b-side single

- ✓ JerUSAlem
- ✓ The Style Council on Film (DVD)

Gardener of Eden (A 3 Piece Suite)

Single	X	Songwriter(s)	Paul Weller
Album	Y	Recorded	1988

10:30
- ✓ Confessions of A Pop Group
- ✓ Complete Adventures of The Style Council (5 CD Box Set)

Ghosts of Dachau

Single	Y	Songwriter(s)	Paul Weller
Album	Y	Recorded	1984

<u>2:48</u> (Vocal)
- ✓ b-side single
- ✓ Here's Some That Got Away
- ✓ Complete Adventures of The Style Council (5 CD Box Set)

Hanging Onto A Memory

Single	X	Songwriter(s)	Dunbar, Wayne and Dumas
Album	Y	Recorded	1983

<u>5:16</u>
- ✓ In Concert

- ✓ The Tube, 1983 (Live)

- ✓ European Tour (October 1983)
- ✓ Council Meetings Part 1 (March 1984)

Harvest For The World

Single	X	Songwriter(s)	The Islay Brothers
Album	X	Recorded	1983

- ✓ Three of A Kind, 1983. Studio (mimed)

Have You Ever Had It Blue

Single	Y	Songwriter(s)	Paul Weller
Album	Y	Recorded	1984

3:24 (Cut version)
- ✓ a-side single
- ✓ Singular Adventures of The Style Council (Vinyl)

4:46 (Uncut version)
- ✓ a-side single
- ✓ Complete Adventures of The Style Council (5 CD Box Set)

5:42 (Soundtrack Mix)
- ✓ Absolute Beginners

5:17 (12" version)
- ✓ Singular Adventures of The Style Council (CD)

There is a Radio Edit from Commercial Radio in March 1986.

- ✓ Video Adventures (Greatest Hits Volume 1)
- ✓ The Style Council on Film (DVD)

- ✓ Terry Wogan, 1986 (Mimed)

- ✓ Council Meetings Part 2 (October 1984)
- ✓ Internationalists '85 (Summer tour)

Headstart For Happiness

Single	Y	Songwriter(s)	Paul Weller
Album	Y	Recorded	1983

<table>
<tr>
<td rowspan="1">icons</td>
<td>
2:48 (acoustic)
✓ b-side single
✓ Introducing The Style Council
✓ Complete Adventures of The Style Council (5 CD Box Set)
3:21
✓ Café Bleu
✓ Complete Adventures of The Style Council (5 CD Box Set)
3:24
✓ Home and Abroad
</td>
</tr>
<tr>
<td>icon</td>
<td>
✓ Far East & Far Out
✓ Showbiz
✓ The Style Council on Film (DVD)
</td>
</tr>
<tr>
<td>icon</td>
<td>
✓ The Switch, 1983 (Live)
✓ Saturday Superstore, 1983 (Live)
✓ The Tube, 1983 (Live)
✓ ORS, 1983 (Live)
</td>
</tr>
<tr>
<td>icon</td>
<td>
✓ European Tour (October 1983)
✓ Council Meetings Part 1 (March 1984)
✓ Council Meetings Part 2 (October 1984)
✓ Internationalists '85 (Winter tour)
✓ Benefit/Festival (off tour)
✓ Paul Weller (solo)
</td>
</tr>
</table>

Heavens Above

Single	X	Songwriter(s)	Paul Weller
Album	Y	Recorded	1987

CD LP MC	6:15 ✓ The Cost of Loving ✓ Complete Adventures of The Style Council (5 CD Box Set) 6:29 ✓ In Concert
	✓ JerUSAlem ✓ The Style Council on Film (DVD)
	✓ Saturday Live, 1987 (Live)
	✓ Cost of Loving Tour (February 1987)

Here's One That Got Away

Single	X	Songwriter(s)	Paul Weller
Album	Y	Recorded	1984

CD LP MC	2:35 ✓ Café Bleu ✓ Complete Adventures of The Style Council (5 CD Box Set) 2:40 ✓ In Concert
	✓ Far East & Far Out
	✓ European Tour (October 1983) ✓ Council Meetings Part 1 (March 1984) ✓ Council Meetings Part 2 (October 1984) ✓ Paul Weller (Solo)

Hey What Do Ya Say

Single	X	Songwriter(s)	Dee C Lee
Album	X	Recorded	1985
NON TSC		Dee C Lee released on *Shrine*	

✓ Red Wedge - Tour 1 (January 1986)

Homebreakers

Single	X	Songwriter(s)	Paul Weller, Mick Talbot
Album	Y	Recorded	1985

5:07
✓ Our Favourite Shop
✓ Complete Adventures of The Style Council (5 CD Box Set)

5:06
✓ Home and Abroad

✓ Showbiz
✓ The Style Council on Film (DVD)

✓ Whistle Test, 1985 (Live)

✓ Internationalists '85 (Summer tour)
✓ Internationalists '85 (Winter tour)
✓ Red Wedge - Tour 1 (January 1986)
✓ Red Wedge - Tour 2 (March 1986)
✓ Cost of Loving Tour (February 1987)
✓ Renaissance Tour (October 1987)
✓ Benefit/Festival (off tour)
✓ Paul Weller (Solo)

(Hope) Feelings Gonna Getcha

Single	X	Songwriter(s)	Paul Weller, Mick Talbot, DC Lee
Album	Y	Recorded	1989

7:13
- ✓ Modernism: A New Decade
- ✓ Complete Adventures of The Style Council (5 CD Box Set)

How She Threw It All Away

Single	Y	Songwriter(s)	Paul Weller
Album	Y	Recorded	1988

4:15
- ✓ a-side single
- ✓ Confessions of A Pop Group
- ✓ Singular Adventures of The Style Council (Extra on CD)
- ✓ Complete Adventures of The Style Council (5 CD Box Set)

- ✓ Confessions of A Pop Group
- ✓ The Style Council on Film (DVD)

- ✓ Paul Weller (Solo)

I Ain't Goin' Under

Single	X	Songwriter(s)	Paul Weller
Album	Y	Recorded	1986

3:17
- ✓ Here's Some That Got Away

I Am Leaving

Single	X	Songwriter(s)	Paul Weller
Album	Y	Recorded	1988

<u>3:36</u>
   ✓ Here's Some That Got Away

I Do Like To Be B-Side The A-Side

Single	Y	Songwriter(s)	Mick Talbot
Album	Y	Recorded	1988

<u>4:45</u>
   ✓ b-side single
   ✓ Complete Adventures of The Style Council (5 CD Box Set)

Internationalists

Single	X	Songwriter(s)	Paul Weller, Mick Talbot
Album	Y	Recorded	1985

3:07
- ✓ Our Favourite Shop
- ✓ Complete Adventures of The Style Council (5 CD Box Set)

3:12 (Unreeased Demo)
- ✓ Our Favourite Shop (Deluxe)

5:40
- ✓ Home and Abroad

- ✓ Showbiz
- ✓ The Style Council on Film (DVD)

- ✓ Lenny Henry Show, 1985 (Mimed)
- ✓ Live Aid, 1985 (Live)

- ✓ Internationalists '85 (Summer tour)
- ✓ Internationalists '85 (Winter tour)
- ✓ Red Wedge - Tour 1 (January 1986)
- ✓ Cost of Loving Tour (February 1987)
- ✓ Renaissance Tour (October 1987)
- ✓ Benefit/Festival (off tour)

It Didn't Matter

Single	Y
Album	Y

Songwriter(s)	Paul Weller, Mick Talbot
Recorded	1986

4:47
- ✓ Singular Adventures of The Style Council
- ✓ a-side single

5:45 (Extended version)
- ✓ a-side single
- ✓ The Cost of Loving
- ✓ Complete Adventures of The Style Council (5 CD Box Set)

5:45 (Instrumental version)
- ✓ a-sided Single

- ✓ JerUSAlem
- ✓ Video Adventures of The Style Council
- ✓ The Style Council on Film (DVD)

- ✓ Rock Around The Dock, 1986 (Mimed)
- ✓ San Remo, Italy, 1986 (Mimed)
- ✓ Fresh & Clean, Italy, 1986 (Mimed)
- ✓ Terry Wogan, 1986 (Mimed)
- ✓ Top of The Pops, 1986 (Mimed)

- ✓ Cost of Loving Tour (February 1987)

It Just Came To Pieces In My Hands

Single	Y	Songwriter(s)	Paul Weller
Album	Y	Recorded	1983

2:32
- ✓ b-side single

2:37
- ✓ In Concert

- ✓ Far East and Far Out

- ✓ European Tour (October 1983)
- ✓ Council Meetings Part 1 (March 1984)
- ✓ Council Meetings Part 2 (October 1984)
- ✓ Internationalists '85 (Summer tour)
- ✓ Paul Weller (Solo)

It's A Very Deep Sea

Single	X	Songwriter(s)	Paul Weller
Album	Y	Recorded	1987

5:32
- ✓ Confessions of A Pop Group
- ✓ Complete Adventures of The Style Council (5 CD Box Set)

5:08
- ✓ In Concert

- ✓ Confessions of A Pop Group

- ✓ Renaissance Tour (October 1987)
- ✓ Paul Weller (solo)

Iwasadoledadstoyboy

Single	X	Songwriter(s)	Paul Weller
Album	Y	Recorded	1988

4:27
- ✓ Confessions of A Pop Group
- ✓ Complete Adventures of The Style Council (5 CD Box Set)

Johannesburg

Single	X	Songwriter(s)	Gil Scott Heron
Album	X	Recorded	1986

- ✓ Benefit/Festival (off tour)

Le Depart

Single	Y	Songwriter(s)	Mick Talbot
Album	Y	Recorded	1983

2:49
- ✓ b-side single
- ✓ Introducing The Style Council (Cassette Only)
- ✓ Complete Adventures of The Style Council (5 CD Box Set)

2:36
- ✓ In Concert

- ✓ Far East and Far Out
- ✓ What We Did On Our Holidays

- ✓ BBC Sight and Sound in Chippenham, 1984 (live)

- ✓ European Tour (October 1983)
- ✓ Council Meetings Part 1 (March 1984)
- ✓ Council Meetings Part 2 (October 1984)

Life At A Top Peoples Health Farm

Single	Y	Songwriter(s)	Paul Weller
Album	Y	Recorded	1988

4:18
- ✓ a-side single
- ✓ Confessions of A Pop Group
- ✓ Singular Adventures of The Style Council

6:00 Spank! (Live At A Top Peoples Health Club (Remix)
- ✓ a-side single

5:48 Um and Argh Mix
- ✓ a-side single
- ✓ Complete Adventures of The Style Council (5 CD Box Set)

- ✓ The Style Council on Film (DVD)
- ✓ Video Adventures of The Style Council
- ✓ Confessions of A Pop Group

- ✓ Festival Bar, Italy (Mimed)

Like A Gun

Single	Y	Songwriter(s)	Truman/Arnold (Paul Weller/Mick Talbot)
Album	X	Recorded	1989

5:37
- ✓ 12" only

3:16
- ✓ Safe Safe Mix

3:55
- ✓ Dub Version

3:12
- ✓ Radio Edit Mix

- ✓ Final Concert (Royal Albert Hall, July 1989)

Little Boy In A Castle

Single	X	Songwriter(s)	Mick Talbot
Album	Y	Recorded	1988

3:01
- ✓ Confessions of A Pop Group
- ✓ Complete Adventures of The Style Council (5 CD Box Set)

- ✓ Final Concert (Royal Albert Hall, July 1989)

Long Hot Summer

Single	Y	Songwriter(s)	Paul Weller
Album	Y	Recorded	1983

3:51
- ✓ a-side single 1983
- ✓ Singular Adventures of The Style Council (Vinyl)

5:26
- ✓ compilation LP - Jezamix
- ✓ b-side single - Tom Mix
- ✓ a-side single 1989

6:58 (Extended)
- ✓ b-side to single (12")
- ✓ Introducing The Style Council
- ✓ Complete Adventures of The Style Council (5 CD Box Set)

6:52 (Club Mix)
- ✓ b-side to single (12")
- ✓ Introducing The Style Council

6:56 (89 mix Extended)
- ✓ a-side Single 1989
- ✓ Singular Adventures of The Style Council (CD)

7:15
- ✓ In Concert

- ✓ Far East and Far Out
- ✓ What We Did On Our Holidays
- ✓ Video Adventures of The Style Council
- ✓ The Style Council on Film (DVD)
- ✓ Showbiz

	✓ Top Of The Pops (Mimed) ✓ The Switch (Live) ✓ BBC Sight and Sound (Live)
	✓ European Tour (October 1983) ✓ Council Meetings Part 1 (March 1984) ✓ Council Meetings Part 2 (October 1984) ✓ Internationalists '85 (Summer tour) ✓ Internationalists '85 (Winter tour) ✓ Benefit/Festival (off tour) ✓ Paul Weller solo

Love of The World

Single	X	Songwriter(s)	Paul Weller
Album	Y	Recorded	1989

8:55
✓ Modernism: A New Decade
✓ Complete Adventures of The Style Council (5 CD Box Set)

10:21 (Free Love Mix)
✓ b-side of Sure is Sure acetate

Love Pains

Single	X	Songwriter(s)	Willie Clayton
Album	Y	Recorded	1986

3:20
✓ Here's Some That Got Away

Love The First Time

Single	Y	Songwriter(s)	Paul Weller
Album	Y	Recorded	1988

3:38
- ✓ b-side single
- ✓ Here's Some That Got Away
- ✓ Complete Adventures of The Style Council (5 CD Box Set)

Luck

Single	Y	Songwriter(s)	Paul Weller, Mick Talbot
Album	Y	Recorded	1985

2:32
- ✓ Our Favourite Shop
- ✓ Complete Adventures of The Style Council (5 CD Box Set)

- ✓ Dee C Lee b-side single (Live)

- ✓ Internationalists '85 (Summer tour)
- ✓ Internationalists '85 (Winter tour)

Me Ship Came In

Single	X	Songwriter(s)	Paul Weller
Album	Y	Recorded	1984

	3:04
	✓ Café Bleu
	✓ Complete Adventures of The Style Council (5 CD Box Set)
	✓ Far East and Far Out
	✓ Council Meetings Part 1 (March 1984)
	✓ Council Meetings Part 2 (October 1984)

Meeting (Up) Over Yonder

Single	X	Songwriter(s)	The Impressions
Album	Y	Recorded	1984

	3:14
	✓ In Concert
	✓ BBC Sight and Sound (Chippenham 1984)
	✓ Council Meetings Part 1 (March 1984)

Mick's Blessings

Single	Y	Songwriter(s)	Mick Talbot
Album	Y	Recorded	1984

1:13
- ✓ Café Bleu
- ✓ Complete Adventures of The Style Council (5 CD Box Set)
- ✓ TSC EP Series

- ✓ Final Concert (Royal Albert Hall, July 1989)

Mick's Company

Single	Y	Songwriter(s)	Mick Talbot
Album	Y	Recorded	1984

2:48

- ✓ B-side single
- ✓ Here's Some That Got Away
- ✓ Complete Adventures of The Style Council (5 CD Box Set)
- ✓ TSC EP Series

- ✓ Red Wedge - Tour 1 (January 1986)
- ✓ Cost of Loving Tour (February 1987)
- ✓ Final Concert (Royal Albert Hall, July 1989)

Mick's Up

Single	Y	Songwriter(s)	Mick Talbot
Album	Y	Recorded	1983

3:10
- ✓ b-side single
- ✓ Introducing
- ✓ Here's Some That Got Away

4:37
- ✓ In Concert

- ✓ Far East and Far Out

- ✓ European Tour (October 1983)
- ✓ Council Meetings Part 1 (March 1984)
- ✓ Council Meetings Part 2 (October 1984)
- ✓ Red Wedge - Tour 1 (January 1986)
- ✓ Red Wedge - Tour 2 (March 1986)
- ✓ Renaissance Tour (October 1987)

Money Go Round

Single	Y	Songwriter(s)	Paul Weller
Album	Y	Recorded	1983

<u>3:25</u>
- ✓ a-side single

<u>7:25</u> Extended, Part 1 & 2
- ✓ a-side single
- ✓ Singular Adventures of The Style Council

<u>7:42</u> Bert Bevans Mix
- ✓ Introducing The Style Council

<u>7:42</u> Club Mix
- ✓ Introducing The Style Council

<u>7:25</u> Bert Bevans Mix 2
- ✓ Complete Adventures of The Style Council (5 CD Box Set)

<u>7:50</u> Dance Mix (Instrumental)
- ✓ Holland 12"

<u>5:56</u> (Part of Medley)
- ✓ In Concert

- ✓ Far East and Far Out
- ✓ What We Did On Our Holidays
- ✓ Video Adventures of The Style Council
- ✓ The Style Council on Film (DVD)

- ✓ The Switch (Live)
- ✓ BBC Sight and Sound (Chippenham, 1984) Live
- ✓ Top of the Pops (Mimed)

- ✓ European Tour (October 1983)
- ✓ Council Meetings Part 1 (March 1984)
- ✓ Council Meetings Part 2 (October 1984)
- ✓ Internationalists '85 (Summer tour)
- ✓ Internationalists '85 (Winter tour)
- ✓ Red Wedge - Tour 1 (January 1986)
- ✓ Cost of Loving Tour (February 1987)
- ✓ Renaissance Tour (October 1987)
- ✓ Benefit/Festival (off tour)

Move (Dance All Night)

Single	X	Songwriter(s)	Robert Howard, DC Lee
Album	X	Recorded	1988

NON TSC	Dee C Lee released *Free Your Feelings*

🚌	✓ Final Concert (Royal Albert Hall, July 1989)

Move On Up

Single	Y	Songwriter(s)	Curtis Mayfield
Album	Y	Recorded	1985

7" 12"	2:34 ✓ b-side single ✓ Complete Adventures of The Style Council (5 CD Box Set)
CD LP MC	2:49 ✓ In Concert

🚌	✓ Freedom Beat

🚌	✓ Internationalists '85 (Summer tour) ✓ Benefit/Festival (off tour)

Mr Cool's Dream

Single	Y	Songwriter(s)	Mick Talbot
Album	Y	Recorded	1986

7" 12" CD LP MC	2:27 ✓ b-side single ✓ Complete Adventures of The Style Council (5 CD Box Set)

My Ever Changing Moods

Single	Y	Songwriter(s)	Paul Weller
Album	Y	Recorded	1984

3:32 (Slow Piano)
- ✓ a-side single
- ✓ Complete Adventures of The Style Council (5 CD Box Set)

4:00
- ✓ a-side single

5:40 (Extended) Fast Version
- ✓ a-side single
- ✓ Singular Adventures of The Style Council (Vinyl)

4.20
- ✓ Café Bleu

4:30
- ✓ Home and Abroad

4:12
- ✓ In Concert

- ✓ What We Did On Our Holidays
- ✓ What We Did The Following Year
- ✓ Video Adventures of The Style Council
- ✓ The Style Council on Film (DVD)

- ✓ The Tube (Live)
- ✓ Pop Goes Xmas (Live)
- ✓ Top of the Pops (Mimed)
- ✓ Saturday Superstore (Mimed)

- ✓ Council Meetings Part 1 (March 1984)
- ✓ Internationalists '85 (Summer tour)
- ✓ Internationalists '85 (Winter tour)
- ✓ Red Wedge - Tour 1 (January 1986)
- ✓ Cost of Loving Tour (February 1987)
- ✓ Renaissance Tour (October 1987)
- ✓ Benefit/Festival (off tour)
- ✓ Paul Weller solo

My Very Good Friend

Single	X	Songwriter(s)	Paul Weller
Album	Y	Recorded	1986

	3:38
	✓ Here's Some That Got Away

Never Stop (A Message)

Single	X	Songwriter(s)	Steve White, Gary Wallis
Album	X	Recorded	1984

NON TSC	6:00
	Mighty Eltham Funk Federation single (Steve White)

	✓ Council Meetings Part 2 (October 1984)

Night After Night

Single	X	Songwriter(s)	David Sea
Album	Y	Recorded	1986

	2:58
	✓ Here's Some That Got Away

One Nation Under A Groove

Single	X	Songwriter(s)	Clinton, Morrison and Shider
Album	Y	Recorded	1984

	4:58
	✓ In Concert

	✓ Council Meetings Part 1 (March 1984)
	✓ Council Meetings Part 2 (October 1984)

Nzuri Beat

Single	X	Songwriter(s)	Steve White, Gary Wallis
Album	X	Recorded	1985

NON TSC	5:25
	Mighty Eltham Funk Federation single (Steve White)

	✓ Council Meetings Part 2 (October 1984)
	✓ Red Wedge - Tour (1986)

Our Favourite Shop

Single	Y	Songwriter(s)	Mick Talbot
Album	Y	Recorded	1985

7" 12"	2:51
	✓ Our Favourite Shop
	✓ Complete Adventures of The Style Council (5 CD Box Set)
	2.48 (Alternative)
	✓ Our Favourite Shop Deluxe
CD LP MC	3:19
	✓ Home and Abroad
	4:12 (Club Mix)
	✓ b-side single
	✓ Our Favourite Shop Deluxe

	✓ Showbiz
	✓ The Style Council on Film (DVD)

	✓ Internationalists '85 (Winter tour)

The Paris Match

Single	Y	Songwriter(s)	Paul Weller
Album	Y	Recorded	1983

3:40 (Paul Weller Vocal)
- ✓ b-side single
- ✓ Introducing The Style Council
- ✓ Complete Adventures of The Style Council (5 CD Box Set)

4.21 (Tracie Thorn Vocal)
- ✓ Café Bleu

Dee C Lee b-side single

- ✓ Far East and Far Out
- ✓ The Style Council on Film (DVD)

- ✓ Top of the Pops (Mimed)
- ✓ The Switch (Live)
- ✓ BBC Sight and Sound (Chippenham, 1984)

- ✓ European Tour (October 1983)
- ✓ Council Meetings Part 1 (March 1984)

Party Chambers

Single	Y	Songwriter(s)	Paul Weller
Album	Y	Recorded	1983

3:19 (Vocal)
- ✓ b-side single
- ✓ Here's Some That Got Away
- ✓ Complete Adventures of The Style Council (5 CD Box Set)

2:48 (Instrumental)
- b-side single

- ✓ BBC Sight and Sound (Live- Instrumental version)

- ✓ Council Meetings Part 1 (March 1984) - Instrumental

Piccadilly Trail

Single	Y	Songwriter(s)	Paul Weller
Album	Y	Recorded	1984

3:44
- ✓ b-side single
- ✓ Here's Some That Got Away
- ✓ Complete Adventures of The Style Council (5 CD Box Set)

- ✓ Cost of Loving Tour (February 1987)
- ✓ Paul Weller solo

Promised Land

Single	Y	Songwriter(s)	Joe Smooth
Album	Y	Recorded	1988

2:50 (Juan Atkins Mix)
- ✓ a-side single
- ✓ Singular Adventures of The Style Council

7:04 (Longer Version)
- ✓ a-side single
- ✓ Complete Adventures of The Style Council (5 CD Box Set)

3:45 (Pianopella Version)
- ✓ a-side single

5:20 (Joe Smooth Alternative Club Mix)
- ✓ a-side single

6:00 (Latin Orchestral Workout)
- ✓ Compilation CD

- ✓ Video Adventures ofhe Style Council
- ✓ The Style Council on Film (DVD)

- ✓ Motormouth (Mimed)
- ✓ Top of the Pops (Mimed)

- ✓ Final Concert (Royal Albert Hall, July 1989)

Razors Edge

Single	X	Songwriter(s)	Defunkt
Album	X	Recorded	1984

✓ The Tube (Live)

✓ Council Meetings Part 2 (October 1984)

Right To Go

Single	X	Songwriter(s)	Paul Weller, Steve White, Dynamic Three
Album	Y	Recorded	1987

5:11
✓ The Cost of Loving
✓ Complete Adventures of The Style Council (5 CD Box Set)

See The Day

Single	X	Songwriter(s)	Dee C Lee
Album	X	Recorded	1983

NON TSC | Dee C lee a-side single

✓ Internationalists '85 (Summer tour)

Shout To The Top

Single	Y	Songwriter(s)	Paul Weller
Album	Y	Recorded	1984

3:18
- ✓ a-side single
- ✓ Singular Adventures of The Style Council

4:14 (Extended)
- ✓ a-side Single
- ✓ Complete Adventures of The Style Council (5 CD Box Set)

4:19 (USA remix 1)
- ✓ Our Favourite Shop

4.12 (USA remix 2)
- ✓ Our Favourite Shop - Deluxe

3:23
- ✓ Home and Abroad

4.08 (Instrumental)
- ✓ a-side single

- ✓ What We Did The Following Year
- ✓ Video Adventures of The Style Council
- ✓ The Style Council on Film (DVD)
- ✓ Showbiz

- ✓ The Tube (Live)
- ✓ Top of the Pops (Mimed) - USA version

- ✓ Council Meetings Part 2 (October 1984)
- ✓ Internationalists '85 (Winter tour)
- ✓ Red Wedge - Tour 1 (January 1986)
- ✓ Paul Weller solo

Soul Deep

Single	Y	Songwriter(s)	Paul Weller, Mick Talbot
Album	Y	Recorded	1984

3:20 (Part 1)
- ✓ a-side single

7.15 (Club Mix)
- ✓ a-side single
- ✓ Complete Adventures of The Style Council (5 CD Box Set)

6.10 (Extended – Parts 1 & 2)
- ✓ a-side single
- ✓ Our Favourite Shop (Deluxe)

5.56
- ✓ In Concert (Part of Medley)

- ✓ Top of the Pops (Mimed)
- ✓ The Tube (Live)

- ✓ Internationalists '85 (Summer tour)
- ✓ Internationalists '85 (Winter tour)

Speak Like A Child

Single	Y	Songwriter(s)	Paul Weller
Album	Y	Recorded	1983

2:47
- ✓ a-side single
- ✓ Introducing
- ✓ Singular Adventures of The Style Council
- ✓ Complete Adventures of The Style Council (5 CD Box Set)

3:14
- ✓ In Concert

- ✓ Far East and Far Out
- ✓ What We Did On Our Holidays
- ✓ Video Adventures of The Style Council
- ✓ The Style Council on Film (DVD)

- ✓ Top of the Pops (Mimed) - version
- ✓ Hotel Suburbia, Denmark (Live)
- ✓ Saturday Live (Live)
- ✓ The Switch (Live)
- ✓ Generation 80, Belgium (Live)

- ✓ European Tour (October 1983)
- ✓ Council Meetings Part 1 (March 1984)
- ✓ Council Meetings Part 2 (October 1984)
- ✓ Benefit/Festival (off tour)
- ✓ Paul Weller solo

Spin Drifting

Single	Y	Songwriter(s)	Paul Weller
Album	Y	Recorded	1987

3:07
- ✓ b-side single
- ✓ Complete Adventures of The Style Council (5 CD Box Set)
- ✓ Our Favourite Shop Deluxe

- ✓ Paul Weller solo

Spring, Summer, Autumn

Single	Y	Songwriter(s)	Jake Fluckery
Album	Y	Recorded	1984

<table>
<tr><td rowspan="3"></td><td>2:22
   ✓ a-side single

2.52
   ✓ In Concert

Also released by Tracie Young on Far From The Hurting Kind</td></tr>
<tr><td>✓ Council Meetings Part 1 (March 1984)</td></tr>
</table>

Stand Up Comics Instructions

Single	X	Songwriter(s)	Paul Weller
Album	Y	Recorded	1985

<table>
<tr><td>1:29
   ✓ Our Favourite Shop
   ✓ Complete Adventures of The Style Council (5 CD Box Set)</td></tr>
<tr><td>✓ Internationalists '85 (Summer tour)</td></tr>
</table>

Story of Someones Shoe

Single	X	Songwriter(s)	Paul Weller
Album	Y	Recorded	1988

3:40
   ✓ Confessions of A Pop Group
   ✓ Complete Adventures of The Style Council (5 CD Box Set)

Strength of Your Nature

Single	X	Songwriter(s)	Paul Weller
Album	Y	Recorded	1984

	4:21 ✓ Café Bleu ✓ Complete Adventures of The Style Council (5 CD Box Set) 5:56 ✓ In Concert (Part of Medley)
	✓ Showbiz ✓ The Style Council on Film (DVD)
	✓ The Tube (Live)
	✓ Internationalists '85 (Summer tour) ✓ Internationalists '85 (Winter tour)

Sure Is Sure

Single	Y	Songwriter(s)	Paul Weller, Camelle Hinds
Album	Y	Recorded	1989

	6:13 ✓ Modernism: A New Decade ✓ Complete Adventures of The Style Council (5 CD Box Set)
	8:22 ✓ Acetate 12"
	✓ Hit International, Japanese TV, 1990
	✓ Final Concert (Royal Albert Hall, July 1989)

Sweet Loving Ways

Single	Y	Songwriter(s)	Paul Weller
Album	Y	Recorded	1988

3:31
- ✓ b-side single
- ✓ Here's Some That Got Away
- ✓ Complete Adventures of The Style Council (5 CD Box Set)

Tender Love

Single	X	Songwriter(s)	Paul Weller
Album	X	Recorded	1989

NON TSC	Dee C Lee released on Slam Slam LP *Free You're Feelings*
	✓ Final Concert (Royal Albert Hall, July 1989)

Thank You (Fallettin Me Be Mice Elf Agin)

Single	X	Songwriter(s)	Sly and The Family Stone
Album	X	Recorded	1986
		✓ Red Wedge - Tour 2 (March 1986)

That Spiritual Feeling

Single	X	Songwriter(s)	Paul Weller, Mick Talbot, DC Lee, Marco Nelson
Album	Y	Recorded	1989

CD LP MC	7:32 ✓ Modernism: A New Decade ✓ Complete Adventures of The Style Council (5 CD Box Set)
(bus)	✓ Final Concert (Royal Albert Hall, July 1989) ✓ Paul Weller solo

The Lodgers

Single	Y	Songwriter(s)	Paul Weller, Mick Talbot
Album	Y	Recorded	1985

7" 12"	3:50 ✓ a-side single ✓ Our Favourite Shop ✓ Complete Adventures of The Style Council (5 CD Box Set) 3:33 (Alternate) ✓ Singular Adventures of The Style Council (CD) 4:56 (Extended) ✓ a-side single ✓ Our Favourite Shop (Deluxe)
CD LP MC	3:46 (Dance Mix/Club Mix) ✓ b-side single 4:12 (Demo) ✓ Our Favourite Shop Deluxe 4:35 ✓ Home and Abroad
(video)	✓ What We Did The Following Year ✓ Video Adventures of The Style Council ✓ The Style Council on Film (DVD)
(TV)	✓ Top of the Pops (Mimed) ✓ Soul Train (Mimed)
(bus)	✓ Internationalists '85 (Summer tour) ✓ Internationalists '85 (Winter tour) ✓ Red Wedge - Tour 1 (January 1986) ✓ Cost of Loving Tour (February 1987) ✓ Renaissance Tour (October 1987)

Times Are Tight

Single	X	Songwriter(s)	Jimmy Young
Album	X	Recorded	1984

✓ Benefit/Festival (off tour)

Up For Grabs

Single	X	Songwriter(s)	Paul Weller
Album	Y	Recorded	1984

3:36
✓ In Concert

✓ European Tour (October 1983)
✓ Council Meetings Part 1 (March 1984)

Waiting

Single	Y	Songwriter(s)	Paul Weller
Album	Y	Recorded	1987

4:27
✓ a-side single
✓ The Cost of Loving
✓ Singular Adventrures of The Style Council (CD only)
✓ Complete Adventures of The Style Council (5 CD Box Set)

4:27 (Instrumental)
✓ a-side single

✓ The Style Council on Film (DVD)

✓ Cost of Loving Tour (February 1987)

Waiting On A Connection

Single	X	Songwriter(s)	Paul Weller
Album	Y	Recorded	1988

CD LP MC	3:05 ✓ Here's Some That Got Away
🚌	✓ Final Concert (Royal Albert Hall, July 1989) ✓ Paul Weller solo

Walking The Night

Single	X	Songwriter(s)	Paul Weller, Mick Tablot
Album	Y	Recorded	1987

CD LP MC	4:29 ✓ The Cost of Loving
📺	✓ Italian TV (Mimed)
🚌	✓ Cost of Loving Tour (February 1987)

Walls Come Tumbling Down

Single	Y	Songwriter(s)	Paul Weller
Album	Y	Recorded	1985

3:22
- ✓ a-side single
- ✓ Our Favourite Shop
- ✓ Singular Adventures of The Style Council
- ✓ Complete Adventures of The Style Council (5 CD Box Set)

3:37
- ✓ Home and Abroad

- ✓ What We Did The Following Year
- ✓ Video Adventures of The Style Council
- ✓ The Style Council on Film (DVD)
- ✓ Showbiz

- ✓ Top of the Pops (Mimed)
- ✓ Italian TV (Mimed)
- ✓ Whistle Test (Live)
- ✓ Terry Wogan (Live)
- ✓ Countdown (Mimed) - Australia

- ✓ Internationalists '85 (Summer tour)
- ✓ Internationalists '85 (Winter tour)
- ✓ Benefit/Festival (off tour)

Wanted

Single	Y	Songwriter(s)	Paul Weller, Mick Talbot
Album	Y	Recorded	1987

3:24
- ✓ a-side single
- ✓ Singular Adventures of The Style Council
- ✓ Complete Adventures of The Style Council (5 CD Box Set)

- ✓ Video Adventures of The Style Council
- ✓ The Style Council on Film (DVD)

- ✓ Top of the Pops (Mimed)
- ✓ The Roxy (Mimed)
- ✓ Festival Bar (Mimed) - Italy

- ✓ Renaissance Tour (October 1987)

(When You) Call Me

Single	Y	Songwriter(s)	Paul Weller
Album	Y	Recorded	1985

3:16
- ✓ b-side single
- ✓ Complete Adventures of The Style Council (5 CD Box Set)
- ✓ Our Favourite Shop

4:24
- ✓ Home and Abroad

2:55
- ✓ Here's Some That Got Away
- ✓ Our Favourite Shop Deluxe

- ✓ Showbiz
- ✓ The Style Council on Film (DVD)

- ✓ Internationalists '85 (Summer tour)
- ✓ Internationalists '85 (Winter tour)
- ✓ Cost of Loving Tour (February 1987)
- ✓ Renaissance Tour (October 1987)
- ✓ Paul Weller solo

Who Will Buy?

Single	Y	Songwriter(s)	Lionel Bart
Album	Y	Recorded	1986

2:42
- ✓ b-side single (Japan only)
- ✓ Here's Some That Got Away

Whole Point II

Single	Y	Songwriter(s)	Paul Weller
Album	Y	Recorded	1985

2:50
- ✓ b-side single
- ✓ Here's Some That Got Away
- ✓ Complete Adventures of The Style Council (5 CD Box Set)

- ✓ Cost of Loving Tour (February 1987)
- ✓ Renaissance Tour (October 1987)
- ✓ Paul Weller solo

Whole Point of No Return

Single	X	Songwriter(s)	Paul Weller
Album	Y	Recorded	1984

2:40
- ✓ Café Bleu
- ✓ Complete Adventures of The Style Council (5 CD Box Set)

3:20
- ✓ Home and Abroad

- ✓ Far East and Far Out

- ✓ Council Meetings Part 1 (March 1984)
- ✓ Council Meetings Part 2 (October 1984)
- ✓ Internationalists '85 (Winter tour)

Why I Went Missing

Single	X	Songwriter(s)	Paul Weller
Album	Y	Recorded	1988

(CD/LP/MC)	4:43 ✓ Confessions of A Pop Group ✓ Complete Adventures of The Style Council (5 CD Box Set)
(cassette)	✓ Confessions of A Pop Group ✓ The Style Council on Film (DVD)

With Everything To Lose

Single	X	Songwriter(s)	Paul Weller, Steve White
Album	Y	Recorded	1985

(CD/LP/MC)	3:50 ✓ Our Favourite Shop ✓ Complete Adventures of The Style Council (5 CD Box Set) 4:09 ✓ Home and Abroad
(cassette)	✓ The Style Council on Film (DVD) ✓ Showbiz
(TV)	✓ Soul Train (Mimed)
(tour bus)	✓ Internationalists '85 (Summer tour) ✓ Internationalists '85 (Winter tour) ✓ Red Wedge - Tour 1 (January 1986) ✓ Red Wedge - Tour 2 (March 1986) ✓ Cost of Loving Tour (February 1987) ✓ Renaissance Tour (October 1987)

World Must Come Together

Single	X	Songwriter(s)	Paul Weller
Album	Y	Recorded	1989

5:18
- ✓ Modernism: A New Decade
- ✓ Complete Adventures of The Style Council (5 CD Box Set)

You'll Find Love

Single	X	Songwriter(s)	Paul Weller
Album	X	Recorded	1989

NON TSC	Dee C Lee released on Slam Slam LP, *Free Your Feelings*

- ✓ Final Concert (Royal Albert Hall, July 1989

You're The Best Thing

Single	Y	Songwriter(s)	Paul Weller
Album	Y	Recorded	1984

4:29 (7" version)
- ✓ a-side single
- ✓ Singular Adventures of The Style Council (Vinyl)

5:40 (Extended Version)
- ✓ a-side single

5:26 (You're The Dub Thing)
- ✓ a-side single

4.59
- ✓ b-side single (live)

5.43
- ✓ Café Bleu
- ✓ Complete Adventures of The Style Council (5 CD Box Set)

4:20 (Alternate Mix)
- ✓ Singular Adventures of The Style Council (CD)

- ✓ Far East and Far Out
- ✓ What We Did The Following Year
- ✓ Video Adventures of The Style Council
- ✓ The Style Council on Film (DVD)

- ✓ Saturday Live (Live)
- ✓ Earsay (Live)
- ✓ St. Vincent Estate - (Mimed) - Italy
- ✓ St. Vincent Estate (Mimed) - Italy. 2nd Performance

- ✓ Council Meetings Part 2 (October 1984)
- ✓ Internationalists '85 (Summer tour)
- ✓ Cost of Loving Tour (February 1987)
- ✓ Renaissance Tour (October 1987)
- ✓ Benefit/Festival (off tour)

HONORARY STYLE COUNCILLOR'S

Honorary: adj: Held or given as a mark of honor.

78 musicians were tagged by The Style Council as an *Honorary Councillor* - This 'honorary' tag was a clever attempt to make musicians appear to be more than just session players. A few did become established and return for live gigs, but the majority performed their piece, took the fee and were never heard from again. A few did go on to perform with major artists - Steve Sidelnyk, Guy Barker, Roddy Lorimer and Anne Stephenson to name a few.

B

Guy Barker (Flugel Horn); *Walking The Night.*
(Trumpet); *Money Go Round, The Lodgers, Fairy Tales, Walking The Night.*
Performed with The Blow Monkeys, The The, Working Week, Grace Jones, Mike Oldfield, Junior, Wham, Tom Robinson, Boomtown Rats, Erasure, Swing Out Sister, Housemartins, Brother Beyond, Deacon Blue, Sting and Will Young.

Rebecca Bell (Backing vocals); *The Paris Match*

Bert Bevans (Remixer); *Long Hot Summer* (Club Mix),
Money Go Round (Club Mix), *Soul Deep.*
Performed with Depeche Mode, Big Audio Dynamite, Paul McCartney and Omar. Bert also produced *The Gospel* which was written by Paul Weller and performed then released by Dizzy Heights.

Chris Bostock (Bass); *Here's One That Got Away.*
Performed with Jo Boxers and Dave Stewart.

Nick Brown (Drums); *How She Threw It All Away.*

Charlie Buchanan (Violin); *A Stones Throw Away.*

C

Cappuccino Kid (sleeve notes); All Style Council single and album releases.

Billy Chapman (Tenor Saxophone); *Me Ship Came In, Dropping Bombs On The Whitehouse, Big Boss Groove, With Everything To Lose, Have You Ever Had It Blue* and *Heavens Above.*
Performed with Animal Nightlife and Tracie Young.

Leonardo Chignoli (Bass); *Soul Deep.*
Performed with Animal Nightlife.

D

Steve Dawson (Trumpet); *Our Favourite Shop*.

Dave Defries   (Flugel Horn); *A Man of Great Promise*.
                      (Trumpet); *Walls Come Tumbling Down* and *Homebreakers*.
Performed with Dream Academy, The The and Annie Lennox.

Martin Drover (Trumpet); *Speak Like A Child*.
Performed with The Jam, Bryan Ferry, Japan, Adam Ant, Orange Juice, Wham, Aztec Camera, Van Morrison, Diana Brown & Barrie K Sharpe and Edwyn Collins.

Jo Dworniak (Bass); *Money Go Round*.
Performed with I Level, The Belle Stars, John Foxx and S Club 7.

Dynamic Three (Rappin); *Right To Go*.

E

Pee Wee Ellis (Tenor Saxophone); *That Spiritual Feeling*.

Gil Evans (Arrangement); *Have You Ever Had It Blue*.

G

Junior Giscombe (Vocals); *Soul Deep*. Was also a successful solo artist.

Robert 'Kush' Griffith (Trumpet); *That Spiritual Feeling*.

Patrick Grundy-White (French Horn); *A Man of Great Promise*.

H

Simon Halfon (Sleeve Design & Artwork); All single and album releases.
In 2008 still producing all of Paul's artwork.

Lenny Henry (Vocals); *The Stand Up Comic's Instructions*.
Performed with Paul Hardcastle and Kate Bush and still has his TV show in 2008.

Paolo Hewitt   (Interviews); *A Miners Point*.
                      (Vocals); *Love of The World*.

Camelle Hinds   (Vocals); *Confessions 1,2,3.*
        (Bass); *Walls Come Tumbling Down, Stand up Comics Instructions, Internationalists, Why I Went Missing, Heavens Above, Angel, Walking The Night, Gardener of Eden, How She Threw It All Away, Confessions 1,2 & 3* and *Confessions of A Pop Group.*
Performed with Central Line, The Quiet Boys, Boyz II Men, Hindsight, The The, Boogie Box High and Paul Weller solo.

Dizzy Hites (Rappin); *A Gospel, Soul Deep.*

Olivier Horet (Translater); *The Paris Match.*

Chris Hunter (Tenor Saxophone); *A Solid Bond In Your Heart.*
Performed with Junior, Guy Barker, David Grant, Gil Evans, Wham, Joe Jackson, Incognito and Sheena Easton.

J

Jezar (Drum programming); *Confessions of A Pop Group* LP.

K

Clark Kent (Bass - Contra); *All Gone Away, Down In The Seine.*

L

Chris Lawrence (Trombone); *Big Boss Groove, Walls Come Tumbling Down, Homebreakers, A Man of Great Promise, The Lodgers, Fairy Tales, Walking The Night, Confessions 1,2,3.* Performed with Tracie Young, The Stranglers and Animal Nightlife featuring Paul Weller.

Dee C Lee (Vocals); *Money Go Round, Strength of Your Nature, Headstart For Happiness, Big Boss Groove, Shout To The Top, Soul Deep, Walls Come Tumbling Down, A Man of Great Promise, Homebreakers, Internationalists, With Everything To Lose* + permanent member for *Confessions of A Pop Group* and *Modernism, A New Decade* LP's.

Alison Limerick (Vocals); *Shout To The Top.* Also a successful solo artist.

Roddy Lorimer   (Trumpet); *The Lodgers, Fairy Tales, Walking The Night.*
        (Flugel Horn); *Walking The Night.*

Performed with The Waterboys, Wham, Nick Kershaw, Bronski Beat, James Taylor Quartet, Lightening Seeds, Suede, Blur, M People, Eric Clapton, Gene and The Lighthouse Family.

M

Zeke Manyika (Drums); *Speak Like A Child, Party Chambers, Money Go Round, A Solid Bond In Your Heart.*

Performed with Orange Juice, The Zeros, The The; Marc Almond and Paul Weller.

Mary, Benita, Derek (Vocals); *Promised Land.* Surnames not known.

John Mealing   (Strings); *Shout To The Top, A Stones Throw Away.*
                (Arrangement); *Confessions of A Pop Group LP.*
                (Orchestration); *Come To Milton Keynes, Cost of Loving.*
Performed with Status Quo, Tracie, The Blow Monkeys and The Walker Brothers.

Kevin Miller (Bass); *Big Boss Groove, Shout To The Top, With Everything To Lose.*

Paul Morgan (Bass - contra); *It's A Very Deep Sea, Changing of The Guard.*
Performed with The Jazz Renegades, Bjork, Nick Cave and Westlife.

Dick Morrisey (Flute); *How She Threw It All Away.*
Performed with Shakatak, Orange Juice, Gary Numan, Peter Gabriel, Peter Wilson and The Blow Monkeys.

Mike Mower (Flute); *All Gone Away, With Everything To Lose.*
                (Saxophone - Tenor); *Walls Come Tumbling Down, Homebreakers.*
Performed with Bjork, Gil Evans, Tina Turner and the BBC Big Band.

P

Maceo Parker (Saxophone - Alto); *That Spiritual Feeling.*

Rupert Parker (Harp); *Gardener of Eden (In The Beginning)*

Jocelyn Pook (Viola); *A Stones Throw Away.*
Performed with The Communards, Massive Attack and Peter Gabriel

Brian J Powell (Vocals); *Everybodys On The Run.*

Paul Powell (Bass); *Wanted, The Cost.*

Stewart Prosser   (Trumpet); *Big Boss Groove, Walls Come Tumbling Down, Homebreakers.*
                (Flugel Horn); *A Man of Great Promise.*

Performed with Tracie, ABC and Animal Nightlife alongside Paul Weller.

R

Paul Renee (Translator); *Down In The Seine.*

Frank Ricottim (Vibraphone); *The Story of Someone's Shoe.*

Audrey Riley (Cello); *A Stones Throw Away.*
Performed with Marc Almond, The Communards, The Go-Betweens, Nick Cave, New Order, Coldplay, Feeder, Muse and Moloko

Jean Louis Roques   (Accordion); *The Paris Match.*
                          (Piano); *The Paris Match.*
Jean was on Polydor's French label at the time and joined the band in Paris. He has appeared on numerous French artists releases.

Jimmy Ruffin (Vocals); *Soul Deep.* Also a solo artist.

Little Jo Ruocco (Percussion); *How She Threw It All Away, Confessions of A Pop Group.*

S

Hilary Seabrook (Tenor Saxophone); *My Ever Changing Moods, A Gospel, Headstart For Happiness* (from *Café Bleu*)

Steve Sidelnyk   (Congas); *Heavens Above, Fairy Tales.*
                       (Percussion); *The Lodgers, Right To Go, Fairy Tales.*

Performed with The Soup Dragons, Coldcut, Yazz, Tracie, The Blow Monkeys, Alison Moyet, ABC, Rolling Stones, Tina Turner, Annie Lennox, Electronic, M People, Kylie Minogue, Madonna, Melanie C, Orbital, PJ Harvey, S Club 7, Richard Ashcroft, All Saints, REM, David Gray, Will Young, Dido, Seal and Robbie Williams.

Sarah Silver (Translator); *Down In The Seine.*

Swingle Singers (Vocals); *The Story of Someones Shoe.*

Ashley Slater (Trombone); *The Lodgers, Walking The Night, Fairy Tales.*

Performed with Freakpower and Fatboy Slim.

Barbara Snow (Trumpet); *Me Ship Came In, Dropping Bombs On The Whitehouse, A Gospel, Headstart For Happiness.*

Performed with The Questions, Maxi Priest, The Blow Monkeys, James Taylor Quartet, Jools Holland, The Waterboys and David Gilmour.

Spegos (Percussion); *Money Go Round.*

Anne Stephenson (Violin); *A Stones Throw Away, Heavens Above.*

Performed with Siouxsie & The Banshees, The Cure, The Undertones, Brian Ferry, Royal Philharmonic Orchestra, Texas, The Manic Street Preachers, The The, The Communards and Kylie Minogue.

T

Pete Thams (Trombone); *The Lodgers, Walking The Night, Fairy Tales.*

Tracie Thorn (Vocals); *The Paris Match.* Tracie is half of Everything But The Girl.

Vaughn Toulouse (Vocals); *Soul Deep.* Lead singer of Department S.

Luke Tunney (Trumpet); *The Lodgers, Fairy Tales, Walking The Night.* (Flugel Horn); *Walking The Night*

Performed with The Teardrop Explodes, Everything But The Girl, Tom Robinson, China Crisis, Swing Out Sister, Boomtown Rats, The Jam and The Farm,

Helen Turner (Piano); *Walls Come Tumbling Down.*

Performed with Tracie and Paul Weller solo.

V

John Valentine (Vocals); *Walking The Night.*

Bobby Valentino (Violin); *Heres One That Got Away.*

Performed with The Bluebells, Billy Bragg, Sam Brown, Christians, Kirsty MacColl, Tom Petty and The Proclaimers.

W

Jeremy Wakefield (Keyboard Sequencing); *Boy Who Cried Wolf.*

Gary Wallis (Percussion); *All Gone Away.*

Performed with Tom Jones, Pink Floyd, Dusty Springfield, Nik Kershaw, Power Station and Westlife. Has been musical director for Il Divo, Girls Aloud and Atomic Kitten.

Ben Watt (Guitar); *The Paris Match* (from *Café Bleu*). Ben is half of Everything But The Girl.

Nicky Weller (Fan Club); Management.

Fred Wesley (Trombone); *That Spiritual Feeling.*

Steve White (Drums); All tracks unless stated.

Annie Whitehead (Trombone); *Money Go Round.*

Performed with Elvis Costello, Fun Boy Three, Joan Armatrading, Working Week, S Club 7 and Paul Weller on Robert Wyatt's Shleep LP.

Jaye Williamson (Vocals); *Big Boss Groove.*

Peter Wilson   (Co-Producer/Producer); Many singles and LP's.
(Bass Synth); *My Ever Changing Moods.*
(Drum Programming); *A Gospel, Strength of Your Nature, You're The Best Thing.*
(Keyboard Sequencing); *Boy Who Cried Wolf.*
(Strings); *Blue Café.*

Performed with The Jam, Sham 69, Fiction Factory, The Blow Monkeys, The Vapors and The Cockney Rejects.

Y

Tracie Young (Backing Vocals); *Speak Like A Child, Boy Who Cried Wolf.*

Also a solo artist. Performed with Kevin Miller, Steve Sidelnyk, Brian Robson, Helen Turner, Billy Chapman, Chris Lawrence, Stuart Prosser, Kevin Miller and Camelle Hinds.

GIGOGRAPHY

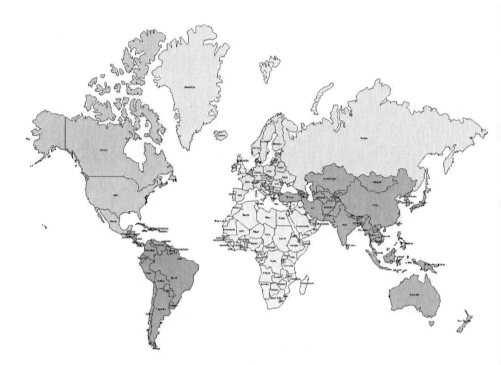

THE STYLE COUNCIL - LIVE
1983 - 1990

AUSTRALIA, AUSTRIA, BELGIUM, DENMARK, FRANCE, GERMANY
ITALY, JAPAN, NETHERLANDS, SWITZERLAND, UK, USA

UNITED KINGDOM

Total - 101 (8 cancelled)

1983 - May 1st - Liverpool, Empire Theatre. Benefit (CND)
1983 - May 7th - London, Brockwell Park. Benefit (Youth CND)
1983 - May 25th - London, The Paris Theatre (Respond Package)
1983 - December 7th - London, Hammersmith Odeon. Cancelled
1983 - December 8th - Southampton, Gaumont. Cancelled
1983 - December 10th - Coventry, The Apollo. Cancelled
1983 - December 11th - Ipswich, Gaumont. Cancelled
1983 - December 12th - Sheffield, City Hall. Cancelled
1983 - December 13th - Halifax, Civic Hall. Cancelled
1983 - December 18th - London ,The Apollo. Benefit (The Big One)

1984 - March 10th - Chippenham, Golddiggers
1984 - March 13th - Southampton, Gaumont
1984 - March 14th - London, Dominion
1984 - March 15th - London, Dominion
1984 - March 16th - Birmingham, Odeon
1984 - March 17th - Ipswich, Gaumont Theatre
1984 - March 18th - Nottingham, Sports Centre
1984 - March 19th - Newcastle, City Hall
1984 - March 20th - Glasgow, Apollo
1984 - April 8th - London, The 100 Club (End of tour gig)
1984 - May 26th - Coventry, Apollo Theatre. Benefit (CND)
1984 - July 7th - Liverpool, Venue ?? Benefit (Miners)
1984 - September 7th - London, Royal Festival Hall. Benefit (Miners)
1984 - October 4th - Wolverhampton, Civic Hall. Benefit (Miners and CND)
1984 - October 6th - Oxford, Apollo
1984 - October 7th - Bristol, Hippodrome
1984 - October 8th - Cardiff, St. David's Hall
1984 - October 9th - St. Austell, Cornwall Coliseum
1984 - October 11th - Sheffield, City Hall
1984 - October 12th - Manchester, Apollo
1984 - October 14th - Edinburgh, The Playhouse
1984 - October 15th - Liverpool, Royal Court Theatre
1984 - October 16th - Leicester, De Montfort Hall

1984 - December 1st - Margate, Winter Gardens. Benefit (Animal rights)
1984 - December 3rd - London, Royal Albert Hall
1984 - December 4th - London, Royal Albert Hall

1985 - June 5th - London, Brixton Academy
1985 - June 6th - Bournemouth, Windsor Hall
1985 - June 7th - Portsmouth, Guildhall
1985 - June 8th - Brighton, The Centre
1985 - June 9th - Birmingham, Odeon Theatre
1985 - June 10th - Birmingham, Odeon Theatre
1985 - June 11th - Sheffield, City Hall
1985 - June 13th - Nottingham, Royal Centre
1985 - June 14th - Manchester, Apollo
1985 - June 15th - Liverpool, Empire
1985 - June 16th - Glasgow, Apollo Theatre
1985 - June 22nd - Glastonbury Festival (Headline act)
1985 - July 13th - London, Wembley Stadium. Benefit (Live Aid)
1985 - October 26th - London, Hyde Park. Benefit (CND)
1985 - December 3rd - Leicester, De Montfort Hall
1985 - December 4th - Gloucester, Leisure Centre
1985 - December 5th - Blackburn, King Georges Hall
1985 - December 6th - Edinburgh, The Playhouse
1985 - December 8th - London, Wembley Arena
1985 - December 9th - London, Wembley Arena
1985 - December 10th - London, Wembley Arena

1986 - January 25th - Manchester, Apollo (Red Wedge)
1986 - January 26th - Cardiff, St. David's Hall (Red Wedge)
1986 - January 27th - Birmingham, Odeon (Red Wedge)
1986 - January 28th - Leicester, De Montfort Hall (Red Wedge)
1986 - January 29th - Bradford, St. Georges Hall (Red Wedge)
1986 - January 30th - Edinburgh, The Playhouse (Red Wedge)
1986 - January 31st - Newcastle, City Hall (Red Wedge)
1986 - March 2nd - London, The Royal Albert Hall. Benefit (GLC jobs)
1986 - March 21st - London, Hammersmith Odeon. Benefit (GLR Farewell)
1986 - June 28th - London, Clapham Common. Benefit (AAA)
1986 - July 20th - London, Shaw Theatre. Secret - The Party Chambers Group
1986 - September ?? - London, venue ?? Benefit

1987 - January ?? London, The Barbican. Benefit (AIDS)
1987 - February 14th - Newport, The Centre
1987 - February 15th - Newport, The Centre
1987 - February 16th - London, The Royal Albert Hall
1987 - February 17th - London, The Royal Albert Hall
1987 - February 18th - London, The Royal Albert Hall
1987 - February 19th - London, The Royal Albert Hall

1987 - February 20th - Bournemouth, International Centre
1987 - February 21st - Birmingham, National Exhibition Centre
1987 - February 22nd - Birmingham, National Exhibition Centre
1987 - February 24th - Brighton, The Centre
1987 - February 25th - Bradford St. George's Hall
1987 - February 26th - Newcastle, City Hall
1987 - February 27th - Newcastle, City Hall
1987 - February 28th - Glasgow, Scottish Exhibition Centre
1987 - April 25th - London, Hyde Park. Benefit (1st Chernobyl anniversary)
1987 - June 8th - Nottingham, Royal Concert Hall (Red Wedge)
1987 - July 19th - London, Brixton Academy. Benefit (Nicaragua)
1987 - October 15th - Glasgow, The Barrowlands (Cancelled)
1987 - October 16th - Dundee, Caird Hall (Cancelled)
1987 - October 17th - Manchester, Apollo
1987 - October 18th - Harrogate, Conference Centre
1987 - October 22nd - Sheffield, City Hall
1987 - October 23rd - Leicester, De Montfort Hall
1987 - October 24th - Crawley, Leisure Centre
1987 - October 25th - Margate, Winter Gardens
1987 - November 24th - London, Hammersmith Odeon
1987 - November 25th - London, Hammersmith Odeon

1988 - March 6th - London, Hackney Empire. Benefit (Fight Alton's Bill)

1989 - July 4th - London, The Royal Albert Hall

1990 - February 11th - London, Dominion Theatre. Benefit (Ambulance)

Australia

Total gigs - 4

1985 - August 18th - Sports and Entertainment Centre, Melbourne
1985 - August 19th- The Venue, Melbourne (Benefit, Children's Charities)
1985 - August 21st - The Hordern Pavilion, Sydney Showground
1985 - August 22nd - The Hordern Pavilion, Sydney Showground

Austria

Total gigs - 2

1984 - October 5th - Lindt
1984 - October 6th - Innsbruck

Belgium

Total gigs - 7

1983 - October 28th - V.U.B. Auditorium Q, Brussels

1984 - March 25th - Ancienne Hall, Brussels
1984 - October - Unconfirmed dates

1985 - July 6th - Torhout Festival, West Flanders
1985 - July 8th - Werchter Festival, Rotselaar
1985 - October 19th - Deinze Brielpoort, Brussels

1987 - March 8th - Cirque Royale, Koninklijk Circus, Brussels

Denmark

Total gigs - 1

1985 - June 28th - Roskilde Festival

France

Total gigs - 4

1983 - October 26th - Le Palace Theatre, Paris

1984 - March 27th - Palais D'Hiver, Lyon
1984 - March 29th - L'Eldorado, Paris

1987 - March 18th - Paris

Germany

Total gigs - 15

1983 - October 30th - Trinity, Hamburg

1984 - March 30th - Zeche, Bochum
1984 - April 1st - Metropol, Berlin
1984 - October 29th - Alabamahalle, Munich
1984 - November 1st - Robert Schumann Saal, Dusseldorf

1985 - October 10th - Laeiszhalle Musikhalle, Hamburg
1985 - October 11th - Tempodrom, Treugast, Berlin
1985 - October 13th - Ludwigshafen, Pfalzbau
1985 - October 17th - Philipshalle, Dusseldorf

1987 - March 10th - Dusseldorf
1987 - March 11th - Munster
1987 - March 12th - The Capital, Hannover
1987 - March 13th - Freitag, Hamburg
1987 - March 15th - Frankfurt
1987 - March 16th - Heidelberg

Italy

Total gigs - 16

1984 - October 22nd - Rome
1984 - October 23rd - Bologna
1984 - October 24th - Teatro Tenda, Milan

1985 - September 8th - Festa De L'Unità, Ferrara
1985 - September 10th - Theatre Tendra, Rome
1985 - September 11th - Palasport, Firenze
1985 - September 12th - Modena
1985 - September 13th - Teatro Tenda, Milan
1985 - September 14th - Parco Pellerina, Torino

1987 - May 6th - Palasport, Firenze
1987 - May 7th - Palasport, Torino
1987 - May 8th - Palasport, Varese
1987 - May ?? - Milan
1987 - May ?? - San Remo
1987 - September 14th - Festa De L'Unità, Reggio Emilia, Italy
1987 - September 7th - Palatrussardi, Milan, Italy

Japan

Total gigs - 15

1984 - April 30th - Koseinenkin Hall, Tokyo
1984 - May 2nd - Joh Hall, Osaka
1984 - May 4th - SunPlaza Hall, Nakano, Tokyo

1985 - August 2nd - Osaka, Castle Hall (Rock in Japan)
1985 - August 4th - Fukuoka Kokusai, Center, Fukuoka
1985 - August 8th - Nagoya Kokusai Tenjiho, Nagoya
1985 - August 10th - Yokohama Stadium
1985 - August 11th - Yokohama Stadium

1987 - April 2nd - World Kinen Hall, Kobe
1987 - April 3rd - Kohichan, Tokyo
1987 - April 4th - Kohichan, Tokyo
1987 - April 5th - Kohichan, Tokyo

1989 - June 7th - Arena, Yokohama
1989 - June 8th - Joh Hall, Osaka
1989 - June 9th - Shiodome, Tokyo

Netherlands

Total gigs - 5

1983 - October 31st - De Meervaart, Amsterdam

1984 - April 3rd - Vredenburg, Utrecht
1984 - November 4th - Carre, Amsterdam

1987 - March 7th - Ahoy, Rotterdam
1987 - May 23rd - Brabauthallen, Den Bosch (KRO Eindexamen Festival)

Switzerland

Total gigs - 1

1983 - October 24th - The Volkhaus, Zurich

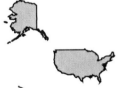

United States of America

Total gigs - 4

1984 - May 7th - Wilshire Theatre, Beverley Hills
1984 - May 8th - Wilshire Theatre, Beverley Hills
1984 - May 10th - The Savoy Theatre, New York
1984 - May 11th - The Savoy Theatre, New York

1985 - Summer - Tour cancelled.

Paul Weller sings The Council 1990 - 2008

Paul has covered many Style Council songs since going solo in 1990. When you discard TSC instrumentals, cover versions and songs no longer lyrically suitable for today then there are not many left to choose from the catalogue.

1990

My Ever Changing Moods
How She Threw It All Away
It's A Very Deep Sea
Waiting On A Connection
Down In The Seine

Homebreakers
A Man of Great Promise
Whole Point II
Headstart For Happiness
Speak Like A Child

1991

My Ever Changing Moods
The Piccadilly Trail
Long Hot Summer
The Cost of Loving

Homebreakers
A Man of Great Promise
Have You Ever Had It Blue
Headstart For Happiness

1992

Long Hot Summer
The Cost of Loving
Headstart For Happiness

(When You) Call Me
All Year Round

1993

Long Hot Summer
The Cost of Loving

That Spiritual Feeling
Headstart For Happiness

1995

Down In The Seine

A Man of Great Promise

1996

Down In The Seine

A Man of Great Promise

1999

A Man of Great Promise

2001

Here's One That Got Away
Down In The Seine

A Man of Great Promise
Headstart For Happiness

2002

Long Hot Summer
Down In The Seine

A Man of Great Promise
Headstart For Happiness

2003

Long Hot Summer
Down In The Seine

A Man of Great Promise
Headstart For Happiness

2004

My Ever Changing Moods
Long Hot Summer
It Just Came To Pieces In My Hands

Shout To The Top
A Man of Great Promise
Headstart For Happiness

2005

My Ever Changing Moods
Long Hot Summer
Headstart For Happiness

Shout To The Top
A Man of Great Promise

2006

Long Hot Summer
A Man of Great Promise

Shout To The Top

2007

My Ever Changing Moods
Speak Like A Child
It's A Very Deep Sea
Long Hot Summer

Shout To The Top
A Man of Great Promise
Down In The Seine
Headstart For Happiness

2008

Shout To The Top

As at 1st September 2008

SONGS RECORDED

The Style Council have 117 known titles to their name. Over 42% of these were written between 1984 and 1985, the 'untouchable' years.

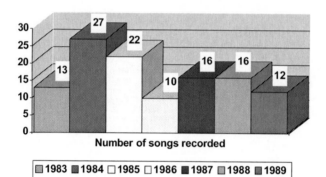

Number of songs recorded

■ 1983 ■ 1984 □ 1985 □ 1986 ■ 1987 ■ 1988 ■ 1989

UNRELEASED SONGS

Although never officially released as The Style Council the following 21 songs have been performed live. For the curious or collector I have detailed where to find The Style Council's performance and the original artists release where applicable.

A Word From Our Leaders
Back To The Chicken Shack
Cover Me With Love
Depth Charge
Don't Do It Baby
Everlasting Love
I Can't Deny Myself
Instrumental (title unknown)
It's Time To Stop Shopping Around
Harvest For The World
Johannesburg

Move (Dance All Night)
Never Stop (A Message)
Now Your Gone
Nzuri Beat
Razors Edge
Tender Love
Times Are Tight
Thank You
(Fallettin Me Be Mice Elf Agin)
That Spiritual Feeling
You'll Find Love

1983

Harvest for the World an Isley Brothers 1976 top 10 hit about World peace was performed by TSC in 1983 on TV show *3 Of A Kind* alongside Tracie and The Questions. As it could not be sung live it was recorded prior to the show and then mimed. Dennis Munday confirmed it still remains in the Weller vault.

Times are Tight performed at the Paris Theatre, London on 25th May 1983 as part of a 4 track acoustic set. Broadcasted on Radio 1. Originally released by US artist Jimmy Young. Look for the 12" vocal version on Delirium Records. Also on Nitelife Records. The BBC still have this show in their vaults.

1984

Don't Do it Baby performed on the October 1984 Council Meetings part 2 tour. Released by Dee C Lee as a single in 1984 and re-surfaced in 1985 on the b-side of her top 5 hit *See The Day*.

It's Time To Stop Shopping Around performed at a miners benefit gig in July with Madness. Originally released on Smokey Robinson's *One Heartbeat* LP.

Never Stop (A Message) performed on the October 1984 Council Meetings part 2 tour. Written by Steve White and Gary Wallis and released as a single under their own band The Mighty Eltham Funk Federation.

Nzuri Beat performed on the October 1984 Council Meetings part 2 tour. Written by Steve White and Gary Wallis and released as a single under their own band The Mighty Eltham Funk Federation.

The Razors Edge performed on the October 1984 Council Meetings part 2 tour and also on *The Tube* in same month. Originally released by Defunkt on a 12" in Europe in 1982. Look for the lengthy 9:20 release on their compilation *Avoid The Funk: A Defunkt Anthology*.

1985

A Word From Our Leaders performed on the Internationalists '85 tour as a video/thumping drum based politically tinged instrumental. Possibly written by Paul Weller and Steve White. Included quotes from then then Tory leader Maggie Thatcher.

1986

Johannesburg performed at the Artists Against Apartheid demonstration at Clapham Common in June. Originally released by US artist Gil Scott Heron on the album with Brian Jackson *From South Africa To South Carolina*.

Back to the Chicken Shack performed on the Red Wedge tour in 1986 with guest Jerry Dammers from The Specials on Keyboards. Originally released by Jimmy Smith on an album of the same name in April 1960 on Blue Note.

Thank You (Falettin Me Be Mice Elf Agin) performed on the 2nd Red Wedge tour in March 1986. Originally released by Sly and The Family Stone in 1969.

1987

Cover Me With Love performed on the Renaissance Tour in October 1987. Sung by Dee C Lee. Songwriter unknown, more than likely Paul Weller.

Everlasting Love performed on the Cost of Loving Tour in February 1987. This is available on the *Full House* DVD which is an exclusive. Sung by Dee C Lee. Not a cover of the well known Love Affair hit.

1988

No tour.

1989

All the following are from the Revue Tours - Japan (June) or the infamous final concert at The Royal Albert Hall (July).

Depth Charge Dee C Lee on lead vocals. This was released on Dee's Slam Slam LP, *Free Your Feelings* in 1991.

I Can't Deny Myself Bassist Camelle Hinds on lead vocals. Songwriter was Camelle Hinds.

Instrumental (Title unknown) Saxophone based instrumental. Songwriter unknown.

Move (Dance All Night) Dee C Lee on lead vocals. This was released as a single by Dee in her Slam Slam project in 1990. Then later on the LP, *Free Your Feelings* in 1991.

Now Your Gone Dr Robert (Blow Monkeys) on lead vocals. Songwriter unknown.

Tender Love Dee C Lee on lead vocals. This was released on Dee's Slam Slam LP, *Free Your Feelings* in 1991.

That Spiritual Feeling was released by The Paul Weller Movement as a b-side on *Into Tomorrow*. It then resurfaced in 1993 as a remix on the *Sunflower* single. Written by Paul, Mick, Dee and Marco Nelson.

You'll Find Love Dee C Lee on lead vocals. This was released on Dee's Slam Slam LP, *Free Your Feelings* in 1991.

The story of many shoe's...

It was a real rollercoaster after The Jam. No one knew what to expect - there were highs and some lows, but it was a ride worth getting on!

Anthony Gardiner

I can still remember hearing about The Jam splitting up, it nearly killed me. I couldn't believe what Paul Weller had done. Then I heard *Speak Like A Child* and for the next few years every song they did was indelibly etched into my mind for ever. Those first few years worth of songs made up for losing the greatest band in the world in 1982, as I had a new greatest band from 1983 onwards!"

Charlie Bravo aka Col Baker

There are Jam fans and there are Paul Weller fans, but my flag has always been firmly planted in The Style Council's camp. During my teens, the Council helped shape my outlook on everything from music to politics to, inevitably, style. With the exception of the Fabs, no other band has had anywhere near as profound an effect on me, and as far as I'm concerned, they're still probably the best band in the world!

Eric Stephenson, Executive Director, Image Comics

Paul Weller has provided the soundtrack to my entire life and I will be forever grateful that The Style Council were there, playing in the background of my late teens. I fell in love to *Long Hot Summer* and *The Paris Match*, later mourning its loss to *Changing Of The Guard* and almost believing that he was writing just for me. Beautiful, haunting, uplifting, swinging and groovy, they had it all, and they dressed well too!

Old Flashy

The first few years were fantastic you never knew who would be playing on the records or what versions they would play live, Weller at his best.

Mark Anthony

Simply the best group so many memories, Keep on Burning. **Ian Dandy**

Magical Times, Magical Tunes, Magic. **Mark Venton**

THE STYLE COUNCIL

Following The Style Council back in the day was not an easy time for the fans...we had all lived through the highs of what The Jam achieved, not only through all the classic tracks and phenomenal gigs, but the fact that they were so close to the fans, and it was so easy for people to relate to the band.

TSC were a different (new) breed - far more experimental, more introverted and doing things for themselves and for the hell of it .. sometimes it was confusing, sometimes frustrating, but perseverance paid dividends - the list of classic PW songs from 83-89 still stand strong today - *Walls Come Tumbling Down, Shout To The Top, My Ever Changing Moods*, I could go on and on.

TSC not only took us on a magical musical mystery tour, with the vastly different styles of music recorded, but they introduced so much more to those who were keeping up with the pace - politics, humour, sarcasm, internationalism! TSC were a massive part of my life, and still are - they keep on burning for me.

Neil Allen, Birmingham

Edinburgh Playhouse 1984, Shout to the top, Deck Shoes & Pringle Jumpers.
Brian Leitch

The Style Council probably defined one of the most important aspects of music history.
Kareem El Farargy

Claudia Konijn (bass player for several TV clips) gets the original The Style Council member pin and that pin I've got these days! **Nick Fray**

Took me a while to get into The Style Council or where Weller was coming from, but when I did it opened whole new avenues or should I say Boulevards. I got into modern Jazz, house music and soul. Just loved the attention to detail, the sleeves & the sleeve notes. If The Jam were black & white the Style Council were definately technicolour! **Simon Franklin**

TSC - Great music, great style, still the best! - **Michael Melvin**

About time TSC were recognised as the pre-eminent English music collective!! Marvelling at Weller's genius transformation from Jam to The Style Council, you could hardly see the join.

Simon Barnes-Davies

Long Hot Summer and *Headstart For Happiness* makes life feel good. *You're The Best Thing* is the love I found, *A Man of Great Promise* is all the people I've loved and lost. Great lyrics, great music, great times.

Mark Hubble

The music is the diary of my young life.
Steve Neale

They put fire in my soul many years ago and it burns just as strong today. Keep the flame burning.

David Page

From the fevered anticipation of the release of *Speak Like A Child*, through to the 1985 appearance at Live Aid and the joy of many classic tunes, The Style Council era gave many memories never to be forgotten.

Martin Ling

THE STYLE COUNCIL

The Great Paul Weller

Imagine you're 24 years old and the lead singer and principle songwriter for Britain's most popular punk band, with a string of chart-topping hits in your wake and your popularity at its absolute peak, and you decide to disband the group to pursuit an entirely new genre of slick, soul and R&B influenced pop music that was the polar opposite of punk, which makes many of your former punk fans call you a traitor, sellout, and total poof. This was exactly what Paul Weller did in late 1982 when he disbanded The Jam and formed The Style Council, alienating tens of thousands of his fans worldwide and confounding millions more.

Strangely, other punk heroes had long ago abandoned punk and changed musical directions in a similar manner, as was the case with Elvis Costello in 1980 when he made *Get Happy*, which was his brilliant homage to Motown and Northern soul. But Weller and The Jam were bigger than Elvis - hell, they were bigger than the Clash too - in the UK and had a firmer grip on the hearts and minds of the working and middle classes, so Weller's defection was seen as a grotesque snubbing of his humble lower-class roots to become a posh and fashionable pop star singing about love and the moon in June instead of being the Pete Townsend and Ray Davies of his generation as he was with The Jam.

And with the opening bars of 1983's brilliant soul-funk, synth bass-driven *Long Hot Summer*, the former Mod revivalist and punk poet laureate embarked upon a new career as a fair-skinned Smokey Robinson, embracing a wide range of styles and influences, all packaged in slick and well-produced records that greatly distanced Weller from his work with The Jam. For a couple of records he still charted well in the UK, as he'd obviously not lost his great pop sense even if the styles had changed so dramatically, and Style Council's music became the soundtrack for the posh cool club kids all over the UK and Europe and suddenly jazz-soul pop bands and acts became all the rage, such as Sade, Everything But The Girl, Level 42, Blow Monkeys, Swing Out Sister and Simply Red, creating music a little less plastic and synthetic than that of the New Romantics, but with the same posh and sophisticated fashion sense. Even new wave stalwart Joe Jackson joined the fray with his brilliant jazz-pop classic, Body and Soul, which captured the moment and all this sophisti-pop madness in 1984 as well as anybody had.

The Style Council's music from 83-87 was timeless and often superb, and it was difficult not to find yourself in a European dance club and not hear at least one of their songs before the night was over. I can't remember all the times I found myself dancing to *Shout To The Top* or *Headstart For Happiness* or *My Ever Changing Moods* in Paris or Venice or Amsterdam or Metz; I'd been one of The Jam fans who thought Paul had gone crazy when he disbanded them, but I was also one of the countless Style Council fans who got his new music too. Posh and pretentious poof music? Maybe. But you could dance your ass off to it and it certainly set the mood for lovemaking. Since when is that such a bad thing?

Headstart For Happiness remains one of my favorite pop songs from that and just about any other era. It's a light and bouncy homage to classic Motown duets by Marvin Gaye and Tammi Terrell, and honestly it was a breath of fresh air right at about the time that synth pop and new wave music started to stink up the place. But even better was the magnificent slow-dance love song *You're The Best Thing*, The Style Council's magnum opus.

By Matthew C Scheck, Freelance writer, Philadelphia.

http://journalofdoubt.net

The Style Council conjured images of summer happiness and at times banished sadness in *The Paris Match*. A joy to grow up with and memories never to forget. Laughing at the *Speak Like A Child* video and feeling its joy. Loving every minute, influencing my thoughts then and now on how to treat people with care and respect. Lyrical inspiration for humanity. *Spin Driftin', Headstart For Happiness, A Man Of Great Promise, (When You) Call Me*, etc. Wonderful! Thank you.

Chris Willman

It has to be said those first few years 1983 -1985 were purely magical. Whether live or on record you just never knew what to expect. Musical direction? Arrangements? Weller not playing guitar! Guest vocalists! Artwork! Different sleeves for 7" and 12" singles! Sleeve notes! Masses of TV! Humour! and above all great songs! Some feelings do last forever.

Mark Anthony

I was 15 when The Jam split and thought my world had ended. Little did I know it had only just begun.
Martin Chubb

The Style Council still to this day are influencing my look. The greatest Mod band ever!
Warren Quigley

THE STYLE COUNCIL

The Style Council happened just at the right time. I was young and they were my life, if they were in it or on it then I had to have it. I am grown up now but Paul Weller still has that effect on me, only difference is I no longer buy Smash Hits! I can truly say The Style Council shaped my life. I became a Mod, got a scooter and live that lifestyle to this day. I met my friends and wife through the mod and scooter scenes and have two beautiful kids who will one day know all about their Uncle Paul.

The Tartan Target

They were a fantastic band and I don't think they got the recognition they deserved. I was at the final gig and although it was totally different to anything they had done and not at all what I was expecting, I really enjoyed it. It was good that The Style Council experimented with as many different music styles as they did. I listen to their stuff all the time and still love it as much today as I did 20 years ago, the lyrics and the music say so much

In 2005 it was great that Paul has the brass section back and we are getting to hear some of those brilliant songs played live again. Shout To The Top!!

Mel O' Toole

THE STYLE COUNCIL

TSC were the best. Not only were the tunes outstanding (they still do it for me now), the band was the complete package, a cult movement in itself. Style, passion and intelligence. Continental cool. Great sleeve notes, immaculate threads, iconic photo shoots, a rocking Hammond, long hot summers... The torch keeps on burning!

Graeme Atkins

Flashbacks of *NME* full page adverts, album and single covers, the great Council Meetin Part 2 gig at Liverpool Royal Court. Watching bewilderd at the *JerUSAlem* film at The Royal Albert Hall, thinking (rightly) how good the *Confessions* album was. Finally a couple of years ago getting *Modernism* on CD - so many great memoirs!!

Paul Brindle

I loved The Style Council. Weller goes pop soul, tremendous lyrically and with melodies that still get me singing along at full throttle. In my opinion easily his best period (an opinion usually met with an 'oh come come' by Weller fans). *Shout To The Top* gets into my top ten singles, I even like *The Cost Of Loving* and I still own a pair of Bass Weejuns.

Steve Rinaldi

The Style Council helped me get through my teenage years. I would hang on every word Weller spoke, so much so that I even joined the young socialists for a time! I remember running to the record shop when every new record was released and running back home even faster to play it on the stereo. It was a gloriously exciting time for me!

Craig Miller, Brisbane, Australia

To me The Style Council meant fun, adventure and experimentation. The quality of music, as in every part of Paul Weller's career, was extremely high and soulful. From the Cappuccino Kid's musings to the pretentious carry-on of *JerUSAlem* it was always interesting. It had its serious side too and that was the music. Some of it worked some of it got lost in the creation process but in the 80's can you think of a band who were that good, that interesting and that challenging?

Robert McNamara

Post TSC with Helen and Camelle

The Style Council up to the orange album! *Café Bleu* I liked, though not all of it worked for me. *Our Favourite Shop* was a classic apart from the Lenny Henry track, it is the one I need to skip all the time, but apart from that that album was an absolute classic. *The Cost of Loving*, I must admit that album for me, I wasn't really into it, I lost interest a little bit I must admit. I got back into TSC again at the *Confessions of a Pop Group* album, some real surprises on that. I thought they were testing themselves, which I think Paul's done with his new album, *22 Dreams* as well.

Gary Crowley

Solo with Style Concillor's - Steve, Camelle, Helen, Paul, (Jacko) and Zeke

THE STYLE COUNCIL

I think that music journalists during the 1990s were very revisionist when it came to writing about The Style Council's part in the 80s music scene, especially those working for Melody Maker, who seemed to slag them off of all the time (even when Paul Weller never had a record out!). It was kind of "everything The Jam did was great and everything The Style Council did was rubbish". Therefore I was quite happy a couple of years ago when I heard ex-*NME* journalist Stuart Maconie and a couple of other panelists on a music singles/roundup radio show say that it was about time that The Style Council were rehabilitated in the general public's eyes and that he wished that the solo Paul Weller would write a new single that was as vibrant and carefree as *Speak Like A Child* was and I sort of agree with him.

Also on BBC Three's recent *Pop on Trial* Miranda Sawyer said that The Style Council were a much underrated band in the 80's. But really they weren't under rated in the 80's, they were pretty damn big, it's just in retrospect that they've been diminished.

Gareth Collins

Great Big Groove!!
Al Stomp

They put fire in my soul many years ago and it burns just as strong today. Keep the flame burning.

David Page

Warsaw, Poland. 1985. The venue for the *Walls Come Tumbling Down* video

I saw The Style Council on the 1st tour in March '84 at the now legendary Glasgow Apollo. Billy Bragg got pelters, your shoes stuck to the carpet and the stage was so high their was never gonna be a crush at the front. Can still recall the whole buzz of how Weller's first gig in Glasgow post Jam was gonna be - Seeing the Council logo on Mick's Hammond (along with his rocking of it), blokes with bowling shoes, boating blazers and Parkas, the girls with the bobs and dogtooth skirts and of course the timeless coolness of Weller. Happy days and still the most under rated band of the time.

Jamie Walker

Very special days. Brixton Academy, Margate Winter Gardens. Mixing great music with politics, Loafers, Blazers and white trousers! Driving all the way from Norwich to Glasgow SECC to hear the opening rift of *The Cost of Loving*. Thanks for those special memories boys and girls. They will live in the memory forever.
Keep on burning.

Kerry Warren

THE STYLE COUNCIL

They got me through the difficult mid teen years after the break up of The Jam with their sound, lyrics and colourful sleeve notes. In short, brilliant. Still as good sounding today.

Paul Taylor

They said Weller had lost his way after The Jam. Oh, how they were wrong !!

Darrell Ambidge

The Tour Band 1984.

Paul Weller wrote some of his best songs during his sabbatical with The Style Council - from savvy, socially-conscious pop to effortless love songs. Between 1983 and 1985, it's as if Paul was happiest (professionally, at least), taking chances, usurping expectations, borrowing magpie-like from the past and re-moulding it for the present (in true Mod fashion)

John Reed

THE STYLE COUNCIL

The Style Council were without doubt the most professional, stylish, and exciting band from what was a musically boring 80's.

Billy Hughes

It is now 25 years since Paul pulled the plug on The Jam and formed The Style Council. History has now proved beyond doubt that it was the right decision.

Dennis Munday

THE STYLE COUNCIL

Hindsight is a beautiful thing and with this in mind I think we can safely say that the songs and spirit of the "Council" have matured to a fine legacy.

Steve White

The Style Council were the best live band around and not a session player in sight!

Helen Turner

TSC were acclaimed and believed we were the hottest band around globally. That's how confident we were and I was tasting it!

Camelle Hinds

For me The Style Council will always represent youth, vitality, sunshine and friendships made that have pretty much endured. I loved it.

Paul Weller

Whatever is said about The Style Council, there is no doubt in my mind that Paul's current solo success owes as much to the Council as it does The Jam.

Dennis Munday

The Style Council was a unique experience. I'm so proud that I was a part of the whole scene and in these days of homogenised pop music, it just emphasises just what a great band The Style Council were!

Steve Sidelnyk

UK DISCOGRAPHY - SINGLES

Detailed as: Song title; Release Code; Release Date; Highest chart position

Speak Like A Child. TSC1. March 1983. Number 4

7" - Speak Like A Child / Party Chambers. Only released on 7"

Money Go Round. TSC(X)2. May 1983. Number 11

7" - Money Go Round (Part 1) / Money Go Round (Part 2)
Initial limited copies with double-sided picture insert.

12" - Money Go Round (Parts 1 & 2) / Headstart For Happiness; Mick's Up
Different sleeve to 7"

À Paris EP. TSC(X)3. August 1983. Number 3

7" - Long Hot Summer; Party Chambers / The Paris Match; Le Départ

12" - Long Hot Summer (Extended Version)/ Party Chambers; The Paris Match;
Le Départ. Different sleeve to 7"

A Solid Bond In Your Heart. TSC4/TSCG4. November 1983. Number 11

7" - A Solid Bond In Your Heart/ It Just Came To Pieces In My Hands;
A Solid Bond In Your Heart (Instrumental). Also gatefold sleeve [TSCG4]
Different sleeve. Only released on 7"

My Ever Changing Moods. TSC(X)5. March 1984. Number 5

7" - My Ever Changing Moods / Mick's Company
Released in cardboard and paper (no gloss) picture sleeves.

12" - My Ever Changing Moods (Long Version)/ Mick's Company; Spring,
Summer, Autumn. Different sleeve to 7"

Groovin'. TSC(X)6. May 1984. Number 5. Double A-Side

7" - You're The Best Thing/ The Big Boss Groove
Released in cardboard and paper (no gloss) picture sleeves.

12" - You're The Best Thing (Long Version);You're The Dub Thing/The Big Boss Groove (Ext). Different sleeve to 7"

Shout To The Top. TSC(X)7. October 1984. Number 7

7" - Shout To The Top/Ghosts Of Dachau

12" - Shout To The Top (Extended); Shout To The Top (Instrumental) / The Piccadilly Trail; Ghosts Of Dachau. Different sleeve to 7"
Label reads, 'Dachau was a Nazi concentration camp, the scene of mass murders.'

Soul Deep. MINE(X)1. December 1984. Number 22
Released under the banner of "The Council Collective"

7" - Soul Deep (Part 1)/ Soul Deep (Part 2)

12" - Soul Deep/A Miners Point
Not credited but this is Part 1 & 2 joined. Code diff: MINE X1.

12" Limited - Soul Deep (Club Mix)/ Soul Deep
Not credited but this is Part 1 & 2 joined. Note code diff: MINEX 1

Walls Come Tumbling Down! TSC(X)8. May 1985. Number 6

7" - Walls Come Tumbling Down!/ The Whole Point II; Bloodsports
b-side credited to "The Council Folk Club"

12" - Walls Come Tumbling Down!; Spin' Drifting / The Whole Point II; Bloodsports. Limited copies included a black & white poster and sticker sleeve.

Come To Milton Keynes. TSC(X)9. July 1985. Number 23

7" - Come To Milton Keynes/ (When You) Call Me
Also available in a gatefold sleeve [TSCG9]. Different picture to 7" & 12"

12" - Come To Milton Keynes; Our Favourite Shop (Club Mix) / (When You) Call Me; The Lodgers (Club Mix). Different sleeve to 7" releases.

The Lodgers. TSC(X)10. September 1985. Number 13

7" - The Lodgers / The Big Boss Groove (Live); You're The Best Thing (Live)

7" double pack - The Lodgers/The Big Boss Groove (Live); You're The Best Thing (Live); You're The Best Thing/Long Hot Summer
Limited double pack [DP1] with extra single in unique sleeve.

12" - The Lodgers (Extended Mix) / The Big Boss Groove (Live); Move On Up (Live); You're The Best Thing (Live); Medley - Money-Go-Round (Live); Soul Deep (Live); Strength Of Your Nature (Live). Double-sided colour insert for 7" & 12". Sleeve credit "Featuring D.C. Lee."

Have You Ever Had It Blue. CINE(X)1. March 1986. Number 14

7" - Have You Ever Had It Blue/ Mr Cool's Dream

7" Cassette - Have You Ever Had It Blue/ Mr Cool's Dream

7" Cassette pack - Have You Ever Had It Blue (Uncut version) / With Everything To Lose (Live in London, Dec. '85). Written on cassette; 'originally recorded March '84.' Limited cassette [CINEC1] in plastic 'blue' embossed wallet & Insert.

12" - Have You Ever Had It Blue (Uncut version) / Have You Ever Had It Blue (Cut version); Mr Cool's Dream

It Didn't Matter. TSC(X)12. January 1987. Number 9

7" - It Didn't Matter/ All Year Round

12" - It Didn't Matter/ It Didn't Matter (Instrumental); All Year Round
Initial copies included circular 'cut out hole' in back of the sleeve.

Waiting. TSC(X)13. March 1987. Number 52

7" - Waiting/ Francoise

12" - Waiting (Vocal); Francoise (Vocal)/ Francoise (Theme from JerUSAlem); Waiting (Instrumental)

Wanted * or Waiter There's Some Soup In My Flies. TSC(X)14. October 1987. Number 20

7" - Wanted/ The Cost Of Loving; The Cost. Plastic & paper labels.
Plastic label notes b-side as 'Instrumental' & 'Vocal' versions.

12" - Wanted/ The Cost Of Loving; The Cost. Glossy inner sleeve with TSC discography.

CD - Wanted; The Cost Of Loving; The Cost

CASSETTE - Wanted/ The Cost Of Loving; The Cost
Not credited, b-sides have an 'Instrumental' version & a new slow 'vocal.'

Life At A Top Peoples Health Farm. TSC(X)15. May 1988. Number 28

7" - Life At A Top Peoples Health Farm/ Sweet Loving Ways

12" - Spank! (Live At A Top Peoples Health Club); Life At A Top Peoples Health Farm (7" version) / Life At A Top Peoples Health Farm (Um & Argh Mix); Sweet Loving Ways

CD - Spank! (Live At A Top Peoples Health Club); Life At A Top Peoples Health Farm (7" version); Life At A Top Peoples Health Farm (Um & Argh Mix); Sweet Loving Ways. Both **7"** & **12"** issued in TSC inner sleeve.

How She Threw It All Away. TSC(X)16. July 1988. Number 41

7" - How She Threw It All Away; Love The First Time / Long Hot Summer;
I Do Like To Be B-Side The A-Side*

12" - How She Threw It All Away; Love The First Time / Long Hot Summer (Tom Mix);I Do Like To Be B-side The A-Side*

CD - How She Threw It All Away; Love The First Time; Long Hot Summer (Tom Mix);I Do Like To Be B-Side The A-Side*

*Credited as being "Performed by Mixed Companions", this is a new version of Mick's Company, originally released in 1984. TSC inner sleeve on **7"** & **12"**

Promised Land. TSC(X)17. February 1989. Number 27

7" - Promised Land (Juan Atkins Mix)/ Can You Still Love Me?

7" Box - Promised Land/ Can You Still Love Me? Limited box set [TSCB17]
Different picture sleeve from 7"; Numbered single; Colour poster; sticker.

12" - Promised Land (Longer version); Promised Land (Pianopella version)/
Can You Still Love Me? (Dub); Can You Still Love Me? (Vocal)

12" Limited - Promised Land (Joe Smooths alternate club mix)/
Can You Still Love Me? (Club vocal); Can You Still Love Me? (12 O'Clock Dub)
Limited club release [TSCXS] in different sleeve to 7" & 12" release.

CD - Promised Land (Longer version); Promised Land (Pianopella version);
Can You Still Love Me? (Dub); Can You Still Love Me? (Vocal)
There are 2 versions of the CD single - Silver and black/white discs.

Long Hot Summer '89. LHS(X)1. May 1989. Number 48

7" - Long Hot Summer '89 mix / Everybody's On The Run*

12" - Long Hot Summer '89 mix (Extended version) / Everybody's On The Run (Version one); Everybody's On The Run (Version two)

CD - Long Hot Summer '89 mix (Extended version); Everybody's On The Run (Version one); Everybody's On The Run (Version two) *Lead vocals by Brian J Powell.

Like A Gun. Acid Jazz. JAZID 9T. Not officially released.

12" - Like A Gun; Like A Gun (Safe Sax Mix); Like A Gun (Dub Version); Like A Gun (Radio Edit)

Recorded by the unknown 'King Truman' but in reality TSC in disguise. Only 200 copies got out before the planned release date. In 2008, this single continues to sell in excess of £150.

E.P. SERIES

A 6 monthly three EP set was planned. Only TSCEP 1 to 3 appeared.

Café Bleu. 7" - TSCEP 1; CD - TSCCD 101. December '87

7" & CD - Headstart For Happiness; Here's One That Got Away/ Blue Café, Strength of Your Nature

The Birds & The B's. 7" - TSCEP 2; CD - TSCCD 102. December '87

7" & CD - Piccadilly Trail; It Just Came To Pieces In My Hands/ Spin' Drifting; Spring Summer Autumn

Mick Talbot is Agent 88. 7" - TSCEP 3; CD - TSCCD 103. December '87

7" & CD - Mick's Up; Party Chambers/ Mick's Blessings; Mick's Company

7" UK PROMOTIONAL SINGLES

All are promotional white labels with sticker sleeve and same tracks on each side unless stated.

Speak Like A Child [TSC DJ1]

The Paris Match [TSC DJ3]
One sided

Long Hot Summer/Paris Match [TSC DJ3]
2 tracks

Long Hot Summer/Paris Match [TSC D3]
2 tracks. No centre. Jukebox

A Solid Bond In Your Heart/It Just Came To Pieces In My Hands [TSC D4]
No centre. Jukebox only. No instrumental version

Walls Come Tumbling Down! [TSC DJ8]

Walls Come Tumbling Down/Bloodsports [TSCD8]
2 tracks. No centre. Jukebox

The Lodgers/Big Boss Groove (Live) [TSC D10]
2 tracks. No centre. Jukebox. No *You're The Best Thing*

Wanted [TSC 14]

Life At A Top Peoples Health Farm/ Sweet Loving Ways [TSC 15]

Life At A Top Peoples Health Farm (Edit)/ Sweet Loving Ways [TSC ED15]
Different label design

How She Threw It All Away [TSC DJ 16]
1 track

12" UK PROMOTIONAL SINGLES

All are promotional white labels with stickered sleeve unless stated.

Money Go Round/Money Go Round (Dance Mix) [TSC X 2]
Dance Mix unreleased in the UK

Long Hot Summer/Long Hot Summer [TSC DM3/X3]
Two x Extended mixes

My Ever Changing Moods [TSC X 5]

Me Ship Came In [Cafe 1] Cafe Bleu Sampler
Me Ship Came In, Dropping Bombs On The Whitehouse and Headstart For Happiness.

You're The Best Thing [TSC X 6]

Shout To The Top [TSC X 7]

Soul Deep [MINE X1- DJ] 1 sided

Walls Come Tumbling Down! [TSC X 8]

Come To Milton Keynes [TSC C9 DJ]
(When You) Call Me, Internationalists, Boy Who Cried Wolf.
Tracks 2 and 3 are not on UK release

The Lodgers (Extended Mix) /The Lodgers (Club Mix) [TSC CM 10]
TSC promotional sleeve. The Extended Mix differs from the actual Extended Mix released in the UK. The Club Mix appeared on the previous singles b-side.

Have You Ever Had It Blue [CINE X1 DJ]

The Style Council Club Mix [TSC CM1]

Club Mix of Our Favourite Shop and The Lodgers; With Everything To Lose. Special TSC purple sleeve.

It Didn't Matter/Right To Go [Cost 1]

Different b-side to standard release. In special TSC sleeve.

Angel/Heavens Above [Cost 2]

Double a-side was never released. In special TSC sleeve.

Spank! (Live At A Top Peoples Health Farm) [TSC X 15 DJ]

Confusing title but this is identical to the UK 12" release of Life At A Top Peoples Health Farm. It does not credit Sweet Loving Ways and the credited Extended Mix is actually the Um & Argh Mix.

I Do Like To Be B-Side The A-Side/ Long Hot Summer (Tom Mix) [TSCX16 DJ]

Different title but this is from the 'How She Threw It All Away' release.

Promised Land [TSC X17 DJ]

Promised Land (Club Mix) [TSCXS 17DJ]

Standard Club Mix, however, Radio Edit replaces the Pianopella version.

Everybody's On The Run [LHS X1 DJ]

Different title but as per standard release of Long Hot Summer 1989

UK SHEET MUSIC

Singles

Speak Like A Child (14076)
Money Go Round (14085)
A Paris EP (14090)
A Solid Bond In Your Heart (14096)
My Ever Changing Moods / Spring Summer Autumn (14110)
Groovin - You're The Best Thing/Big Boss Groove (14132)
Shout To The Top (14154)
Walls Come Tumbling Down (14245)
The Lodgers (14258)
Have You Ever Had It Blue (14280)
It Didn't Matter (14320)
Wanted (14358)
Life At A Top Peoples Health Farm (14379)

Albums

Café Bleu (14109)
Our Favourite Shop (14249)
Our Favourite Shop (14249) Updated folio - 3 extra singles added;
    (You're The Best Thing, Long Hot Summer, My Ever Changing Moods)
The Cost of Loving (14326)
IMP Presents The Style Council (14339) 8 singles
The Singular Adventures of The Style Council (14423)
Confessions of A Pop Group (21344)

ADDITIONAL RELEASES

The Style Council Fan Club Flexi Disk (LYN 15344/45)

7" - It Just Came To Pieces In My Hands (live Coventry)/ Speak Like A Child (live London). Limited edition fan club only flexi disk. 1984

Le Club Rouge (Australia only, 1984)

12" - Speak Like A Child, A Solid Bond In Your Heart, Big Boss Groove / Money Go Round (Club Mix 7:42)

Australia only live single (September 1985)

(When You) Call Me (Melbourne, Australia, 18th August 1985)

The Hit Magazine (Hot 001; Sept 1985)

7" - Walls Come Tumbling Down (Manchester Apollo, 14th June 1985) Free with *The Hit* magazine, Issue 1.

New Musical Express (GIV2; Sept 1985)

7" - My Ever Changing Moods (Liverpool Empire, 15th June 1985) Free with *New Musical Express*, September 1985.

An Afro-Euro Compilation (AELP1)

The compilation album, *A Taste of Summer* was released on Polydor with a new version of *Long Hot Summer* (JezaMix). There is also a 4 track promo 12" (taste1). This was an exclusive Mix at the time though since then an exact version was released under a different name (Tom Mix).

Unofficial interview (STYLE 7; April 1988)

7" **picture disc** - Limited to 2000 copies
7" **blue vinyl** - Limited to 1000 copies
7" **x 2 clear vinyl** - 1 sided clear vinyl double pack - Limited to 100 copies and exclusive to Adrian's Records, Wickford.
7" **black vinyl** - Limited to 25 copies. Initial test press

1988 Interview LP (TSCIN-1)
Confessions of A Pop Group promo interview LP with Paul and Mick.

Promised Land. DMC Mixes 1 (March 1989)

12" - Promised Land (Latin Orchestral Workout) 6:00
ReMixed by Brothers In Rhythm. String arrangement and all instrumentation by Steve Anderson. Latin riddims and boomin bass by Dave Seaman.

'DMC Mix records are available exclusively to club members for use in their discotheques and bars and to Radio programmes for their information and convenience.'

Old Gold series

7" - Speak Like A Child/Long Hot Summer
Part of the 'Old Gold' series (Old Gold. OG9924;1990) No TSC picture sleeve.

7" - You're The Best Thing/My Ever Changing Moods
Part of the 'Old Gold' series (Old Gold. OG9929;1990). No TSC picture sleeve.

Rare 4 trax EP (Modernist Music 001; 1991)

7" - Sure Is Sure.

Limited 'bootleg' 4 track EP featuring The Style Council, Paul Weller, The Jam & Bruce Foxton. Available in 3 picture sleeves. Limited to 25, 75 and 400 copies. At the time of its release *Sure Is Sure* had never been released. This version was straight from the acetate recording.

Days of Speed (SPEED 2. Independiente)

Headstart For Happiness (Conrad Sohm, Dornbin, 15th May 2001)
Down In The Seine (Olympia, Dublin, 19th March 2001)

The 2nd CD released to promote Paul's live album, 'Days of Speed'

Extracts from the Complete Adventures of The Style Council (SCBS 1)

CD - Speak Like A Child, Long Hot Summer, My Ever Changing Moods, The Whole Point of No Return, Headstart For Happiness, You're The Best Thing, Shout To The Top, Down In The Seine, Have You Ever Had It Blue, Heavens Above, The Cost of Loving (12" version), It's A Very Deep Sea, Can You Still Love Me?, That Spiritual Feeling, Sure Is Sure.

NON STYLE COUNCIL [BUT LINKED]

The following releases feature Paul Weller or Mick Talbot during TSC years.

Animal Nightlife - Mr Solitaire
Paul sings backing vocals. Reached number 25 in August 1984

Band Aid - Do They Know It's Christmas
Featuring Paul on vocals. Number 1 in December 1984. Personal Christmas message from Paul on the b-side.

Various artist compilation - Son of Jobs For The Boys
A 14 track compilation released for awareness of unemployment in Merseyside. '112 jobs for 32,000 school leavers.' The exclusive TSC track was *Come To Milton Keynes* (instrumental). Limited copies contained a bonus 7" EP featuring Dee C Lee as part of the Dust Choir on *Another Fly Network* (lies1).

Dizzi Heights - A Gospel! (Tell it like it is)
With his named changed from Dizzy and the song title extended, this Weller penned track from *Café Bleu* was released in 1985 on Parlophone (12Dizz1). It is the only place to find these versions and an instrumental mix of the song.

The Gospel! (Tell It Like It Is)/ The Gospel! (Tell It Like It Is) (Dub Mix), The Gospel! (Tell It Like It Is) (Instrumental)

Chairman Of The Board - Loverboy
Featuring Paul & Mick. Reached number 56 in 1986

Jazz Defektors - LP
Ooh! This Feeling was recorded at Solid Bond Studios and four of the songs were Mixed by Paul and Mick. The Jazz Defektors appeared in the *Absolute Beginners* movie and TSC's *Have You Ever Had It Blue* promotional video.

Dizzi Heights - Would I Find Love
The b-side to this single has another version of *The Gospel*, the Weller penned track from *Café Bleu*. This version was remixed by Bert Bevans who also mixed for TSC. Released in 1986 on Parlophone.

Boogie Box High - Jive Talkin
Rumoured to feature Mick on keyboards. Reached number 7, July 1987

Lisa M - Going Back To My Roots
Going Back To My Roots (Dynamite Mix) Going Back To My Roots (Back To The Beats Mix)/ Make It Right. All versions were produced by Paul and Mick and engineered by Brendan Lynch at Solid Bond Studios. Released by Zomba records in 1989. JIVE(T) 221.

COVERED

The following artists have covered Style Council songs.

Tracie Young - Spring, Summer, Autumn

From Tracie's debut LP *Far From The Hurting Kind* in 1984

Dee C Lee - The Paris Match

From the b-side of her single *See The Day* in 1985

Tracie Young - (When You) Call Me

Single released on Polydor in 1986. From the unreleased 2nd LP.

Fire Island featuring Loleatta Holloway - Shout To The Top

A top 25 UK single and a massive number 1 hit on the US Club play singles chart. Released in April 1998 on Junior Boys Own records. Fire Island are a dance duo of Pete Heller and Terry Farley with Loleatta (born 1946), who has had UK top 40 hits. The well known David Morales played on drums.

There are a multitude of Mixes available, eight at the last count. Radio Edit, Industry Standard Radio Edit, Extended Mix, Industry Standard Uprising Mix, Club 69 Vocal Mix, Frankie Knuckles Classic Club Mix, Industry Standard No Smoke Without Fire Mix and Roach Motel Ruff & Raw Mix.

911 - You're The Best Thing

From their top 10 LP *Their It Is* in 1999. The first boy band to cover TSC

The Lodgers
An unknown Japanese band on a compilation CD.

Lato - It Just Came To Pieces In My Hands

German band Lato on Firestation Tower Records in 2001 (FST031)

Gazzara - Homebreakers

Italian Gazzara released this on his *Spirit of Summer* LP in 2002 on Imra.

Les Cappuccinos - Our Favourite Shop

Excellent reproduction by the Japanese Mod band Les Cappuccinos.

UK DISCOGRAPHY - LONG PLAYERS

Introducing The Style Council. Mini LP, September 1983. Dutch/Japanese

<u>LP/CD</u> Long Hot Summer*; Headstart For Happiness; Speak Like A Child/Long Hot Summer (Club Mix); The Paris Match; Mick's Up; Money Go Round (Club Mix). *Though not stated, this is the 'extended version.'
LP Code: 815277-1. CD Code: 815-277-2

<u>CASS</u> Long Hot Summer; The Paris Match; Mick's Up; Party Chambers; Speak Like A Child/Long Hot Summer (Club Mix); Headstart For Happiness; Le Depart; Money Go Round (Club Mix). Play order changed.
Code: 815-531-4. Two extra tracks Party Chambers and Lè Depart.

Café Bleu. TSC (LP) (MC) 1. March 1984. Number 2

<u>LP/CASS/CD</u> Mick's Blessings; The Whole Point of No Return; Me Ship Came In!; Blue Café; The Paris Match; My Ever Changing Moods; Dropping Bombs On The Whitehouse/A Gospel; Strength of Your Nature; You're The Best Thing; Here's One That Got Away; Headstart For Happiness; Council Meetin'.

Whole Point of No Return is not credited on sleeve, but is credited on the record label. With inner sleeve and a 16 page booklet.
CD Code: 817-535-2. CASS: Different sleeve to LP & CD

Our Favourite Shop. TSC (LP) (MC) 2. May 1985. Number 1

<u>LP/CASS/CD</u> Homebreakers; All Gone Away; Come To Milton Keynes; Internationalists; A Stones Throw Away; The Stand Up Comics Instructions; Boy Who Cried Wolf/ A Man of Great Promise; Down In The Seine; The Lodgers*; Luck; With Everything To Lose; Our Favourite Shop; Walls Come Tumbling Down! *The Lodgers (or She Was Only A Shopkeepers Daughter) was added to title on lyric sheet on LP & CASS only.

<u>LP</u> Inner lyric sleeve; Black & white picture dated February 1985.
<u>Cass</u> Side B. 'Gary Crowley meets the Council' - Full track by track interview with Paul & Mick at Solid Bond Studios. Different sleeve to the LP/CD.
CD Code: 825-700-2. Shout To The Top (USA Mix) is an extra track.

Our Favourite Shop - Deluxe
26th February 2007. Polydor 9838703

'Deluxe' edition was released a year after the planned 21 year anniversary. It contained the original LP and a CD of bonus songs, including unreleased demos. No other LP has yet had the 'deluxe' edition treatment.

CD 1
Homebreakers; All Gone Away; Come To Milton Keynes; Internationalists; A Stones Throw Away; The Stand Up Comics Instructions; Boy Who Cried Wolf; A Man of Great Promise; Down In The Seine; The Lodgers*; Luck; With Everything To Lose; Our Favourite Shop; Walls Come Tumbling Down! Shout To The Top (New Mix); Shout To The Top (Instrumental)

CD 2
The Piccadilly Trail, Ghosts of Dachau ("Dachau was a Nazi concentration camp, the scene of mass murders"),Spin' Drifting, The Whole Point of No Return, Bloodsports, (When You) Call Me, Our Favourite Shop, The Lodgers (or She Was Only a Shopkeeper's Daughter) (Club/Dance Mix),The Lodgers (or She Was Only a Shopkeeper's Daughter) (Extended Single version), The Big Boss Groove (live), Move On Up (live), You're The Best Thing (live), Money Go Round/Soul Deep/Strength of Your Nature medley (live), A Stones Throw Away (Demo), (When You) Call Me (Demo), A Casual Affair, Soul Deep, The Lodgers, Internationalists (Demo), Everything To Lose (Blue Remix), Our Favourite Shop (Alternative)

Home & Abroad. TSC (LP) (MC) 3. May 1986. Number 8

LP,CASS My Ever Changing Moods; The Lodgers; Headstart For Happiness; (When You) Call Me; The Whole Point of No Return/With Everything To Lose; Homebreakers; Shout To The Top; Walls Come Tumbling Down!; Internationalists.

LP Initial copies with discography on an obi wrap-around; inner sleeve.
CD Code: 829 143-2: Includes two extra tracks, Big Boss Groove and Our Favourite Shop.

The Cost of Loving. TSC (LP) (MC) 4. February 1987. Number 2

LP,CASS,CD It Didn't Matter; Right To Go/ Heavens Above; Fairy Tales/ Angel; Walking The Night/ Waiting; The Cost of Loving; A Womans Song.*
*Not credited on the sleeve.

LP Initial copies with 2x12" (45rpm). Orange Gatefold sleeve with two glossy inner lyric sleeves. Later released as a single LP.

CD & CASS Different sleeve to initial LP release.

Confessions of A Pop Group. TSC (LP) (MC) 5. June 1988. Number 15

LP,CASS,CD It's A Very Deep Sea; The Story of Someone's Shoe; Changing of The Guard; The Little Boy In A Castle; The Gardener of Eden (a Three Piece Suite)/ Life At A Top Peoples Health Farm; Why I Went Missing; How She Threw It All Away; Iwasadoledadstoyboy; Confessions 1,2 & 3; Confessions of A Pop Group. LP Fold out lyric sheet showing the Dan Davis paintings.

The Singular Adventures of TSC. TSCTV1. March 1989. Number 3

LP You're The Best Thing*; Have You Ever Had It Blue*; Money Go Round*; My Ever Changing Moods*; Long Hot Summer*; The Lodgers*; Walls Come Tumbling Down/Shout To The Top!; Wanted; It Didn't Matter; Speak Like A Child; A Solid Bond In Your Heart; Life At A Top Peoples Health Farm; Promised Land.

* Have a different version to the CD - The original 7" single versions.

CD/CASS You're The Best Thing (Alternate Mix); Have You Ever Had It Blue (12" version); Money Go Round (12" version); My Ever Changing Moods (12" version); Long Hot Summer '89 (12" version); The Lodgers (Alternate Mix); Walls Come Tumbling Down; Shout To The Top; Wanted; It Didn't Matter; Speak Like A Child; A Solid Bond In Your Heart; Life At A Top Peoples Health Farm; Promised Land; How She Threw It All Away$; Waiting.$

2 extra tracks$; Alternate versions or 12" versions indicated are different to those on the LP and Cassette.

Modernism: A New Decade. TSCLP6; TSCLP6-1 & 2 (double). 1998

LP That Spiritual Thing; Everybodys On The Run; Love of The World; Sure Is Sure/ A New Decade; Can You Still Love Me; The World Must Come Together; Hope (Feelings Gonna Getcha')

This was the rejected 1989 album. Released exclusively as CD 5 within TSC box set in 1998. Promotional LP's were released, single and double. Identical tracks on each.

The Style Council: In Concert. 533 143-2. February 1998.

CD/CASS Meeting (Up) Over Yonder; Up For Grabs; Long Hot Summer; One Nation Under A Groove; Le Depart; Spring, Summer, Autumn; Hanging Onto A Memory; It Just Came To Pieces In My Hands; Here's One That Got Away; My Ever Changing Moods; A Man of Great Promise; Boy Who Cried Wolf; A Stone's Throw Away; Speak Like A Child; Mick's Up; You're The Best Thing; Move On Up; Down In The Seine; It's A Very Deep Sea; Heavens Above.

The Complete Adventures of The Style Council
5 CD Box Set. 1998. Universal. 557790-2 to 557794-2

Each CD was in a cardboard picture sleeve. Box contains lyric sheet, Polydor book. Initial copies from HMV stores contained a strictly limited and rare **special edition** of *Mr Cool's Dream: The Complete History of The Style Council.*

CD 1 Speak Like A Child; Party Chambers (Vocal Version); Money Go Round (Bert Bevans Alternate Remix); Headstart For Happiness; Mick's Up; Long Hot Summer; The Paris Match; Le Départ; A Solid Bond In Your Heart; It Just Came To Pieces In My Hands; My Ever Changing Moods; Mick's Company; Spring Summer Autumn; Mick's Blessings; The Whole Point of No Return; Me Ship Came In!; Blue Café; The Paris Match; My Ever Changing Moods; Dropping Bombs On The Whitehouse; A Gospel.

CD 2 Strength of Your Nature; You're The Best Thing; Here's One That Got Away; Headstart For Happiness; Council Meetin'; The Big Boss Groove; Shout To The Top; Ghosts of Dachau; The Piccadilly Trail; Soul Deep (Bert Bevans Remix); Walls Come Tumbling Down!; The Whole Point II; Bloodsports; Spin' Drifting; Homebreakers; All Gone Away; Come To Milton Keynes; Internationalists; A Stones Throw Away; The Stand Up Comic's Instructions; Boy Who Cried Wolf.

CD 3 A Man of Great Promise; Down In The Seine; The Lodgers (or She Was Only A Shopkeepers Daughter); Luck; With Everything To Lose; Our Favourite Shop; (When You) Call Me; Have You Ever Had It Blue (Uncut Version); Mr Cool's Dream; It Didn't Matter; All Year Round; Right To Go; Heavens Above; Fairy Tales; Angel; Walking The Night; Waiting; The Cost of Loving; A Womans Song; Françoise.

CD 4 Wanted * or Waiter Theres Some Soup In My Flies; The Cost of Loving (12" version) {Slow Version}; Life At A Top Peoples Health Farm (Um & Argh Mix); Sweet Loving Ways; It's A Very Deep Sea; The Story of Someone's Shoe; Changing of The Guard; The Little Boy In A Castle; A Dove Flew Down From The Elephant; The Gardener of Eden (A Three Piece Suite); In The Beginning; The Gardener of Eden; Mourning The Passing of Time; Why I Went Missing; How She Threw It All Away; Iwasadoledadstoyboy; Confessions 1, 2 & 3; Confessions of A Pop Group; In Love For The First Time; I Do Like To Be B-Side The A-Side - The Mixed Companions.

CD 5 Promised Land (Longer version); Can You Still Love Me? Long Hot Summer '89; Everybody's On The Run.

Modernism: A New Decade Running time 49.33

A New Decade; Can You Still Love Me? The World Must Come Together; Hope (Feelings Gonna Getcha'); That Spiritual Thing; Everybodys On The Run; Love of The World; Sure Is Sure.

COMPILATIONS/OTHERS

Track titles and spelling shown are exactly as they appear on the release.

Interview picture disc. LP. BAK 2032. 1985.

<u>LP</u> Interview from the Australian tour, 1985. Colour double sided picture disc.

The Songs of Paul Weller 1982 - 1988. EMI Music. CDWELLER3. 1989.

<u>CD</u> Long Hot Summer*, Waiting*, Spring Summer Autumn~, Why I Went Missing, A Womans Song#, You're The Best Thing, Just My Type^, Walking The Night#, The Paris Match^, Boy Who Cried Wolf*

One of the singers Noel McCalla told Wholepoint this was, 'an album that was made for the purpose of music publishers who might be able to place TSC material with other artists. We sang against the original backing tracks.'

Only 2 are TSC originals. The others were sung by;

*Noel McCalla; ~Tracie Young; # Faylene Brown; ^ Dee C Lee

Headstart For Happiness. PWKS 4090 P. 1991.

Subtitled - 'The Style Council Collection'

<u>CD/CASS</u> Long Hot Summer; Why I Went Missing; Angel; Waiting; Move On Up (live recording); Spring Summer Autumn; Blue Cafe; Come To Milton Keynes; Wanted; Heavens Above; Everybody's On The Run (Version One); Spin Drifting; It Just Came To Pieces In My Hands; Mr Cool's Dream; Headstart For Happiness.

Here's Some That Got Away. 519 372-2/4. 1993. Number 37.

Subtitled - 'Contains 22 rare & unreleased recordings'

<u>CD/CASS</u> Love Pains; Party Chambers; The Whole Point II; The Ghosts of Dachau; Sweet Loving Ways; A Casual Affair; A Woman's Song; Mick's Up; Waiting On A Connection; Night After Night; The Piccadilly Trail; (When You) Call Me; My Very Good Friend; April's Fool; In Love For The First Time; Big Boss Groove; Mick's Company; Bloodsports; Who Will Buy; I Ain't Goin' Under; I Am Leaving; A Stone's Throw Away.

The Style Council Collection. 529483-2/4. Feb 1996

<u>CD/CASS</u> Speak Like A Child; Headstart For Happiness; Long Hot Summer; The Paris Match; It Just Came To Pieces In My Hands; My Ever Changing Moods; The Whole Point of No Return; Ghosts of Dachau; You're The Best Thing; Big Boss Groove; Man of Great Promise; Homebreakers; Down In The Seine; A Stones Throw Away; With Everything To Lose; Boy Who Cried Wolf; The Cost of Loving; Changing of The Guard; Why I Went Missing; It's A Very Deep Sea.

Master Series. 539 841-2. 31st December 1999

<u>CD</u> Shout To The Top!, It Didn't Matter, Life At A Top Peoples Health Farm, You're The Best Thing (Long Version), Speak Like A Child, Angel, All Gone Away, Changing of The Guard, Blue Café, Walls Come Tumbling Down! (live), Headstart For Happiness (live), The Cost of Loving, Here's One That Got Away, The Story of Someone's Shoe, Boy Who Cried Wolf, Waiting, How She Threw It All Away, My Ever Changing Moods (live).

Greatest Hits. 549 134-1 (LP). 557 900-2 (CD). 2000 & 2006 (slidepack)

<u>LP /CD</u> Speak Like A Child, Money Go Round - Parts 1 & 2, Long Hot Summer, A Solid Bond In Your Heart, My Ever Changing Moods, You're The Best Thing, Big Boss Groove, Shout To The Top! Walls Come Tumbling Down!, Come To Milton Keynes, Lodgers, Have You Ever Had It Blue, It Didn't Matter, Waiting, Wanted, Life At A Top Peoples Health Farm, How She Threw It All Away, Promised Land.

Talents Du Siecle. The Style Council. France. 16th July 2001

<u>CD</u> You're The Best Thing; It Didn't Matter; Life At A Top People's Health Farm; Shout To The Top!; Speak Like A Child; Angel; All Gone Away; Changing of The Guard; Blue Café; Headstart For Happiness; Walls Come Tumbling Down; The Cost of Loving; Here's One That Got Away; The Story of Someone's Shoe; Waiting; Boy Who Cried Wolf; How She Threw It All Away; My Ever Changing Moods.

The Best of Style Council. Superstar Collection. Japan. UICY-1076. 2001

<u>CD</u> You're The Best Thing; It Didn't Matter; Life At A Top People's Health Farm; Shout To The Top; Long Hot Summer; Speak Like A Child; Angel; All Gone Away; Changing of The Guard; Blue Café; Headstart For Happiness; Walls Come Tumbling Down; The Cost of Loving; Here's One That Got Away; The Story of Someone's Shoe; Waiting; Boy Who Cried Wolf; Come To Milton Keynes; How She Threw It All Away; My Ever Changing Moods.

Café Best. Japan. October 2002

<u>CD</u> My Ever Changing Moods (12" version); With Everything To Lose; Me Ship Came In!; Headstart For Happiness; (When You) Call Me; Piccadilly Trail; It Just Came To Pieces In My Hands; Down In The Seine; Blue Café; Paris Match (album version); All Gone Away; How She Threw It All Away; You're The Best Thing; It's A Very Deep Sea; Spring, Summer, Autumn; Whole Point of No Return; Spin' Drifting; Story of Someone's Shoe; Blood Sports; Whole Point II; Le Depart; My Ever Changing Moods (album version)

20th Century Masters: Classic Style Council. The Millennium Collection. Polydor, 589 097. 3rd March 2003

<u>CD</u> It Didn't Matter; My Ever Changing Moods (Single Version); You're The Best Thing (Single Version); Shout To The Top (Extended Version); Boy Who Cried Wolf; Speak Like A Child; Money Go Round; Long Hot Summer (Single Version); Call Me, (When You) (live); Have You Ever Had It Blue? (From "Absolute Beginners"); Walls Come Tumblin' Down.

The Sound of The Style Council. 065643-1/2 (LP/CD). 17th March 2003

<u>LP/CD</u> Speak Like A Child, Money Go Round (Part 1) (Original Single Edit), Headstart For Happiness (Album Version), Long Hot Summer (Single Edit), The Paris Match (Album Version), It Just Came To Pieces In My Hands, My Ever Changing Moods (Single Edit), The Whole Point of No Return, You're The Best Thing (Single Edit), Shout To The Top (Full Version), Ghosts of Dachau, The Piccadilly Trail, Walls Come Tumbling Down, Spin' Drifting, Homebreakers, A Man of Great Promise, Have You Ever Had It Blue, Waiting, It's A Very Deep Sea, Changing of The Guard, Spring, Summer, Autumn.

It is worth noting that, How She Threw It All Away and Promised Land were on the 2 CD promotional acetate but not on the final CD. A decision was made to reduce the release from the original plan of 2 CD's down to the 1.

The Style Council - The Ultimate Collection. Universal: CCM9813991. May 2004

<u>CD 1</u> Speak Like A Child, Money Go Round (Part 1), Long Hot Summer, A Solid Bond In Your Heart, The Paris Match, You're The Best Thing, My Ever Changing Moods, Shout To The Top, Come To Milton Keynes, Walls Come Tumbling Down, The Lodgers, Have You Ever Had It Blue, It Didn't Matter.

<u>CD 2</u> Waiting, Wanted, Life At A Top Peoples Health Farm, Promised Land, Who Will Buy?, Waiting For A Connection, The Cost of Loving (12" version), My Ever Changing Moods (12" Version), Shout To The Top (Live), Walls Come Tumbling Down (Live), The Lodgers (Live), Our Favourite Shop (Live), My Ever Changing Moods (Live)

CD 3 (bonus disc) - Start! [The Jam], Going Underground [The Jam], Town Called Malice [The Jam], Beat Surrender [The Jam], Wild Wood [Paul Weller], Sunflower [Paul Weller], Hung Up [Paul Weller], You Do Something To Me [Paul Weller]

The Style Council - Gold. 17th April 2006

CD 1 You're The Best Thing, A Stones Throw Away, Have You Ever Had It Blue, Blue Cafe, Money Go Round (Parts 1 & 2), Headstart For Happiness, My Ever Changing Moods, Here's One That Got Away, Long Hot Summer, Internationalists, A Man of Great Promise, Our Favourite Shop, The Lodgers (or She Was Only A Shopkeeper's Daughter), Walls Come Tumbling Down, The Cost of Loving, Wanted (or Waiter, There's Some Soup In My Flies), The Paris Match - The Style Council Tracey Thorn, The Big Boss Groove

CD 2 It Didn't Matter, The Whole Point of No Return, Speak Like A Child, Why I Went Missing, A Solid Bond In Your Heart, Love Pains, Life At A Top Peoples Health Farm, Sweet Loving Ways, Night After Night, Promised Land, Shout To The Top, Who Will Buy?, How She Threw It All Away, Waiting, (When You) Call Me, Waiting For A Connection, Come To Milton Keynes

Zoom Karaoke - Platinum Artists 115: The Style Council & Paul Weller Zoom Entertainments. 29th November 2006

The 1st Karaoke CD to feature TSC. Featuring music and on screen lyrics.

My Ever Changing Moods, You're The Best Thing, Long Hot Summer, Speak Like A Child, Shout To The Top, Walls Come Tumbling Down

Includes Paul Weller songs; You Do Something To Me, Broken Stones, Peacock Suit, The Changing man, Out of The Sinking, Wild Wood and Hung Up.

Sweet Loving Ways - The Collection. 14th May 2007

CD 1 Speak Like A Child, Party Chambers, Money Go Round (Part 1), Headstart For Happiness, Mick's Up, Long Hot Summer, Le Depart, The Paris Match - The Style Council Tracey Thorn, A Solid Bond In Your Heart, It Just Came To Pieces In My Hands, My Ever Changing Moods, Mick's Company, Strength of Your Nature, Here's One That Got Away, Spring, Summer, Autumn, You're The Best Thing, The Big Boss Groove, Shout To The Top

CD 2 The Piccadilly Trail, Walls Come Tumbling Down, The Whole Point II, Homebreakers, A Man Of Great Promise, Boy Who Cried Wolf, (When You) Call Me, The Lodgers (or She Was Only A Shopkeeper's Daughter), Have You Ever Had It Blue, All Year Round, Francoise, Wanted (or Waiter, There's Some Soup In My Flies), Sweet Loving Ways, Changing of The Guard, Why I Went Missing, Promised Land, Can You Still Love Me?

Keeps On Burning - The box set. Japan only
Universal 421517-0-E07M-FP. 16th May 2007

<u>DELUXE BOX - 10 CD's</u> - Japanese limited edition box set.

Contains all 10 Polydor releases;

Introducing; Cafe Bleu; Our Favourite Shop; Home & Abroad;
The Cost of Loving; Confessions of A Pop Group; Modernism: A New Decade;
Greatest Hits; Heres Some That Got Away; In Concert.

Each CD is within a mini-LP type of sleeve. There are also 2 additional sleeves for Internationalists and My Ever Changing Moods to replicate the USA releases. A total of 135 songs are contained within this ultimate package. All packed in an excellent custom box with Japanese obi-strip. In addition there is an Our Favourite Shop black & white picture and a full set of obi-strips which were on the original vinyl's. Currently selling at a large mark up anywhere between £130 at £300. Not aware of the original retail price upon release in Japan.

Paul Weller - Days of Speed. 8th October 2001

Days of Speed featuring live versions of *Headstart For Happiness* and *Down In The Seine*.

Paul Weller - Fly On The Wall: B Sides & Rarities 1991-2000 (3CD) 25th August 2003

All Year Round (from 'More Wood' Japanese Import Album)

Paul Weller - Catch Flame: Live At The Alexandra Palace 12th June 2006

Live LP featuring *Long Hot Summer* and *Shout To The Top*

Paul Weller - Hit Parade (4 CD Box Set) 6th November 2006

CD 2 featuring the music of TSC. Song titles are listed below as they appear.

Speak Like A Child, Money Go Round Pts. 1 & 2 (Original Full 12" Version), Long Hot Summer (Single Edit), Solid Bond To Your Heart, My Ever Changing Moods (Single Edit), You're The Best Thing (Single Edit), Big Boss Groove (Full Version), Shout To The Top (Full Version), Walls Come Tumbling Down, Come To Milton Keynes, The Lodgers (Or She Was Only A Shopkeeper's Daughter) (Extended Single Version), Have You Ever Had It Blue (Single Version), It Didn't Matter (Single Edit), Waiting, Wanted, Life At A Top People's Health Farm, How She Threw It All Away, Promised Land (Radio Edit)

TRANSCRIPTION DISCS

Transcription discs were high-quality live recordings intended for radio broadcast only. They were made in very limited quantities, and extremely rare. Usually no more than 50 copies were pressed and they went to BBC world stations in Canada, New Zealand, Australia, etc. Finding these in 2008 is a near impossible or expensive task.

BBC

In Concert ~ 330. CN 04364/S
Venue: The Dominion, London, 15th March 1984. Issued week 23

Meeting (Up) Over Yonder; Heres One That Got Away; My Ever Changing Moods; It Just Came To Pieces In My Hands; Micks Up; Up For Grabs; Dropping Bombs On The Whitehouse; Long Hot Summer; Money Go Round; Speak Like A Child; Hanging Onto A Memory.

In Concert ~ 365. CN 04652/S
Venue: The Glastonbury Festival, 22nd June 1985. Issued week 41

Internationalists; Homebreakers; See The Day; The Lodgers; Whole Point of No Return; Our Favourite Shop; Long Hot Summer; (When You) Call Me; Walls Come Tumbling Down; Money Go Round; Soul Deep; Strength of Your Nature; It Just Came to Pieces In My Hands; The Big Boss Groove.

In Concert ~ 409. CN 04960/S
Venue: The Royal Albert Hall, February 1987.

It Didn't Matter; Waiting; Walking The Night; The Cost of Loving; The Piccadilly Trail; Everlasting Love; A Woman's Song; Whole Point II; Mick's Company; Heavens Above; Fairy Tales; Angel; The Lodgers; My Ever Changing Moods; Homebreakers; You're The Best Thing; With Everything To Lose; Money Go Round; Internationalists; (When You) Call Me.

Actual running order TBC.

UNITED STATES OF AMERICA

In the USA the following vinyl LP's were intended for radio broadcast only.

Geffen Records - My Ever Changing Moods
Official 1 Sided interview LP. 1984

The King Biscuit Flower Hour. ABC. 24th March 1985. KB 568
Venue: The Savoy Theatre, New York 10th/11th May 1984.

The Big Boss Groove; Here's One That Got Away; You're The Best Thing; My Ever Changing Moods; Speak Like A Child and Headstart For Happiness.

USA SINGLES & PROMOTIONALS

 The following were released in the USA

Long Hot Summer (Don't Matter What I Do)

7" - Long Hot Summer (Don't Matter What I Do)
815 276-7 DJ. Same both sides.

7" - Long Hot Summer (Don't Matter What I Do)/ Le Depart
815276-7 83 NP 6486

12" - Long Hot Summer (Don't Matter What I Do)
Pro 241-1. Same both sides.

My Ever Changing Moods [Geffen]

7" - My Ever Changing Moods (4:02)
7-29359 BAA 2269VIS. Same both sides.

7" - My Ever Changing Moods / Mick's Company 7-29359 BAA 2269VIS.
Exclusive picture sleeve.

12" - My Ever Changing Moods (5:42) / You're the Best Thing (5:45); A Solid Bond in Your Heart (3:13)
Geffen sleeve Promo (Ref: PRO A-2130)

You're The Best Thing [Geffen]

7" - You're The Best Thing (ReMix/Fade)/ You're The Best Thing (ReMix/Fade)
729248 CAA 2422VIDJS.

7" - You're The Best Thing / The Big Boss Groove.
7-29248 CAA 24222VIS. Unique picture sleeve.

Internationalists [Geffen]

12" - Internationalists (3:04) / Walls Come Tumbling Down (3:11)
PRO A. 2319. Geffen Records sleeve.

Boy Who Cried Wolf [Geffen]

7" - Boy Who Cried Wolf (Edit) / Boy Who Cried Wolf (Edit)
7-28941 CAA 3016VIS. Short Version.

7" - Boy Who Cried Wolf / Our Favourite Shop.
7-28941 CAA 3016VIS. Short Version. Unique picture sleeve.

12" - Boy Who Cried Wolf / The Lodgers (Dance remix)
0-20366. Geffen picture sleeve.

Have You Ever Had It Blue [EMI America]
7" - Have You Ever Had It Blue (3:22) / Have You Ever Had It Blue (3:22)
Ref: P-B 8331.

12" - Have You Ever Had It Blue (Edited version) / Have You Ever Had It Blue
(Extended) SPRO9683 stickered sleeve or SPRO 9690 (Promo)

(When You) Call Me [Geffen]
7" - (When You) Call Me (Live-fade) / (When You) Call Me (Live-fade)
7-28674-A.

7" - (When You) Call Me / Internationalists (5:30)
7-28674. Unique picture sleeve.

12" - (When You) Call Me (Live) / (When You) Call Me (Live).
PRO - A.2490. Geffen picture sleeve.

Heavens Above [Polydor]
7" - Heavens Above (4:08) / It Didn't Matter. 855707-7

7" - Heavens Above (4:08)
885 707-7 DJ. Promo. Red Polydor label. Same both sides.

12" - Heavens Above (Long) / Heavens Above (Short)
PRO 495.1 Polydor sleeve.

How She Threw It All Away [Polydor]

7" - How She Threw It All Away (4:17)/ How She Threw It All Away (4:17)
887 753-7 DJ. Unique picture sleeve. Same both sides

7" - How She Threw It All Away (4:17)/ The Long Hot Summer (3:49)
887 753-7. Polydor label. Picture sleeve.

12" - How She Threw It All Away (Edit; 3:49)
PRO 617-7. Promotional. Same both sides.

Promised Land [Polydor]

12" - Promised Land (Club Mix) 7:05 / Can You Still Love Me? (Club Mix) /
Promised Land (Pianopella); Can You Still Love Me? (Dub)
A darker orange sleeve than the UK sleeve. Promo stamped.

COMPLETE VIDEO

The following refers to releases for Video Cassette Recorders

What We Did On Our Holidays. Polygram 040189-2. 1983

Speak Like A Child; Money Go Round; Long Hot Summer; A Solid Bond In Your Heart; Lè Depart.

The Style Council – The first 6 Singles. Polydor promotional release

The first 6 video singles. Limited to 250 copies.

Far East & Far Out. Polygram 040369-2. 1984

Subtitled *Council Meeting in Japan*, this was from May 1984, Nakano Sun-plaza Hall, Tokyo.

Intro; Me Ship Came In; The Big Boss Groove; Here's One That Got Away; You're The Best Thing; It Just Came To Pieces In My Hands; Mick's Up; Dropping Bombs On The Whitehouse; Long Hot Summer; My Ever Changing Moods; Le Depart; The Whole Point of No Return; Money Go Round; Headstart For Happiness; Speak Like A Child; Le Depart (Reprise).

LIVE Post Modern in Tokyo Night. Japan 1984

The Japanese edition of *Far East & Far Out*, includes an extra 35 minutes.

The Big Boss Groove, Here's One That Got Away, You're The Best Thing, It Just Came To Pieces In My Hands, Mick's Up, Dropping Bombs On The Whitehouse, Long Hot Summer, My Ever Changing Moods, Le Depart, The Whole Point of No Return, The Paris Match, Party Chambers, Money Go Round, Speak Like A Child, Headstart For Happiness, Me Ship Came In, My Ever Changing Moods.

Video Aid. 1985

Big Boss Groove promotional video. Donated to Band Aid until the 2004 DVD.

What We Did The Following Year. Polygram 041 322-2. 1985

You're The Best Thing; Shout To The Top; The Lodgers; My Ever Changing Moods; Boy Who Cried Wolf; Walls Come Tumbling Down!; Come To Milton Keynes. Includes the Rupert Everett voice over advert for *Our Favourite Shop*.

Showbiz! The Style Council Live. Polygram 041 371-2. 1986

Opening Sequence; The Big Boss Groove; (When You) Call Me; Shout To The Top!; Homebreakers; With Everything To Lose; Our Favourite Shop; Headstart For Happiness; Long Hot Summer; Walls Come Tumbling Down; A Stones Throw Away; Medley - Soul Deep & Strength of Your Nature; Internationalists.

Red Wedge, Days Like These. 1986

Documentary on the road with *Red Wedge* in January 1986. Featuring various interviews with TSC and live on-stage footage. The most worthy a cover of *Don't Look Any Further*.

Curtis Mayfield Live At Ronnie Scott's. 1988

This is a 10 track concert at Ronnie Scott's in 1988. What is not credited in the sleeve notes is that in-between the songs a bleached Paul Weller asks Curtis questions in an interesting interview. Features *Move On Up*. Described as, 'this rare recording captures the full power in performance and conversation of one of the giants of black American music.'

JerUSAlem. Palace PVC 3014 M. 1987

TSC movie! 'Pursued by the law, spurned by their Friends, and short of a bob or two, those four sturdy sillies of The Style Council take to the road to prove their worth as Britain's premiere outfit and in the process discover the Royal Family, Stravinsky, JerUSAlem, football hooligans and a brand new wardrobe. Jerusalem! Never has so much been created by so few and with such a little budget too! A Short that will grab you by the shorts.'

Live At The Full House. Germany. 1987

A Japanese video/Laserdisc filmed in Germany during the 1987 *Cost of Loving* Tour. Later released on DVD in Germany and imported into the UK. Includes the unreleased *Everlasting Love* and an interview with Paul & Mick.

Confessions of A Pop Group. Channel 5 CFV 07512. 1988

Recorded at Pinewood Studio's, London, 'from the original sound recording.' Featuring studio recordings of It's A Very Deep Sea; Why I Went Missing; Life At A Top Peoples Health Farm; Changing of The Guard; How She Threw It All Away; Confessions of A Pop Group.

Life At A Top Peoples Health Farm compilation. Polydor Promo. 1988

Promotional 'instore'. Includes the title track 3 times alongside; Have You Ever Had It Blue, Speak Like A Child, Come To Milton Keynes and You're The Best Thing. Released in a custom sleeve.

The Video Adventures (Greatest Hits Vol.1) Channel 5 CFV 07842. 1989

You're The Best Thing; Have You Ever Had It Blue; Money Go Round; My Ever Changing Moods; Long Hot Summer; The Lodgers; Walls Come Tumbling Down!; Shout To The Top!; Wanted; It Didn't Matter; Speak Like A Child; A Solid Bond In Your Heart; Life At A Top Peoples Health Farm; Promised Land.

Paul Weller Movement. Live At The Brixton Academy 1991

Released in 1991 and 1997. Featuring *Headstart For Happiness*, *The Piccadilly Trail*, *Long Hot Summer*, *Homebreakers* and *My Ever Changing Moods*.

Paul Weller. Highlights and Hang Ups. 1994

This is an official, excellent 72 minute production by Pedro Romhanyi, Paolo Hewitt and Steven Elliot detailing Paul's career to 1994. Featuring a healthy section on The Style Council and various interviews with Mick, Steve, Dee and others. Includes live footage. 'The definitive visual documentary.'

MOVIES FEATURING TSC MUSIC

Absolute Beginners - Have You Ever Had It Blue

Vision Quest/Crazy For You - Shout To The Top

Business As Usual - The Cost; Incidental music

Angus, Thongs and Perfect Snogging - You're The Best Thing (Instrumental)

CD VIDEO SINGLES

 In the mid 1980's the CD Video was invented. Described as, 'the latest development in the compact disc system, uniting the extraordinary sound of the compact disc with the highest possible video quality.' This was long before the invention of CD-R's. A CD video single is a 5" gold coloured disc (part laser disc, part audio CD). Up to 6 minutes of analogue video was allowed (16 bit digital soundtrack) and a maximum of 20 minutes digital audio.

À Paris. Polydor 080 206-2. 1988.

Long Hot Summer; Party Chambers; The Paris Match; Le Depart; Long Hot Summer (Promotional Video)

Have You Ever Had It Blue. Polydor 080 336-2. 1988.

Have You Ever Had It Blue (Uncut Version); Mr Cool's Dream; Have You Ever Had It Blue (Promotional Video)

Life At A Top People's Health Farm. Polydor 080 560-2. 1988.

Life At A Top Peoples Health Farm (Extended Mix); Spank! (Live At A Top Peoples Health Club); Sweet Loving Ways; Life At A Top Peoples Health Farm (Promotional Video)

How She Threw It All Away. Polydor 080 400-2. 1988.

How She Threw it All Away; Love The First Time; Long Hot Summer (Tom Mix); How She Threw it All Away (Promotional Video)

CD VIDEO ALBUMS

A CD Video album is an 8" or 12" laser disc (full video). It can be either single or double sided and is compatible in laserdisc players but not on the majority of todays DVD players.

Far East & Far Out. Polygram 040 369. 12" single sided.

Identical to the *Far East & Far Out* video release but recorded in stereo on a long play silver disc. Running time 58 minutes.

Showbiz! The Style Council Live. Polygram 080 038. 12" single sided.

Identical to the *Showbiz* video release but on a 12" gold disc playing digital sound and video together.

Confessions of A Pop Group. Polygram 080 384. 8" double sided.

Identical to the *Confessions of A Pop Group* video release. This differs from the other CD videos in two ways. Firstly, it is an 8" gold disk and secondly it is double sided. Running time 33 minutes.

COMPLETE DVD

Excerpts from The Style Council on Film. (PROMODVD 1)

Showbiz! (Intro / Big Boss Groove / When You Call Me / Shout To The Top); **Confessions Of A Pop Group TV Special 1988** (It's A Very Deep Sea / Life At A Top Peoples Health Farm). **JerUSAlem** 3 minutes. **Promo Clips** for 13.30 minutes (Promised Land / Long Hot Summer / Speak Like A Child / Walls Come Tumbling Down). UK Promo only DVD Sampler in card sleeve.

The Jigsaw Man including exclusive footage from TSC on Film

UK magazine DVD Monthly gave this away free. Includes the Jigsaw Man movie and an episode of Men Behaving Badly. Featuring extracts from **Showbiz!** (Headstart For Happiness); **Confessions of A Pop Group TV Special 1988** (Changing Of The Guard). **Promo Video** (Shout To The Top).

The Style Council on Film. 2 DVD Deluxe Edition. 2004

Showbiz (Wembley Arena, December 1985). The Big Boss Groove, (When You) Call Me, Shout To The Top, Homebreakers, With Everything To Lose, Our Favourite Shop, Headstart For Happiness, Long Hot Summer, Walls Come Tumbling Down, A Stone's Throw Away, Soul Deep medley, Strength of Your Nature, Internationalists.

JerUSAlem (February 1987) Short film.
Angel, It Didn't Matter, Heavens Above, Fairy Tales. Incidental music.

Confessions of A Pop Group (July 1988). It's A Very Deep Sea, Why I Went Missing, Life At A Top People's Health Farm, Changing of The Guard, How She Threw It All Away, Confessions of A Pop Group.

Promotional videos (1983 - 1989). Speak Like A Child*, Money Go Round*, Long Hot Summer$, A Solid Bond In Your Heart*, My Ever Changing Moods$, You're The Best Thing*, Big Boss Groove, Shout To The Top*, Walls Come Tumbling Down*, Boy Who Cried Wolf, Come To Milton Keynes, The Lodgers, Have You Ever Had It Blue$, It Didn't Matter*, Waiting, Wanted$, Life At A Top People's Health Farm*, How She Threw It All Away*, Promised Land*.

The Style Council on Film features

Alternative promo versions of tracks marked $
10 track Jukebox selection of tracks marked *

> Never before released interview with Paul and Mick by Paolo Hewitt from 1988
> Hidden live track.

The Complete Live Aid. November 2004

After nearly 20 years the Live Aid concert was released on DVD. It features 2 of the 4 Style Council tracks performed in July 1985, *Internationalists* and *Walls Come Tumbling Down*.

Style Council - The Universal Masters DVD Collection. April 2005.

You're The Best Thing, It Didn't Matter, Life At A Top People's Health Farm, Shout To The Top!, Speak Like A Child, Walls Come Tumbling Down, Boy Who Cried Wolf, How She Threw It All Away, My Ever Changing Moods, Long Hot Summer.

Live at The Full House. 1987

Originally a Japanese laserdisc from 1987 *Cost of Loving* German tour. Trimmed down to 37 minutes. Includes the unreleased *Everlasting Love* and an interview with Paul & Mick.

Paul Weller, Into Tomorrow. 5th November 2006

Another excellent, official production detailing Paul's career up to 2007. Featuring a decent section on The Style Council and various interviews with Mick, Dee and Steve amongst many others. Iain Munn contributed to this DVD and receives a title credit.

Paul Weller, Live at Braehead, Glasgow, Oct 2002

The 2nd night at Braehead described as 'arguably one of the best solo-shows he's ever committed to film.' Featuring *Down In The Seine* and *A Man Of Great Promise*.

Paul Weller - Studio 150. 28th August 2006

My Ever Changing Moods (Live)

Paul Weller - Hit Parade: 2 DVD. 6th November 2006

Speak Like A Child, Money Go Round, Long Hot Summer, Solid Bond In Your Heart, My Ever Changing Moods, You're The Best Thing, Big Boss Groove, Shout To The Top, Walls Come Tumbling Down!, Come To Milton Keynes, The Lodgers, Have You Ever Had It Blue, It Didn't Matter, Waiting, Wanted, Life At A Top Peoples Health Farm, How She Threw It All Away, Promised Land

Far East & Far Out. Cherry Red PPCR013. 4th August 2008

Intro; Me Ship Came In; The Big Boss Groove; Here's One That Got Away; You're The Best Thing; It Just Came to Pieces In My Hands; Mick's Up; Dropping Bombs On The Whitehouse; Long Hot Summer; My Ever Changing Moods; Le Depart; The Whole Point of No Return; Money Go Round; Headstart For Happiness; Speak Like A Child; Le Depart (Reprise).

Subtitled 'Council Meeting in Japan', this is from May 1984, Nakano Sun-plaza Hall, Tokyo. This did not appear on the *TSC on Film* DVD. Great news is that it includes the previously unreleased (in the UK) extra 35 minutes from the equivalent Japanese release! However, the sleeve notes only list the tracks from the UK release and the DVD title screen has a few spelling mistakes and wrong title names. Did anyone actually check this before release? Did they mean to include the extra footage? Worth the £6 though as first time on DVD.

RADIO SESSIONS

In the early years The Style Council recorded 5 exclusive radio sessions amounting to 18 live tracks. None have been released but hopefully that will change in the future as high quality recordings of these shows are scarce.

1983

BBC Radio 1, London, 5th May @ Maida Vale 4 BBC studios; Mick's Up, Here's One That Got Away, Headstart For Happiness and The Paris Match.

BBC Radio 1, London, 13th August @ Studio S2 BBC studios; Le Depart and The Paris Match.

BBC Radio 1, London, 31st December @ Studio S2 BBC studios; My Ever Changing Moods, Mick's Blessings, The Paris Match, Headstart For Happiness and Long Hot Summer.

1985

Piccadilly Radio, Manchester, 11th December; The Lodgers.

Capitol Radio, London, 12th December @ Red Hot Club; (When You) Call Me, You're The Best Thing, The Lodgers, Homebreakers, A Stones Throw Away and Headstart For Happiness.

2008

Paul Weller at the BBC 1990 - 2008; 4 CD Set; 3rd November 2008.

Although outwith TSC years the following tracks will feature, all recorded by the BBC. Exact venue or dates are still unknown at the time of writing but the 4 tracks, all 'concert footage' (not a Radio Session), from CD 3 will be;

My Ever Changing Moods, A Man of Great Promise, Speak Like A Child and Headstart For Happiness

'*Weller at the BBC* is a stunning 74-track, digitally-remastered, 4-CD Hardback book set of exclusive BBC sessions and live concert tracks from 1990 – 2008, including a lavish 64-page booklet with extensive sleeve notes, new interviews with Paul and others with scores of rare photos from the archive.'

TOUR PROGRAMMES

Contrary to popular belief, The Style Council did not go on many tours in the UK. Touring was a 'no' for 4 of the 7 years (1983, 1986, 1988 and 1989), apart from Red Wedge or one off benefit concerts. There were six UK Tours, two per year, in 1984, 1985 and 1987. The following is a run down of the tour programmes for each tour. Initial tour programmes were very worthwhile and a lot of work went into their creation. They contained an abundance of pictures, news and letters from Paul & Mick, all for a staggering £1.50. However, by 1987 colour glossy pictures replaced the text and the price had nearly quadrupled. One surprising release was for the final concert at The Royal Albert Hall in July 1989.

[x] = page number

Council Meetings, Part 1; 20 pages. 20 x 25 cm. £1.50. March 1984
Produced: Modern Works.
Photographs: Peter Anderson. Design: Simon Halfon & Paul Weller.

[1] Handwritten letters, 'Hoping to bring you something new and different...I'm sick of all the boasts.' (Paul) 'Thank you for coming to tonight's meeting - Yeah a meeting, not a mega laser extravawassname.' (Mick) [3] Photo of Paul and Mick at the bar as used on cover of Issue 1 of fan club magazine Style Population. [4/5] Cappuccino Kid, 'I have heard some of the music he (Paul) made previously (Jam) and was indeed caught tapping my foot when its strong tones came through, but compared to the tunes he makes now, well! so moved was I that I began writing notes for him which have now appeared on the back of his new records.' [5] Paul applying make-up in *The Switch* dressing room (*Speak/Solid Bond* live session) [6] The negatives of photo session by a tree as per *Money Go Round* 7" insert/12" sleeve [7] Full page Paris picture [8] Solid bond/Paris pictures [9/10] Full colour centerfold in Paris (Introducing LP cover) [11] Diary from March '83 to Feb '84 [12/13/14] Cafe Bleu pictures during recording (cassette cover) [15/16] My Ever Changing Moods promo video pictures [17] 'Here come the classics' (Cafe Bleu advert) [18] Respond advert/pictures of forthcoming releases [20] Full colour, 'lost in Poppy fields photo' and pictorial discography.

Council Meetings, Part 2; 24 pages, 20 x 25 cm. £1.50. October 1984
Produced: Modern Works. Photographs: Peter Anderson. Design: Simon Halfon.

[2] History of The Style Council & Paul/Mick pictures and quotes [3] MEFF advert, tour band detailed and Cappuccino Kid notes from Italy, Japan & New York [4] Diary from March '83 to Oct '84 [5] Merchandise (t-shirts, programmes, sweatshirts, badges, postcards and posters) alongside an advert for "Spongers/A new book of poems" from Riot Stories [6] Imaginary 'Best of' 12 track TSC LP by Paul [7] Live photo of Paul/Mick [8/9] *Speak Like A Child* thoughts and pictures [10/11] *Money Go Round* thoughts and pictures [12/13] Colour centrefold of A' Paris thoughts and pics. [14/15] A Solid Bond thoughts and pics. [16/17] My Ever Changing Moods thoughts and pictures.

[18/19] *You're The Best Thing* thoughts and pictures [20/21] *Shout To The Top* thoughts and pictures [22] Advert for *Shout To The Top* [23] Advert for *Far East & Far Out* video. Note the projector in the 'Keeps on Burning' logo [24] Small colour back page picture.

Internationalists '85; 24 pages, 20 x 25 cm. £3.00. June '85
Produced: Modern Works.
Photographs: Nick Knight, Tom Sheehan, Olly Ball and Jason Pevovar.

[2] Looking through shop window & Explaining what new LP is about [3/4] Track by track thoughts of Paul/Mick/Steve [5] Mick photo [6] Paul & Tim Pope in Warsaw [7] Views on Poland and pictures [8] Paul/Mick Feb '85 promo shot & views on Politics and pop [9] Full colour Paul picture [10] Full colour Mick picture [11] International Youth year & 3 photos [12/13] Colour centrefold of Our Favourite Shop sleeve [14] Photo of the shop from a distance. Council Collective [15] Full colour Paul/Mick picture [16] For your listening pleasure, releases so far [17] Full page Steve photo [18] Full page shop advert (as per Milton Keynes 12" cover) [19/20] On tour with TSC [21/22/23] Paul/Mick Feb '85 promo photos [24] Tour dates.

Internationalists '85; 24 pages, 20 x 25 cm. £3.00 Nov/Dec 1985
Produced: Modern Works.
Photographs: Nick Knight, Tom Sheehan, Olly Ball and Jason Pevovar.

Identical to the June 1985 tour programme apart from; *What We Did The Following Year* advert and back page with the current tour dates detailed.

General Election; 24 pages, 20 x 25 cm. £5.00. February 1987
Produced: Modern Works. Photographs: Clare Muller

[2] Band photo from *It Didn't Matter* video shoot [3] ReMix of *Waiting* cover photo [4/6/7/10/11] 'Case of the missing cucumber.' A Sherlock Holmes type tale of, 'one November day the sudden disappearance of Master Stephen White sticksman and parradidler of the highest standard.' [5] Colour picture of Paul with white lip-stick (Jerusalem). Colour picture of Paul/Mick (Jerusalem) [12/13] Colour picture of Paul/Mick/Steve/Dee on Scooters (Jerusalem) [14] Mick (Jerusalem) [15] Dee (Jerusalem) [16/17] Colour photos of band (Jerusalem) [18/19] *Heavens Above* promo video pictures on windmill [20] Colour photos of band (Jerusalem) [21] Paul (Jerusalem) [22] Band photo from *It Didn't Matter* video shoot. Advert for JerUSAlem.

Renaissance; 16 pages. £5.00. October/November 1987
Produced: Modern Works.

The majority is photographs from the Wanted, video shoot. A few interviews.

Royal Albert Hall/Review edition 1; 45 x 30 cm. £7. 4th July 1989

Exclusively for this 1 night. Includes masses of pictures, record sleeves, passes, bands memorabilia in a scrap book layout. However, the 'Edition 1' on the cover indicated that TSC expected to tour in 1989 after the release of *Sure Is Sure* and *Modernism: A New Decade*. Only a few thousand were printed and with many of these torn up on the night it is now the most sought after tour programme.

Other UK releases where programmes were available are; 'Brockwell Park CND Festival' in May 1983, the first ever-live gig. 'Live Aid' in July 1985 and the Red Wedge 1986 tours. Outside the UK each Japanese tour in 1984, 1987 and 1989 all resulted in exclusive colour programmes.

UK MAGAZINE COVERS

The following are collectable Style Council front covers.

Smash Hits
17th March 1983
22nd May 1985

Melody Maker
13th August 1983
24th March 1984
13th July 1985
25th January 1986

New Musical Express
10th March 1984
20th October 1984
1st June 1985
10th January 1987

International Musician
February 1987

Cover
28th September 1988

Record Mirror
13th August 1983
13th October 1984
28th September 1985
7th September 1987

The Face
April 1983

Zig Zag
March 1984

Sounds
24th Sept 1983

No 1
13th August 1983
13th July 1985

BOOTLEG DISCOGRAPHY (NO CD-R)

In 2008 there are many bootlegs and file shares around but the following were all released before the explosion of the home PC, CD-R's or MP3 downloads.

All are professional pressings.

Live in Chippenham [UK: SC-1] Chippenham. 10th March 1984. Vinyl.
Picture disc (Limited to 300 copies); Picture sleeve (Limited to 100 copies)

Dancing [UK: SC-1] Chippenham. 10th March 1984. Vinyl.
Black & clear vinyl. Different picture sleeve to the original.

Live With Style [Italian: RFCD 1049] Chippenham. 10th March 1984. CD.
Removes Hanging Onto A Memory.

Live in Chippenham, March 1984 [Italian: CD/ON 2335]
Includes Hanging Onto A Memory.

The following tracks are in the above 4 releases unless stated;

Meeting (Up) Over Yonder; My Ever Changing Moods; Speak Like A Child; Whole Point of No Return; Le Depart; The Paris Match; Party Chambers; Money Go Round; Headstart For Happiness; Hanging Onto A Memory; Headstart For Happiness†; The Paris Match† [† BBC In Concert, 11/6/83]

Altered States. Rome 22nd October, 1984 [Italian: STY-01 & STY-01] Vinyl.
Single and gatefold sleeve versions are available. Both are double albums.

Cappuccino Kid. Rome 22nd October 1984 [Italian: CD/ON 2336] CD.
Recording from the Altered States LP, omits five tracks all from LP side 4.

The following tracks are in all the above 2 releases unless stated;

Big Boss Groove; My Ever Changing Moods; A Man of Great Promise; It Just Came To Pieces In My Hands; Mick's Up; Long Hot Summer; Shout To The Top; Speak Like A Child; Nzuri Beat; Le Depart; The Paris Match; Whole Point of No Return; Have You Ever Had It Blue; Me Ship Came In; Money Go Round; Headstart For Happiness; Strength of Your Nature; Wont Give In*; One Nation Under A Groove.   * The actual title is Razors Edge.

Live At Wembley Arena. 10th December, 1985 [UK: 13-003 & 23-003] Vinyl.
Full colour picture sleeve. Double album.

You're The Best Thing; The Lodgers; Big Boss Groove; Luck; (When You) Call
Me; Homebreakers; Boy Who Cried Wolf; Shout To The Top; See The Day; With
Everything To Lose; Whole Point of No Return; A Word From Our Leaders; Our
Favourite Shop; Move On Up; Headstart For Happiness; My Ever Changing
Moods; Walls Come Tumbling Down; Long Hot Summer; Money Go Round;
Strength of Your Nature; Speak Like A Child; Internationalists.

Walking The Night. 2nd April, 1987, Kohichan, Tokyo [Japan: 870 204-1]. Vinyl
Picture sleeve of Paul & Mick staring at trombones, Denmark 1985. Double LP.

The Lodgers; Shout To The Top; (When You) Call Me; It Didn't Matter; Walking
The Night/ Angel; Homebreakers; The Cost of Loving; With Everything To Lose;
A Woman's Song/ Whole Point II; Down In The Seine; Money Go Round; You're
The Best Thing/ My Ever Changing Moods; Fairy Tales; Heavens Above;
Internationalists.

Di Milano. 25th April, 1987 at Lobe, near Osaka, North Japan [DAT label]. CD
Actual date was 7th

Internationalists; With Everything To Lose; You're The Best Thing; Money Go
Round; Shout To The Top; A Woman's Song; Fairy Tales; Heavens Above.

In 2008 there are numerous websites/forums/blogs devoted to Paul Weller's
career. Many of these offer downloads from The Jam's 1st gig right through to
the latest Paul Weller concert or TV show. They usually come with an excellent
custom CD sleeve to download and print. It would be impossible to list them all
here as potentially any Style Council performance can be made available on
these sites.

RESPOND RECORDS - COMPLETE DISCOGRAPHY

Courtesy of *Boys About Town* fanzine.

As Paul & Mick were closely involved with Respond Records the following has been included to complete the activity during The Style Council years.

SINGLES

RESP 1 - **DOLLY MIXTURE** - Been Teen/Honky Honda/Ernie Ball (7"; 11/81)

RESP 2 - **THE QUESTIONS** - Work 'n' Play/Work 'n' Play Pt 2 (7"; 2/82)

Both tracks produced by Paul Weller.

RESP 3 - **THE RIMSHOTS** - Sweet Talk/What's The Matter Baby? (7"; 2/82)

RESP 4 - **DOLLY MIXTURE** - Everything and More/You And Me On The Sea Shore (7"; 3/82)

RESP 5 - **URBAN SHAKEDOWN** - The Big Wolf/Rap The Wolf (7"; 6/82)

RESP 7 - **THE QUESTIONS** - Work And Play/Saved By The Bell (7"; 10/82)

All tracks produced by Paul Weller.

RESPX 7 - **THE QUESTIONS** - Work And Play (Extended)/Saved By The Bell (Extended) (12"; 10/82)

RESP 8 - **THE QUESTIONS** - Someone's Got To Lose/The Groove Line (7"; 1/83)

RESPX8 - **THE QUESTIONS** - Someone's Got To Lose (Extended)/ The Groove Line/Someone's Got To Lose (Instrumental) (12"; 1/83)

K0B 701 - **TRACIE** - The House That Jack Built/ Doctor Love (7"; 3/83)

KOBX 701 - **TRACIE** - The House That Jack Built/ Tracie Talks/ The House That Jack Built (Instrumental) (12"; 3/83)

All tracks produced by Paul Weller, Doctor Love written by Paul Weller, sleeve co-designed by Paul Weller, backing band includes Paul Weller and Tracie Talks in her being interviewed by Paul Weller.

KOB 702 - **THE QUESTIONS** - Price You Pay/The Groove Line (7"; 4/83)

KOBX702 - **THE QUESTIONS** - Price You Pay/Price You Pay (Instrurmental)/ The Groove Line (12"; 4/83)

KOB 703 - **MAIN T POSSEE** - Fickle Public Speakin'/Version (7"; 5/83)

KOBX 703 - **MAIN T POSSEE** - Fickle Public Speakin' (Extended)/Version (12"; 5/83)

All tracks co-written and co-produced by Paul Weller and features Paul Weller and Mick Talbot.

KOB 704 - **TRACIE** - Give It Some Emotion/The Boy Hairdresser (7"; 7/83)

KOBX 704 - **TRACIE** - Give It Some Emotion (Extended) /Tracie Raps/Give It Some Version (12"; 7/83)

All tracks produced by Paul Weller, *The Boy Hairdresser* is co-written by Paul Weller, sleeve is co-designed by Paul Weller. *Tracie Raps* is her being interviewed by Paul Weller and the backing band includes Paul Weller.

KOB 705 - **THE QUESTIONS** - Tear Soup/The Vital Spark (7"; 9/83)

Sleeve is co-designed by Paul Weller.

KOBX 705 - **THE QUESTIONS** - Tear Soup (Extended)/The Vital Spark (Extended). (12"; 9/83)

K0B 706 - **A CRAZE** - Wearing Your Jumper/She Is So (7"; 10/83)

KOBX 706 - **A CRAZE** - Wearing Your Jumper/She Is So/Dub But Not Mate (12"; 10/83)

Wearing Your Jumper, produced by Paul Weller. Mick Talbot plays Wurlitzer.

K0B 707 - **THE QUESTIONS** - Tuesday Sunshine/No One (7"; 2/84)

KOBX 707 - **THE QUESTIONS** - Tuesday Sunshine (Jock Mix)/ Tuesday Sunshine (Sass Mix)/The House That Jack Built/No One (Long Version) (12"; 2/84)

Sleeve co-designed by Paul Weller.

KOB 708 - **TRACIE** - Soul's on Fire/You Must Be Kidding (7"; 3/84)

KOBX 708 - **TRACIE** - Soul's on Fire (Long Version)/Soul's on Fire/You Must Be Kidding (12"; 3/84)

Soul's on Fire co-written by Paul Weller, all tracks co-produced by Paul Weller, sleeve co-designed by Paul Weller and Jake Fluckery plays guitar on all tracks.

KOB 709 - **THE QUESTIONS** - Building On A Strong Foundation/ Dreams Come True (7"; 5/84)

KOBX 709 - **THE QUESTIONS** - Building On A Strong Foundation (Long Version)/ Dreams Come True/ Acapella Foundation (12"; 5/84)

K0B 710 - **TRACIE -** (I Love You) When You Sleep/Same Feelings Without The Emotion (7"; 5/84)

KOBX 710 - **TRACIE** - (I Love You) When You Sleep/Moving Together (Club Mix) (12"; 5/84)

(I Love You) When You Sleep co-produced by Paul Weller.

KOBX 711 - **MEFF** - Never Stop (A Message)/ Nzuri Beat/ Non-Stop Electro (12"; 9/84)

Never Stop (A Message) produced by Paul Weller and sleeve co-designed by Paul Weller.

K0B 712 - **THE QUESTIONS** - Month of Sundays/ Belief (Don't Give It Up) (12"; 9/84)

K0BX 712 - **THE QUESTIONS** - Belief (Don't Give It Up) (Extended)/ Month of Sundays (12"; 9/84)

SBS 1 - **TRACIE YOUNG** - I Can't Leave You Alone/19 - The Wickham Mix (7"; 7/85)

SBSK 1 **TRACIE YOUNG** - I Can't Leave You Alone (Pick 'n' Mix)/ 19 - The Wickham Mix/ I Can't Leave You Alone (12"; 7/85)

19 - The Wickham Mix co-written by Paul Weller.

SBS 2 - **VAUGHAN TOULOUSE** - Cruisin' The Serpentine/ You See The Trouble With Me (7"; 8/85)

SBSX 2 - **VAUGHAN TOULOUSE** - Cruisin' The Serpentine (Version Excursion)/ You See The Trouble With Me (Extended) / Cruisin' The Serpentine (Club Mix) (12"; 8/85)

SBS 3 - **TRACIE YOUNG -** Invitation/The Country Code (7"; 10/85)

SBSX 3 - **TRACIE YOUNG -** Invitation (RSPV Mix) / The Country Code/ Invitation (12"; 10/85)

LONG PLAYERS

Various - Love The Reason, A Selection of Songs
(RRC 501) October 1983

Work 'n' Play (The Questions); She Is So (A Craze); Give It Some Emotion (Tracie); Peace Love and Harmony (ND Moffatt); Mama Never Told Me (Tracie and The Questions); Building On A Strong Foundation (The Questions); Fickle Public Speaking - Remix (The Main 'T' - KO); Keeping The Boys Amused (A Craze); History of The World (Big Sound Authority); The House That Jack Built (Tracie); Give It Up Girl (The Questions)

The Questions - Belief
(RRL/RRC 503) October 1984

Belief; All The Time In The World; The Bottom Line; Month of Sundays; Someone's Got To Lose; Body And Soul; Tuesday Sunshine; December; The Learning Tree; Drop That Burden; Everything I See.

Tracie - Far From The Hurting Kind
(Respond RRL 502) June 1984

(I Love You) When You Sleep; Souls on Fire (Young/Weller); Nothing Happens Here But You (Weller); I Can't Hold on Till Summer; Dr. Love (Weller); Thank You; Moving Together; Spring, Summer, Autumn (Weller); What Did I Hear You Say; Far From The Hurting Kind (Weller)

Paul Weller co-produced, co-sleeve designed and played Guitar.

THE LOST TRACIE LP - TRACK BY TRACK

Exclusive review by Tracie Young for *Mr Cool's Dream*

Only Tracie and a few other trusted friends have this album. It is complete and was at the time ready for release. In September 2008 it is not available anywhere in any shape or form. Tracie is the only one who can change this.

TRACIE: "Here is a blow by blow review of my own album, exclusively for *Mr Cool's Dream*."

1. **No Smoke Without Fire.** A blinding song which sounds a little dated now, but I still like it. Obviously, I pick holes in the vocals but that's just me - I do think I could have done better. Anyway, it was written by Don Snow, who was keyboard player with Squeeze (post Jools Holland) and a friend of his worked at EMI and gave me a tape of some of his songs. I loved it all (and still listen to it today) but Alan (from EMI) and I were keen for me to record one. The best thing was when he came to the studio to work on it with me. He's one of those blokes who can play every instrument really well and can sing brilliantly as well, I mean a really brilliant voice - a cross between Michael McDonald and John O'Kane. He spent all day and night working on that song with us, and I loved his voice so much that I asked him to do some vocals on Call Me as well. We got on great, he was a huge Steve Martin fan and we went for an Indian afterwards. Never seen him since!! But I like the track, and at the back of our minds we always had it figured as the kind of song that would be a good US release.

2. **Me and Jimmy Stone**. This is truly terrible because I can't remember the name of the guy who wrote this. But it's a nice laid back track and I do think the vocals are good, although my voice on this (as on a lot of this album) is much deeper than previously. John (Weller) had this earmarked as a single.

3. **Invitation**. I still prefer the demo! I've just listened to it again while writing this, and Camelle sounds fab, I sound crap and it's all too much in places. Good song, bad version.

4. **Love Without Jealousy**. Written for me by Billy Franks from the fabulous Faith Brothers. I can't remember how that came about, but I'd heard a couple of their songs, loved them (particularly *Country Of The Blind* - if you've never heard it, you don't know what a joy you've missed) told the right people (I guess) and then this song was sent to me. Funnily enough, I've just been checking out Billy's website as he sent me an email, thanks to Wholepoint! Anyway, this is special. It could never be a single (well, I'm not a good judge about that kind of thing) but it is a wonderful song. The words are the most heartfelt Mix of tenderness and bitterness and desperation so I think I give one of my best performances.

Very different to Billy's version (which he tells me is back in his live set) and different for me too! I don't remember how we came to do it in the style we did (no doubt, much to do with Brian Robson) but it is rather good and different and I don't know how else to describe it. Just an amazing song - but it needs time to grow on you, and you have to listen to the words.

5. **(When You) Call Me**. Well, probably a bad move, as I frequently recorded songs that Paul had written or sung. But when you know one of the best songwriters in the country it's too big a temptation! Just not clever if you're trying to be independent. I like this a lot, still. I like the way I sing it, I like the arrangement, which starts with very little and builds wonderfully like the really wild guitar and vocals at the end, I like the fact that it's about 5 and a half minutes long because it couldn't do what it does if it was shorter (so...crap single). I love Don Snow's vocals - it's a thrill when you sing with someone who's great and your voices go together well. The high parts are him, not me!!! A bit rocky for Paul's liking, I'd say, but I love it!

6. **We Should Be Together**. Trash rock - very bad taste on my behalf. What was I thinking????

7. **The Country Code**. This had been a b-side. My guitarist, Sav, had a piece of music he'd written and we needed a b-side urgently so I sat down and wrote some words to it in about half an hour. The original was just piano and vocal. We got such a good response to it that I wrote an extra verse and we re-recorded it with a harp. A bit fanciful really, and deep down I still prefer the original, but I think it's good. The problem with being vehemently opposed to fox-hunting (which I still am) and then writing songs about it (in much the same way as I did about vivisection) is that people always thought I was just spouting opinions put in my mouth by Paul. Interesting story about that. When I'd been working with Paul for a few months, he informed me one day that we were appearing at a CND gig in Finsbury Park. I hit the roof because Paul and I had never really discussed my political views and I was offended that he would just assume I would get involved in something like that without asking how I felt about it. It was a point of principal really - of course I supported CND - but why did he assume that? Anyway, he was very apologetic and withdrew me from the gig - yet another example of us clashing for no good reason and I took it too far. I would have done it but I was incensed at his presumptuousness!! I always felt a bit touchy after that about issues I was supportive of, because Paul was so politically motivated. I didn't want to be perceived as spouting whatever he told me to.

8. **Italian Girl**. This is actually very good. It's an album track only, written by Paul Barry and I asked him to co-produce it with Brian. It's a very upbeat poppy track, with typical Paul Barry grooviness just in there somewhere. But it was hell to record. I made this album with Brian, who I'd worked with virtually from day one. Brian was laid back, easy to work with and non-confrontational (he had a subtle way of getting his ideas forward or telling you something was rubbish.) Paul was the exact opposite of that.

But the track still sounds good so the hell was worth it. The song suits me and I didn't attempt to use my "mature" voice for this. I sound young and fresh and the song is in a similar vein to dancey, poppy Culture Club stuff, a bit like It's A Miracle.

9. **Dark Horse/Fingers Crossed**. Never did decide on a title for this. I wrote this with Kevin Miller, my bass player and (then) boyfriend and apart from some of the words, I think this sounds good. Laid back, summery, easy to listen to, fresh. Brian referred to this as "Dark Horse" throughout the recording of the album because he felt it had something a bit special about it. Listening to it today, I can hear what he meant - it's a very happy track. If ever I was going to sing again, I would use this song but re-write some of the lyrics.

10. **I Think You're Lucky**. If I was going to release a single tomorrow, this would be a contender. Another Paul Barry song and I still love it. It's up, without being too rocky, a good, unfussy vocal, solid drumming courtesy of Simon, the Higsons' drummer, which drives the song, and some lovely guitar and brass work (it goes very Motown unexpectedly in the instrumental break, thanks to some great sax). It's just happy and simple!

11. **I Can't Leave You Alone**. Still breaks my heart that this wasn't a hit. A song I loved that we'd worked live since 1983. It just developed into a climax on stage. One night in Scotland, a guy came up to me and told me I'd be nuts if I didn't release it as a single and I knew it was true. Don't know why it didn't catch on, but it broke my heart. If there was a moment when I felt sad, it was the day this single dropped from sixty-something. I felt alive singing this song, that I was doing something I wanted to do and I was giving it my all. Maybe we messed with it too much in the studio - it was quite different to the live version - but I don't think so. I still think this was one of my best moments.

TRACIE: "So, there you have it. It was a bit of fun and nostalgia for me to listen to it again. I have listened to one or two of the songs recently, but not all of it. It's amazing what you remember after all this time!"

DEE C LEE

Since joining The Style Council in 1983 Dee C Lee released and appeared on a surprising amount of solo singles and LP's. Here is an overview of what has been released.

There are still gaps so any additional information is welcomed.

SINGLES

1984
Don't Do It Baby/Yes [CBS (T) A4838]

Selina Wow Wow (Extended Mix)/Hey What Do You Say (Extended Version)/ Ain't Nothing Missing [CBS (T)A4192]

Yippee-Yi-Yay/Space and Time/ Yippee-Yi-Yay (Dub Mix) [CBS (T) A4377]

1985
See The Day/The Paris Match/Luck (live)/ Don't Do It Baby (Remix) [CBS (T) A6570]

Dust Choir - Another Fly Network. EP with *Son of Jobs For The Boys* LP

1986
Come Hell or Waters High/I Don't Mess 7" + poster [CBS (T) A6869]

Hold On/Welcome, Shrine (Club Mix) [CBS (T) A7179]

Hey What'd Ya Say/Selina Wow Wow [CBS (T) A7294]

1989
Move (Dance All Night)/Smooth, Move (Dance All Night) (Club Mix), Move (Dance All Night) (Big Fat Dub Mix), Dream On [MCA 1346]

1990
Something Ain't Right, Something Ain't Right (Slammin' Club Mix), Something Ain't Right (Jammin' Urban Mix), Something Ain't Right (D Beat Slammin' Mix), What Dreams Are Made of, Free Your Feelings [MCA 1444]

Move (Dance All Night) (Extended Version), Move (Dance All Night) (Zanzibar Dub)/ Move (Dance All Night) (Zanzibar Instrumental) [MCA-23998]

1991

Move (Dance All Night) (Slammin' 12"), Move (Dance All Night) (Red Zone Mix), Move (Dance All Night) (The If Mix), Move (Dance All Night) (Tony Humphries Mix), Move (Dance All Night) (Movin' Mix) [MCSTD 1503]

Free Your Feelings, Free Your Feelings (Xtra Feeling Mix), Free Your Feelings (Gifted Mix), Free Your Feelings (Instrumental) [MCS(T) 1533]

1992

Paul Weller - Feeling Alright? From the b-side of *Above The Clouds*. 'Recorded drunk at Comfort's Place.'

1993

Guru, featuring D.C. Lee - No Time To Play [Cooltempo Cool 282]

1994

Things Will Be Sweeter/Things Will Be Sweeter (12")/Wherever You Run [Cleartone; CTNCDS 004]

New Reality Vibe/New Reality Vibe (Dub Version) 12" [MW 019; Mo Wax]

Mother Earth - Vocals on Jesse.

LONG PLAYERS

1986

Shrine. Shrine, Hey What Do Ya Say?, That's When Something Special Starts, See The Day, He's Gone/Come Hell or Waters High, What about Me, Still The Children Cry, Just My Type, Hold On [CBS 26915]

1991

Free Your Feelings (Slam Slam) Move (Dance All Night); Something Ain't Right; Free Your Feelings; What Dreams Are Made of; Giving It Up; You'll Find Love; Depth Charge; Round & Round; Tender Love; Nothing Like It.
[MCA 10147]

1992

Paul Weller (LP). Vocals on Bull-Rush, Remember How We Started, Kosmos and Bitterness Rising.

1993

Guru. No Time to Play on Jazzmatazz Volume 1 [Cooltempo CD 34]

1994

Things Will Be Sweeter. How Far?; I'm Somebody; Wherever You Run; Set Your Spirit Free; It's Gonna be Alright; Things Will Be Sweeter; Definitive Love; Wherever You Run (version); Walk Away From the Floor; Can You Lead Me? [Cleartone. CTN 001]

Mother Earth - Jesse and Mr Freedom from The People Tree [Acid Jazz CD 83]

Nobukazu Takemura - Vocals on Searching from his Child's View LP.

1995
Guru. Choice of Weapons from Jazzmatazz Volume 2 (The New Reality)

Jamiroquai. Just Another Story from Return of The Space Cowboy.

1998
Smiles. I Will Wait, I Won't Break Your Heart, In This Life, Don't You, To Have & To Hold, I Love You, No-one Needs to Know, When You Were Mine, You Were The One, Cajun Moon, How Far (Martin Luther King Speech Version) [Japan only, Pony Canyon. PCCY-1223]

2002
D'Influence. La Dee Dah from their D-Vas LP.

2006
Rabbit Fever released 22nd September was a movie about the Rampant Rabbit Vibrator! Dee is said to have had a small part in this as a club singer and is credited on the movie's website.

See The Day - An update on Dee's biggest hit.

As well as being a massive hit for Dee in 1985 *See The Day* has recently had a lot of exposure, probably resulting in good royalties for the songwriter, Dee.

Girls Aloud released this on Polydor as their Christmas single in 2005 which peaked at number 9. From it they won the Heart Award at the O2 Silver Clef Lunch which honours songwriting and performance in aid of Nordoff-Robbins Music Therapy. They also released the 'Soundhouse Masterblaster Mix', a Karaoke video and a ringtone before it appeared on their LP *Chemistry* and in their live set.

In 2006 the well known Eastenders actress Lucy Benjamin performed a version on the *X Factor: Battle of The Stars*. Benjamin won the final.

Dee appeared on lunchtime chat show, Loose Women on 26th Sept 2007 (Season 12, Episode 18) to discuss her career and sing *See The Day*.

4th April 2008 - 17 year old finalist Samantha performed *See The Day* live to the nation on the BBC's popular show *I'd Do Anything*. The Graham Norton and Andrew Lloyd Webber show to find Nancy.

Wholepoint Publications would be delighted to interview Dee C Lee and discuss all areas of her career for a future release of this publication.

MICK TALBOT

Mick did not pursue a solo career and seemed content in the early days to be a session musician on an astounding number of projects. The first being on Steve White's *Certain Kind Of Freedom* 1990 project where he went under his own name for *That Guy Called Pumpkin* as well as assisting on other tracks. He also appeared on 6 of the 9 tracks from the outstanding Young Disciples *Road To Freedom* LP, playing on Keyboards, electric Piano, Moog and Clavinet and also on *Top of the Pops* with them.

Other notable guest appearances were with Diane Brown and Barrie K Sharpe (singles and LP); the popular Des'ree LP *Mind Adventures*; Slam Slam (singles and LP), Dodge City and Paul Weller (solo LP's). He has also played live with Paul and contributed alongside Chris Bangs and Camelle Hinds on the 1992 Acid Jazz Quiet Boys release *Can't Hold The Vibe*, playing Fender Rhodes and clavinet on four of the ten tracks. Mick assisted Graham Parker on *Burning Questions* (Demon Records, 1992) taking keyboard credits for the whole album and also on the Boogie Box High LP. His most notable long-term project was with Talkin Loud favourites Galliano. He guested on *In Pursuit of The 13th Note*, and by the next he was a full-time member appearing at all live gigs and on the LP's *A Joyful Noise Unto The Creator* and *The Plot Thickens*. Mick wrote tracks and produced/Mixed a number of singles for Galliano before parting in 1993 to concentrate on other projects.

1993 saw Mick Talbot and Steve White join forces under Talbot and White for the excellent vocal/instrumental LP *United States of Mind* (for a long time a Japanese only release). A follow up 100% instrumental, *Off The Beaten Track*, was released in the UK on 30th September 1996.

In 1996 with the group Changing Man, Kenny Jones and Mick Talbot recorded *Afterglow* on the Small Faces tribute CD *Long Agos And Worlds Apart*. The Yada Yada and Subculture projects were an adventurous duo with Chris Bangs on the 2Kool Label and they released an amazing number of LP's in a very short space of time.

Mick and Steve teamed up again for a bigger project with The Players, releasing two solid LP's by October 2005. Mick also took part in Dexy's Midnight Runners and The Bureau re-union dates.

Wholepoint Publications would be delighted to interview Mick Talbot and discuss all areas of his career for a future release of this publication.

STEVE WHITE

Steve White quit The Style Council in 1987 to concentrate on the Jazz Renegades. He re-joined Paul for the 'Movement' dates in 1990 and stayed for nearly 18 years until Paul and Steve decided it was time for a new, fresh start. However, during these 18 years Steve was busy with many other projects.

He was with The James Taylor Quartet late in 1988 and after playing well over 100 gigs in UK and Europe and recording an album Steve left in the autumn of 1989. He went on to guest with Galliano and on various Acid Jazz compilation LP's with The Jazz Renegades. He appeared on one track, *As We Come (To Be)* from the Young Disciples *Road To Freedom* LP alongside Paul and Mick but the major release for Steve was *A Certain Kind Of Freedom*, a project compiled, produced and Mixed by him in 1990.

A Certain Kind Of Freedom was an ambitious project bringing together top Acid Jazz/session players of the time and also his Style Council sidekick Mick Talbot whose masterpiece *That Guy Called Pumpkin* also featured Steve and Gary Wallis both Honorary Councillor's and Paul Francis who would bass with the Paul Weller Movement. Steve appears on 6 of the 10 tracks. There are 34 musicians on the album, including Lenny Peterson, Paul Carr Quartet, Sarah Jane Morris and Gary Husband.

Steve has remained very close friends with Mick Talbot and the pair created the *United States Of Mind* and *Off The Beaten Track* LP's under the Talbot and White banner and were both heavily involved in The Players. Look out for the forthcoming entire back catalogue of Talbot & White and The Players releases.

In 2008 White, Minchella and Beaghan formed Trio Valore who release their debut album on 6th October. This follows on from a cover of Amy Winehouse' *Rehab*. A fine mix of Funk, Nu Jazz and Soul.

His excellent website is **www.whiteydrums.com**

BIBLIOGRAPHY

Porcelain God - Darren Eales
978-0955570407 (Paperback, 2007)

Heaven's Promise - Paolo Hewitt
978-0952072119 (Paperback, 1994)

The Changing Man - Paolo Hewitt
978-0593058756 (Hardback, 2007); 978-0552156097 (Paperback, 2008)

Paul Weller, The Unauthorised Biography - Steve Malins
978-0753500873 (Paperback, 1997)

Shout To The Top, The Jam and Paul Weller - Dennis Munday
978-1846094019 (Hardback, 2006); 978-1846098574 (Paperback, 2008)

Internationalists, Introducing The Style Council - Andrea Olcese
B0007C6U8C (Paperback, 1985)

My Ever Changing Moods - John Reed
978-0711954953 (Hardback, 1996); 978-0711963795 (Paperback, 1997)
978-0711988668 (Paperback, 2002); 978-1844494910 (Paperback, 2005)

Paul Weller & The Jam - John Reed
978-0711968189 (Paperback, 1999)

Long Hot Summer - Eric Stephenson & James McKelvie
978-1582405599 (USA, Paperback, 2005)

A Thousand Things - Paul Weller
978-1905662050 (Hardback, 2008)

Suburban 100 - Paul Weller
978-1846052897 (Hardback, 2007); 978-0099515661 (Paperback, 2008)

WHOLEPOINT PUBLICATIONS

2006 Paperback

The paperback edition of *Mr Cool's Dream* was released on 2nd January 2006 to excellent reviews from the press, Style Council members and fans alike.

In 2008 it went 'out of print' and is no longer available in store. It is now a Style Council fans collectors item, rarely appearing on Ebay or Amazon marketplace, retaining at the least its RRP.

ISBN: 0955144302
196 pages
RRP: £10.99

HMV - 1998 STYLE COUNCIL BOX SET EDITION

In 1998 one of the world's leading music stores, HMV, struck an exclusive deal with Wholepoint Publications when they printed a cut down, strictly limited edition of the book for inclusion within The Style Council 5 CD box set. Advertisements appeared in *NME* promoting the book and as no other outlet was offering any incentive it was a simple choice when deciding where to buy it from.

If you have a copy then it is worth noting that it sold without the box set on Ebay, 26th July 2001 for an amazing £101, making it one of the highest priced Style Council items to date. It has rarely appeared for sale since its release in 1998.

CONTACTING IAIN MUNN

Phone/Fax

08712 115510
Leave a message, review or request
Service available 24x7x365

email

info@wholepoint.co.uk

Web

www.wholepoint.co.uk
www.paulwellerbook.com
www.mrcoolsdream.co.uk

Social

www.myspace.com/wholepoint
www.facebook.com
www.linkedin.com

An IKON footwear promotion

BBC London DJ and contributor to *Mr Cool's Dream,* Gary Crowley, features in a new range from **IKON footwear** - A Desert Boot aptly named **The Crowley**.

Further information and ordering details at

www.ikonfootwear.co.uk
www.myspace.com/ikonfootwear

Photograph by Jordan McLachlan

PHOTOGRAPH CREDITS

Graeme Atkins	267
Karl Bedingfield	262 (top)
Paulu Cuccurullo	266
Andy Davis	264, 265, 270
Rene De Hey	265 (bottom), 321
Dodger	All illustrations
Anthony Harty	257, 260 (top), 264 (bottom), 265 (top) 268, 269 (top)
Debbie Kruger	262 (bottom), 264 (top)
Mike Mower	260 (bottom)
Dennis Munday	269 (bottom)
Iain Munn	11
Mel O'Toole	270 (top)
Tony Pacey	270 (middle), 270 (Bottom)
John Verity	258 (bottom)
Steve White	322
Tracie Young	258 (top), 259, 268

INDEX (HISTORY PAGES)

THE STYLE COUNCIL

MR COOL'S DREAM

WWW.WHOLEPOINT.CO.UK

0 0 5 5

THE STYLE COUNCIL